*The Making
of a Library*

THE MAKING
OF A LIBRARY

THE ACADEMIC LIBRARY IN TRANSITION

ROBERT S. TAYLOR

HAMPSHIRE COLLEGE WORKING PAPER NUMBER TWO

A WILEY-BECKER-HAYES PUBLICATION

BECKER AND HAYES, INC., a subsidiary of
John Wiley & Sons, Inc.
New York · London · Sydney · Toronto · Bethesda

A/027.7744'23

To Leni

Information Sciences Series

Information is the essential ingredient in decision making. The need for improved information systems in recent years has been made critical by the steady growth in size and complexity of organizations and data.

This series is designed to include books that are concerned with various aspects of communicating, utilizing, and storing digital and graphic information. It will embrace a broad spectrum of topics, such as information system theory and design, man-machine relationships, language data processing, artificial intelligence, mechanization of library processes, non-numerical applications of digital computers, storage and retrieval, automatic publishing, command and control, information display, and so on.

Information science may someday be a profession in its own right. The aim of this series is to bring together the interdisciplinary core of knowledge that is apt to form its foundation. Through this consolidation, it is expected that the series will grow to become the focal point for professional education in this field.

Preface

A book like this is a cumulation of experience, thought, error, and, hopefully, learning of many years. It did not start, like a water faucet, at precisely that moment in 1967 when the Office of Education so kindly awarded a grant to Hampshire College for the development of the concept of the extended and experimenting library, although the grant was certainly the means for, and a spur to, its formalization. In reality the idea for this book started when I heard Jesse H. Shera address the Eastern College Librarians Conference Thanksgiving Weekend in 1954. I cannot now remember what he said, but I do know that his words were my trigger of serendipity. I owe Dr. Shera my gratitude for saying the right things at the right time—for one listener at least. Fortunately, Jesse Shera's effect on me did not end at that moment and I am indebted to him for opportunities and ideas that helped to build the base for this book. Another such person is James D. Mack, librarian of Lehigh University, for and with whom I worked for many years. He once called me a "metalibrarian," and that, in a very real sense, is what this book is all about. I wish to acknowledge both his support in helping to lay a base and his patience in letting me unscramble some of my ideas. So much for prolegomenon.

For the work on this specific project I am indebted to the generous financial support for three years by the Office of Education. I am especially grateful to Eugene Kennedy, Frank Curt Cylke, and Lawrence Papier, successively project monitors, whose suggestions, patience, courtesy, and occasional but necessary bullying aided and spurred the process.

If merit exists in the ideas, the plans, and the operations described here, then much of that merit is attributable to the Trustees and Officers of Hampshire College, who had the foresight, even temerity, to provide a home base for this project—a project that may pay off only sometime in the future. I wish in particular to acknowledge with gratitude the support of the first President of the College, Franklin Patterson, and the present President, Charles Longsworth, whose concern and imagination not only provided the context for a redefinition of the library in liberal arts education but whose interest sustained a constant flow of ideas and constructive criticism.

To my colleagues within the Library Center I am especially indebted; in fact some of the prose and many of the ideas are directly derived from their discussions and reports. Susan Severtson, assistant project director in the early project phase, provided imagination and ideas for the design of the building. Chapter 5 on systems and processes rests in good part on the work and ideas of Judith Watts, Assistant Director for Technical Processes. Estelle Jussim, Associate Director for Media Resources and Services, gave creative input for the acquisition and exploitation of non-print media and for the planning of the Gallery function. Chapter 6 could not have been written without the hard work and articulate effort of Richard Muller, Director of Educational Technology. Gai Carpenter, Media Resources Adviser, aided in the writing of Chapter 4. The physical production of the report would not have been possible without the capable assistance of Christiana Newton and Chahnaz McRae.

I wish especially to acknowledge the contribution of several of the project consultants listed in Appendix B. Richard C. Oldham provided extensive assistance in the writing of Chapter 6 on educational technology and Chapter 7 on library networks. George E. Piper educated me on the problems and operation of the college bookstore. Vincent E. Giuliano chaired the Hampshire Conference on the Relationship of Information Transfer Systems and Experimentation to the Design and Function of the Library. Frederick Kilgour chaired the Hampshire Conference on Planning for Automated Systems in College Libraries. Both conferences, under their respective chairmanships, were essential and rich sources of information in our early thinking. Richard Trueswell helped and advised us in our early struggles with PERT and systems analysis. Anne C. Edmonds and Newton F. McKeon, librarians respectively of Mount Holyoke and Amherst Colleges, were generous in their help and advice. The assistance of all these consultants is reflected throughout these chapters and is gratefully acknowledged. Errors in fact and misinterpretations, however, are my responsibility, a burden I gladly accept in exchange for the discussions and ideas which all who have touched this project have provided.

Acknowledgment would not be complete without mention of the personal support of Leni Taylor. Her patience, good humor, and cheerful absorption of household responsibilities provided the personal context without which concentrated work would not have been possible. I thank her.

ROBERT S. TAYLOR

Amherst, Massachusetts
August 1971

Acknowledgments

Grateful acknowledgment is made to McGraw-Hill Book Company for permission to reprint excerpts from *Schedule, Cost, and Project Control with PERT* by Robert W. Miller, 1963, from *Innovation, the Basis of Change* by H. G. Barnett, 1953, and from *Present Tense* by Norman Cousins, 1967; to the Harvard University Press for permission to reprint excerpts from *Run, Computer, Run* by Anthony Oettinger, 1969; to Harper & Row, Publishers, Inc., for permission to reprint excerpts from *The Age of Discontinuity* by Peter Drucker, copyright (c) 1968, 1969 by Peter F. Drucker, from *Self-Renewal* by John W. Gardner, 1963; to Basic Books, Inc., for permission to reprint excerpts from *Scientists: Their Psychological World* by Bernice T. Eiduson, 1962, from *The Parsons College Bubble* by James Koerner, 1970, and from *The Art of Conjecture* by Bertrand de Jouvenal, 1967; to Doubleday & Company for permission to reprint an excerpt from *The Academic Revolution* by Christopher Jencks and David Riesman, 1968; to the Shoe String Press, Inc., for permission to reprint an excerpt from *Libraries and the Organization of Knowledge* by Jesse H. Shera, 1966; to the M.I.T. Press for permission to reprint excerpts from *Men, Machines and Modern Times* by Elting Morison, 1966; and to the Princeton University Press for permission to reprint an excerpt from *The Production and Distribution of Knowledge in the United States* by Fritz Machlup, 1962.

Contents

The Making
of a Library

Introduction

This book is written in rondo form. Now, Webster's Third Unabridged defines a rondo as "an instrumental composition or movement in which the principal theme or first subject occurs at least three times in the same key with contrasting themes or sections in between and which is often the last movement of a sonata." This introduction and the first two chapters serve to present the rondo theme. The remaining chapters pick up the theme in various instruments and develop, orchestrate, or explicate them. Some of the themes are not fully developed because the instruments do not yet exist to provide the sounds we would like to hear. In some cases the players were too expensive, in others the orchestration was too difficult. There are no trumpets—or if there are, they are muted. We are not satisfied that we have *the* answer. An answer, yes. A direction, yes.

The theme is basically this. All institutions of higher learning have a place called the library, usually spelled with a capital L. A great deal of money, time, and effort have been poured into the library. Because of an aura of mistaken veneration and misplaced emphasis, however, its potential for education has been largely neglected and its potential for providing the environment for an effective community has been overlooked. It is suggested that those who plan libraries during the 1970's examine rather closely what the library does and what it could do, to become a productive participant in the learning process and in the community it serves. This will be the last library of the kind with which we are familiar to be built on a campus. It will bear the burden of being a transition instrument to a new type of institution.

This book is the result of a project begun in June 1967 and supported by the U. S. Office of Education under Grant 1-7-071180-4351 and its continuation. Its objective was to develop the concept of an experimenting and extended library, and to oversee its physical and operational design in a new college—Hampshire College in Amherst, Massachusetts. In the original proposal, written in the spring of 1967, the proposed activities were described as follows:

Hampshire College proposes . . . to define and design a library for

Hampshire College, which would serve as a prototype design to demonstrate to other undergraduate colleges an integrated set of solutions to the problems that beset colleges and college librarians, particularly as they attempt to be relevant to rapidly changing student needs and emerging techniques.

The traditional library, by consciously acting merely as a passive store of knowledge, is neglecting opportunities to contribute directly and dynamically to the educative process. Hampshire intends to take advantage of its opportunity to create a new library program by designing a library to function as a vital element in the total commitment of the College to that process.

Three areas of concern were discussed in the proposal. The first was that students must be given a larger role and greater responsibility in the functioning of the library. We wished, therefore, to develop a series of systems and interfaces which could, in good part, be student-operated. The second concern grew out of this desire for student involvement—that this new library should be an experimenting library. The student and faculty member, and in fact the librarian, should become more than mere users of a service. They should interact, test, and observe both themselves and the system. In short, the user should begin to see himself as generator, user, and communicator of knowledge in an on-going communications system. The third area of concern was to extend the library into activities not normally considered part of its domain. Such an extension was posited on the assumption that as merely a storage house the library was destined to become a more expensive and less effective appendage in the educational process. Consequently it was felt that the library should be extended to collect, make available, and exploit all available channels and media of communication.

The second proposal, written in late 1968, requested support for continuing the project. The original objectives were refined and may be illustrated by the following excerpts:

> . . . the major objective is to provide an intellectual and empirical base for new and enriched departures in the interaction between a college library and its academic environment.
>
> . . . specifically it is our purpose to issue a report . . . which will be the basis for college library planning during the Seventies: a summary of what is known now, what the significant questions are, and what the parameters are for seeking solutions.

One of the major aims of Hampshire College has been and will be to state its plans and analyze its progress as clearly and as publicly as possible, both for its own benefit and as a contribution to the improvement of undergraduate education in the large. The setting for the development of this concept of the library and its physical expression is significant.

Hampshire College, more than most institutions, has had time and talent to plan and design its curriculum, posture, sense of community, and library system.

There are mistakes in the library. We hope that in this book they are discussed candidly and honestly in the belief that the record of failure is at least as important as—if not more important than—the record of success. Some mistakes are frozen in the bricks and mortar of the building. Some are implicit in the assumptions—frequently differing assumptions—of librarians, faculty members, and administrators. Some will not be apparent until the library is operational. We did not, however, design the perfect library of the future. We do not quite know what that Nirvana would be like. We did design a library in a real situation with all the constraints of reality: financial, political, human, and the current image of what a library is.

Evelyn Waugh once said that a writer must never tell a reader where he is going, for he may never get there. That risk is taken in the next few paragraphs in the expectation that the reader will understand the spirit in which the book is written. It is written both in the past tense of decisions made, and the future tense of decisions yet to come. It is in writing about decisions yet to be made that most people get into trouble, for, as Betrand de Jouvenal has so aptly remarked, ". . . the wish to predict and the wish to persuade conspire to impress on the minds of men the idea of a line of the future . . ."[1] We become persuaded by the obvious correctness of our own rhetoric and by the obvious perfection of the universe we predict to the point that not only will these things come about but they have already done so.

There may be an element of this in this report. If this is true, then it grows out of the conviction that the library may be the only social institution which can combine into a new synthesis the tradition of print, that "second chain of human inheritance," with the brashness of the varied and incandescent media culture which surrounds us. This can happen, however, only if the library profession can make a quantum jump in its goals and in its abilities.

Chapters 1 and 2 describe the setting in the belief that the environment and conscious and unconscious assumptions establish both the opportunities and boundaries within which the concept of the Hampshire Library Center will either prosper or wither away.

It is important to note and repeat that by the very act of designing and constructing a building, and by making decisions on systems and operations, we limit future options. In a way the first two chapters deal rhetorically with ideals and goals. The remainder of the book is concerned with decisions about the Library which have compromised those goals. This is an overstatement, of course, for one of the constraints on decision-making was that, wherever possible, decisions should be made that will leave as many options open in the future as are feasible, economical and practical. This is not mere procrastination (although an element of this may exist) but a realistic estimate of the present state (or nonstate) of library thinking. It is also a reflection of both changing technologies and changing patterns of liberal education.

The background and program of Hampshire College are described in Chapter 1, an attempt to establish the environment, the setting for the remainder of the book. On the College itself there are three principal statements and this chapter is extracted from them.

> S. McCune, C. L. Barber, D. Sheehan, and S. M. Stoke. *The New College Plan: A Proposal for a Major Departure in Higher Education.* Amherst, Mass., The Four Colleges, 1958, reprinted 1965.
>
> F. Patterson, and C. R. Longsworth. *The Making of a College: Plans for a New Departure in Higher Education.* Cambridge, The M. I. T. Press, 1966. (Hampshire College Working Paper Number One.)
>
> *Hampshire College 1970: A Catalog for a New College.* Amherst, Mass., Hampshire College, 1970.

In essence the simple description of these three documents illustrates the 13-year history of the institution. The first, published in 1958, was principally the work of a committee of interested faculty members from the four area institutions: Amherst, Mount Holyoke, and Smith Colleges, and the University of Massachusetts. It is worth noting that, at that time, the college existed only on paper and had no name but "new college." The second document was written in 1966 by the President and Vice-President of Hampshire College. By this time the institution was incorporated and had a name, planning money, land, and a president and vice-president. The third document, a handsomely printed and profusely illustrated publication, was a collective effort, the work of some 30 Hampshire College officials and faculty members, but the College still lacked a most important ingredient—students. By 1970 the College also had a motto—*Non Satis Scire*—To Know Is Not Enough. The key words in each of the document titles also illustrate the formalization of an idea: 1958—"A Proposal"; 1966—"Plans"; 1970—"A Catalog."

In Chapter 2 we discuss the restructuring necessary if the academic library is to survive as a viable and vital part of the educational process. It draws together the various strands which must be interwoven to define the library of the future: the tradition of print, the culture of communication technology, the impact of display, and changing student cultures and learning patterns. This chapter is based on several already published papers and documents written during the course of the project.

R. S. Taylor. "Planning a College Library for the Seventies." *Educational Record*, **50** (4) 426–431 (Fall 1969).

————. "Toward the Design of a College Library." *Wilson Library Bulletin*, **43** (1) 44–51 (September 1968).

————. The Hampshire College Library. March 1969. (Hampshire College Planning Bulletin No. 3.)

These papers, and consequently the chapter itself, represent both a formalization of concepts and a process of self-education, of becoming. These two, almost antithetical, tendencies perform a sort of intricate dance throughout the book: the need to stabilize and formalize operational systems, and the need to innovate and therefore remain flexible.

Chapter 3 is about translation, the translation of the concept of the experimenting and extended library into bricks and mortar. What compromises were made? As we see it now, what mistakes were made? That is to say, if we could do it over again, what would we change? It is a complex building because it attempts to bring together the gamut of images, technologies, and services discussed in Chapter 2, within the setting of a specific college—Hampshire College.

The planning of a library for a new college does not stop with the design of a building. In fact, that is only the beginning. This is particularly true of an experimenting college such as Hampshire where a prime condition is the open-endedness of systems, curricula, and the whole educational process; for example, the Hampshire Library Center not only includes the conventional book and media library, but also a bookstore, a display gallery, and the Information Transfer (INTRAN) Center which implies computer support for education and film and television studios with support facilities. In addition, the building is connected by conduit to every student room, faculty office, and library reading space on the campus.

Chapters 4 through 6 discuss another form of translation—translation of ideas into operating systems. In truth one should say into almost operating systems, for we lacked that most important element of our environment—students. Also by 1970 we had certain financial constraints not foreseen in 1967. It is necessary to register this difference here between what is and what we hope will happen. Too many pieces, particularly on libraries and related communication systems, have confused future hopes with present realities. We hope the reader accepts this as fair warning and that, should he visit us, he will not be surprised or disappointed that all the ideas and systems described here are not operational. The process of change is much slower than one might wish—or suspect. Mere change in rhetoric, or in external form, does not, by some abracadabra, create a new social institution—a goal toward which this book is dedicated, even though it may be some ways down the road.

Originally Chapters 4 and 5 were reversed from the order in which they now appear. That is to say that "Systems and Processes" came before "Resources and Services." It suddenly became apparent that, if the sequential order of chapters meant anything, then a discussion of services should precede a chapter on processes. Why? Because it is the process of matching resources with users, both current and potential, which defines, limits, and sets systems. It is the user who defines systems, not the physical object. The very fact that we thought of these things in the other order indicates the perfidious and unconscious assumptions of the whole profession. Everyone—the librarian, the information scientist, the documentalist—is concerned with the handling of materials, rather than with the needs of people: their needs must match the packages. This is an insidious form of forcing ideas into straitjackets. This is exaggerated of course, but it serves to emphasize the problem, and, like all good and correct things, it is more easily said than done. It is in this context and with this spirit that Chapters 4, 5, and 6 are written.

Chapter 4, entitled "Resources and Public Services," describes our effort to change the posture of the library from facing inward to facing outward. The chapter is concerned with the combination of bookstore, reference and information services, display gallery, orientation activities, and the development of resources. At first glance to many this will appear as a disparate and nondescript group of activities. But there are several threads of similar color running through them. The major thread is that these activities are the points of contact, the interfaces between user and the artifacts—did someone once call them "mentifacts"?—of communication which the Hampshire Library will acquire, organize, store, lend, sell, display, and distribute electronically. It is shocking, for example, that with very few exceptions the academic library and the bookstore have never been combined. One lends ond one sells, but both serve the purpose of moving books (and other media) from shelves to people who want or need them. It is this kind of boxed-in thinking that the Hampshire Library Center—and other college libraries—must overcome.

Another among the public services we plan is the display gallery. Such a juxtaposition is not entirely new among libraries; however, in most colleges the gallery is the domain of the art department, which usually restricts its use. We intend to use the gallery to provide space and facilities for experimenting with all forms of expression in a public manner—to tempt, to challenge, to suggest, and to communicate. We expect the gallery to serve as a laboratory for students, where projects can be developed within the full gamut of gallery organization and three-dimensional communication. We envision the gallery alive with coordinated interdisciplinary exhibits, exploiting all the new media for the elaboration of specific concepts. We see the gallery as an important link between the Hampshire students and the community needs of cities and towns around us, particularly for the development of useful portable displays.

This chapter then discusses the many faces a library turns toward a user. Librarians concerned with this interface are middlemen between resources and users—negotiators, merchandisers, communicators, and generators of *both* questions and answers.

Chapter 5 is concerned with technical processes, with the design of systems to match the needs of users. This includes the acquisition, processing, organization, storage, and distribution of all materials; not only the materials normally processed by a conventional library such as books and periodicals, but also the much broader and more diffuse range of nonprint materials: discs, tapes, slides, video tapes, and films. A beginning is being made in controling these materials on a national scale. For the individual library, however, the open-ended questions are numerous and in some cases unknown. A candid discussion of the questions we asked and the answers we made, fluid though they may be, will be useful to anyone concerned with similar problems. The organization and storage of these materials, both physically and intellectually, pose analogous problems when we insist, as we did, that all media be accessed through similar means; that is, the public catalog and any computer-based system we can justifiably foresee. Decisions on these questions of storage, organization, and processing have an effect on, and vice versa are affected by, our needs for distribution of materials. We are not, for example, concerned only with the electronic distribution of images— print, sound, and visual—throughout the campus. Can this variety of constraints, requirements, and hopes be integrated into a workable and economic system? We do not know. Undoubtedly we have more questions than answers, but an open-ended discussion of those questions, together with our tentative answers amid the range of possible answers, is useful.

Chapter 6 deals principally with our concern (a) to make the library and its contents ubiquitous on the campus through electronic means, and (b) to help faculty define and develop teaching contexts within a range of media which can be creatively designed and used. To accomplish these ends requires energy, tact, imagination, and, in some cases, considerable monetary support. More than anything else, it requires an environment, an ongoing context, in which feedback and, concomitantly, evaluation can take place.

Hampshire College in 1970 will not have a full-blown communication system, although the skeleton of physical facilities exists for it. As in any other private college, however, we are acutely aware of both original and continuing costs inherent in any system of this size and complexity. Consequently a thorough analysis of the assumptions, questions, criteria, and costs will be of value to other institutions who find themselves at the point of decision. In a sense, we are concerned with the structure of a central nervous system for the College. We must be careful with this metaphor, however, because it implies flesh and blood, and the one thing electronic circuits lack is flesh and blood. They are substitutes, and very primitive ones at that, for the real thing. Once we concede that metaphor and fact are not the same we can begin to explore its potential. In spite of the rhetoric we really know very little about the real uses to which technology can be put. The eventual result of widespread use of educational technology will be subversive to traditional modes of teaching and learning. Because of its cost and pervasiveness it will force both teacher and student to examine rather closely what the processes and modes of education are supposed to accomplish. This will be the real revolution, not the use of technology merely to perpetuate traditional forms. The process will be painful and traumatic, and terribly uneconomic; but we cannot know what these systems and devices can do until we have tried and evaluated them. This is the dilemma of all new technology, indeed of change itself.

Chapter 7 is concerned with the role and impact of the Hampshire College Library Center within the context of four other academic libraries, and with other five-college communications activities. The discussion is concerned not only with the potential of library networks, but with those decisions a new library must make now so that it will not limit itself in the future. There are some rather fundamental and cherished notions about education and research which need to be examined when we ask the question—cooperation for what and for whom? It may be that such questions are not ours to answer, but rather that they exist in a larger context. But if the thesis of this book has validity, then we must ask these questions. It is not that an answer will necessarily be forthcoming, but it is important that the questions be asked and their context understood.

The last chapter in the book is entitled "Innovation: Implications and Alternatives."[2] Here we are concerned principally with the exploration of the hypothesis that "adopting new means in order to better accomplish old ends very often results in the substitution of new ends for old ones."[3] It is neither daring nor unconventional—in fact it's rather banal—to assert that libraries have changed, are changing, and will change. The point is that such assertions stop when this has been said, except for those flights of fancy that tell us what the library will be like some time in the future. And by the way, these imaginative flights closely resemble today's libraries, making such fancies rather suspect. Neither these assertions nor future fancies tell us anything about the road between "here" and "there."

This chapter then is an exploration of the kinds of questions we should ask and of the options open or closed to the profession as the institutional base changes. Our problem is not only one of defining the pertinent questions, but also of formulating the framework of those questions and the types of answers we can anticipate—what we know with reasonable assurance and what we do not know—because this is the only basis on which we can plan future libraries *and* present education.

There are obvious implications for librarianship and its professional education in this chapter, indeed in the whole book. The librarian must become a modern generalist, concerned and knowledgeable about print, sound, and image, about automation and computer technology, and about formal and informal communication systems. He must become much more sophisticated about the processes of communication, in contrast to the artifacts of communication. Library education does not yet reflect these qualities. This chapter explores and suggests possible alternatives.

REFERENCES

1. Bertram De Jouvenal, *The Art of Conjecture*. New York, Basic Books, 1967, 103.
2. In addition to Office of Education support, work on this topic was also supported by a grant from the Educational Facilities Laboratories.
3. E. G. Mesthene, How Technology Will Shape the Future, *Science*, 161:141 (July 12, 1968).

Chapter One

Educational Setting: Hampshire College

We do not expect that Hampshire College will be a fully defined institution in the months just ahead, or even in its early years. We are involved in "the making of a college," a new and re-newing institution, and the "making" will be a continuing process in which many, many people will play a part.

Hampshire College 1970, p. 3

As we said in the Introduction, this chapter consists principally of extracts from three documents.[1-3] Because of the uniqueness of Hampshire's vision of its relationship to the urban and rural communities of Western Massachusetts a fourth document should be added.[4]

BACKGROUND AND PHILOSOPHY OF HAMPSHIRE COLLEGE

Hampshire College is a new, independent, experimenting liberal arts college which opened for students in September 1970. It is intended specifically as a national pilot enterprise for innovation in American higher education. Hampshire was brought into being through the initiative of faculty and administrative leaders of four institutions in the Connecticut Valley of Massachusetts: Amherst, Mount Holyoke, and Smith Colleges, and the University of Massachusetts. It is the result of planning begun in 1958, and its establishment was approved by the Trustees of its four neighboring institutions. In 1965 the new college received a pledge of six million dollars from Harold F. Johnson, an Amherst alumnus, and was incorporated under a charter granted by the Commonwealth of Massachusetts. Exemption from federal income taxes as a charitable institution was granted in December 1965, and eligibility to borrow or receive grants-in-aid from the federal government was established in January 1967. In addition to Mr. Johnson's original gift, the most significant support has come from the Ford Foundation, which has given Hampshire a three million dollar grant on a two-for-one matching basis, the largest Ford Foundation grant ever given to a college, and the only one given to a college which at that time was not yet accepting students.

The College owns 555 acres of land in the towns of Amherst and Hadley, and is in the process of constructing a campus and buildings. The first academic building, the first residential and dining unit, and the Library Center were ready for the first class in September 1970. The architects are Hugh Stubbins and Associates and Ashley/Myer/Smith. Sasaki, Dawson, DeMay Associates, Inc., are the master planners, and Pietro Belluschi is architectural consultant.

Hampshire plans to have a student body of approximately 1500 by the middle of the 1970's, and may expand in time to 3600 students. The history and character of the early planning for Hampshire College are detailed in Working Paper Number One, *The Making of a College*, by Franklin Patterson and Charles R. Longsworth, and are brought up-to-date in the first Hampshire College catalog. These volumes, which elaborate the intentions of Hampshire College, are not considered static blueprints, but a thorough approximation of all aspects of the College's planning.

The Hampshire College program introduces a number of departures from conventional academic procedures; among them a three-School academic structure instead of the more fragmented departmental arrangement, a flexible time schedule of three sequential divisions in lieu of the usual four-year rule, and replacement of fixed graduation requirements based on prescribed course credits by a system of comprehensive examinations and independent research or creative projects. Time off campus is encouraged for travel, work periods, independent research, and community service.

Hampshire College will undertake an innovative role in several broad interrelated realms of higher education. The College seeks, through continuing experiment, consultation, and review, to redesign liberal education so that it

> . . . better serves the growth in every human dimension—intellectual, emotional, intuitive, sensuous—of those who comprise its community, and thus offers a more substantial ground for continuing self-education and self-expression;

. . . becomes a more effective intellectual and moral instrument of responsibility for the quality of life in America.

Hampshire also seeks new ways of securing the economic viability of the private liberal arts college in an era in which the demand for quality education is confronted with rapidly rising costs. And Hampshire intends to spur the further development of interinstitutional cooperation in education in the Connecticut River Valley of Western Massachusetts— thereby serving the interests both of educational vitality and sound economy. Hampshire hopes to demonstrate the advantages of a regional complex of closely cooperating public and private institutions.

Hampshire College is explicitly designed to serve as a source of innovation and demonstration for American undergraduate education. The implications of this fact are threefold. First, although determined to avoid the kind of "laboratory school" role that so often compromises the institution's primary responsibility for its own students, Hampshire intends to develop and conduct its programs with a careful eye to their transferability: many of the lessons learned should be applicable to other settings. Second, the College will develop new techniques for institutional self-evaluation, so that its experimenting character does not devolve into just one more narrow, rigid "experimental" orthodoxy. Third, through a continuing series of conferences, consultations, and publications, Hampshire has and will solicit other relevant experience and make widely known the results and review of its own efforts. The subtitle of *The Making of a College*—Working Paper Number One—implies a series of monographs dealing with different and successive aspects of the College's life as it unfolds.

No major departure, no new and consequential venture, is made without a context and a vision. The general context of Hampshire College is an experimental society in which the paces of change accelerate yearly. The particular context for Hampshire is a time of difficulty for undergraduate education when new possibilities are needed and being sought.

The first students of the College will live out a quarter or more of their lives in the morning of the twenty-first century. One cannot tell what living fully and well will come to mean for them and the students who come after them. We can at least guess that they may encounter more change, more options, more complex dilemmas, more possible joys, and more chance of surprise and wonder than men have known before. We have simultaneously given them the unthinkable in destructiveness, the unlimited in abundance, the chemistry to control reproduction and completely alter the social conditions and consequences of mating, the technology that will make work obsolete as man has known it, the transport and telecommunications that annihilate distance, and a flood of knowledge which would make the position of the sorcerer's apprentice seem high and dry. Living fully and well will only be defined as our descendants, now living and yet to come, wrestle with the reality they both encounter and create. The same is true of the content of the society they will experience. It will be up to them. The College cannot give them any handy new prescriptions that will do the trick.

This means that the College must help them acquire the tools with which to build lives and a society they consider worthy. The most continually experimental thing about Hampshire College will be its constant effort, in collaboration with its students, to discern what these tools are and how best they may come to fit one's hand. The success of Hampshire will be significantly affected by the quality of the contribution its students make to its reality. To this end the College will begin by seeking to help each student in every useful way

> to gain a greater understanding of the range and nature of the human condition—past, present, and possible future;
>
> to gain a greater sense of himself in a society whose meaningfulness and quality depend in significant degree on him;
>
> to gain a greater command of the uses of his intellect in order to educate and renew himself throughout life;
>
> to gain a greater feeling for the joy and tragedy that are inherent in life and its mirror, art, when both are actively embraced.

The realization of self, and engagement with the life of society, are hardly novel ends for education. Two things, however, make their restatement and renewed pursuit a major departure. The first is that these ends are only nominal ones in most of liberal education today, and the ways institutions have sought to follow them have too often become worn, irrelevant, hollow, and lacking in coherence. Second, although these ends have atrophied into nominality and emptiness in many college programs, the world around the college has changed in directions that cry out for their reassertion.

The problem of intellectual substance in liberal education, as Hampshire College defines it, is to determine as best we can what experience with inquiry, materials, and ideas will contribute most to understanding such central and difficult matters. The operating assumption is that, if students can get at ideas, principles of inquiry, and information of relevance to these things, they will have a better chance to comprehend life and live it well.

The campus culture needs to be considered instrumental to the ends of education. The distinctive objectives of the College involve conscious decisions which will affect its culture, and in doing so recognize that the student is a person, not simply a classroom fixture. The obligation seen by Hampshire College leadership is to spur the development of a strong institutional culture which will be distinctive not for the sake of distinctiveness, but for its relevance to Hampshire's view of liberal education. Hampshire aims to make the out-of-classroom life at the College vitally related to what occurs in the classroom, rather than separated from it.

Another Hampshire aim is to expect students, from the beginning, to share in shaping decisions about the College, and to take principal responsibility for making decisions about themselves as individuals. To say that students should share in the shaping of decisions is not to say that they can share in *making* all decisions.

Higher education is increasingly an instrument of the specialized, professionalized, technological social order. Even its operations, to say nothing of its curriculum, increasingly require the apparatus (computer scheduling, scientific management, cost accounting, etc.) of organizations in a technological society. Higher education is an instrument of the humanities, too; but given the student's consciousness of self as experience-validated and autonomous, and given the growing thrust of nihilism in both high and mass culture, the humanities do not provide the balance they once did. Many students, particularly those still mobile upward from modest circumstances and attending institutions of modest quality, will settle for the technocratic life without asking questions. Many others will settle for competent professionalism in their public lives, but be alienated and radically subjective in their private worlds. Others, and some of them the best, will disaffiliate themselves altogether, or as far as they can, from any norms at all, having come to feel that not only is the given social order absurd, but that indeed all social orders are.

Against this tendency the College pits itself to help students find acceptable meaning in both society and self. It will expect students to become strong enough to help shape the way society is to be, in politics, the arts, education, race relations, or any field. The culture of the College will be a principal educative element aiming to help students find a complementarity in self and society. The culture of Hampshire as a community lived and worked in by younger and older people, by students and faculty, by people occupying different roles and statuses, will be distinctive in important ways. In this quest Hampshire will be an experimenting college, a laboratory seeking ways the private, liberal arts college can be a more effective intellectual and moral force in a changing general culture.

SOME BASE POINTS OF HAMPSHIRE'S PLANNING

The Idea That Hampshire's Campus is the World. Without intended pretentiousness or melodrama, the curriculum of Hampshire aims at overcoming a dichotomy between "academic" and "real" life, which may seem irrelevant and unimportant to an older generation, but is very much a reality for many undergraduates.

The Idea of Academic Coordination with Related Colleges. In practice, Hampshire's academic program is planned to complement in useful ways the programs of the other Valley institutions (Amherst, Mount Holyoke, and Smith Colleges, and the University of Massachusetts), to offer their students certain distinctive opportunities at Hampshire, to avoid wasteful duplication of offerings, and to enable Hampshire students to pursue certain advanced or special studies on the other campuses.

The Idea of Academic Program Flexibility and Student Responsibility. Hampshire College's academic program will offer students work in a variety of basic, intermediate, and advanced studies. But an accumulation of any given combination of courses is neither compulsory nor equivalent to satisfactory completion of the collegiate phase of education. While preserving essential coherence and continuity, the academic program will provide students great freedom and equivalent responsibility in determining how they can make best use of what the College offers. Students will play a large role both in the design of their examinations and in the planning of their program of studies.

The Idea of the Student as Teacher. A principal concern of Hampshire's academic program is the active and practical preparation of students to teach *themselves*. Students will also be engaged in teaching *others* through leading discussion seminars, acting as assistants to faculty in classes, and serving as tutors and research associates.

The Idea of the Teacher as Teacher. The faculty at Hampshire, as at any college worth the name, will be more important than the organized curriculum. The real teacher is never an intellectual or moral cipher. Nor does he ignore the full complexity of his relationship to students who need to be helped toward independence. He must be an example of man thinking, man concerned, man acting.

The Idea of Technology and Learning. The College proposes to be bold in exploring the potential educational and economic advantages of new technologies for the support of learning. The College intends not only to use new technologies where it is sensible and economically possible to do so, but to introduce its students to their meaning and use as a part of liberal education in the present age. Among other specific things this means that Hampshire College is concerned through the instrumentality of its INTRAN (Information Transfer) Center and Library Center with open and closed circuit television and radio, films and tapes, recordings, computer-assisted instructional programs, simulation games, graphics displays, and facilities for language study.

The Idea of Successive Approximations. Curriculum development is a continued process. It is not possible to prescribe a fixed curriculum which will remain adequate for the demands liberal education must meet in a world of revolutionary change.

The Idea of Continuing Self-Study. Hampshire subscribes to the view that continual evaluation of all its work is essential. For an experimenting college to be what it claims to be, there must be provision for steady observation, assessment, and interpretation of the consequences of the enterprise.

The Idea of Maintaining an Innovative Climate. What starts as an experimenting college should continue to be one. An initial innovative stance can too easily soften into institutional stasis.

THE DIVISIONS

Students at Hampshire College will progress in their studies through three consecutive divisions: Basic Studies, School Studies, and Advanced Studies. The traditional designations for the four years of college— namely, the freshman, sophomore, junior, and senior years—will not be used. Each of these divisions marks a stage in the student's progress toward understanding and mastery of the subjects he chooses for study, and each of them has its own distinctive purposes and procedures.

Division I: Basic Studies. A major purpose of the first division is to introduce the student to the intentions and process of liberal education at Hampshire College, giving him limited but direct and intense experience with the use of the disciplines in all three of Hampshire's Schools. The lectures, seminars, and workshops of this division are not the customary introductory survey courses. Students come to close quarters with particular topics which bring into sharp focus the characteristic concerns and procedures of scholars and artists in diverse fields. Basic

Studies is designed not only to introduce the student to the variety of ways in which men may understand the world, but also to acquaint him with the skills of self-directed inquiry. Development of the desire and capacity for independent study constitutes a second major objective of all work in Division I.

Division II: School Studies. The principal aims of this division are to enable a student to explore in depth one or more disciplines within one of the three Schools or in the Program in Language and Communication, and to broaden his knowledge of the linkages among disciplines. The work of Division II will be carried out in accordance with a particular study plan or concentration designed by the student in consultation with his adviser and members of the faculty. The student's work in this division may be within the province of one School only, or he may choose to continue his studies in the other Schools as well through courses and projects related to his concentration or taken as free electives. Work in the second division will be increasingly independent, with more time allotted to individual projects, reading programs, and special outside studies.

Division III: Advanced Studies. In Division III the student will be occupied at least half of his time with an intensive single inquiry leading to the presentation of a completed thesis or project—perhaps a report on laboratory or field work experiments or a long essay, play, book of poems, film, or solution of a design problem. In addition he will involve himself in one or more integrative seminars, in which he will encounter a broad and complex topic requiring the application of several disciplines. The work of Division III will usually be completed in one year.

At the end of each school year a one-week reading period and a two-week examination period bring faculty and students together in a variety of ways for evaluation of the student's progress in his studies. The examinations assess the student's readiness for more advanced work and enable his instructors to determine the kinds of study he might best pursue to shore up his weaknesses and develop his strengths. A student's performance during this period determines his advance from one division to the next.

Each student participates throughout the year in the process of designing his examinations, formulating questions or problems which will permit him to demonstrate the subjects and skills he has mastered in his studies at Hampshire. Additional questions, also based on each student's individual study program, are submitted by the student's instructors and by College examination committees. Early in each school year the College will open an examination file for each student.

SCHOOLS AND PROGRAMS

The School of Natural Science and Mathematics

The program in natural science and mathematics at Hampshire bridges and combines the several disciplines in order to study most directly man in the context of his natural environment. To a large extent each student's picture of modern science will be one in which he sees himself as participant: perhaps as contributing to the growth of science itself or as playing an informed and responsible role in a culture served by science.

The planning for studies in science is characterized by modes of teaching which emphasize independent study, small groups, accommodation to the variety of backgrounds and interests, mixtures of disciplines, student participation in significant problems, conscious study of the methods of science, and connections to the social sciences, the humanities, and the arts. A program in human biology will be the first to mature in our curriculum of natural sciences. Foundations are also being laid for development in geography, history of science, and astronomy. At the same time studies in pure mathematics form an essential part of the School.

One of the most important challenges that Hampshire College has set for itself is to provide its advanced undergraduate science students the opportunity to concentrate on human ecological studies. To meet the challenge we must work with a set of disciplines, mainly but not exclusively within biology, which are normally separate. Geography will be a point of emphasis within the school, in order to create a disciplinary link between the natural and social sciences. In a similar way the study of history of science suggests itself as the most attractive way of joining ourselves to humanistic discipline.

Our plans for pure mathematics aim once again toward the support and enhancement of disciplines most appropriate to the purposes of the College. The best choices are among the newest and youngest fields of study, branches of mathematics accessible to young students, rich in connection to other disciplines, supplementary to mathematical activity in our sister institutions, and attractive to our faculty. There are several fields suitable in all such respects, covering a wide range of theory and application, and tending to concentrate in the foundations of mathematics: logic, set theory, and axiomatics.

With all of the physical sciences before us we have focused on astronomy as especially attractive for early development at Hampshire. There are strong local justifications for this. Our community holds one of the nation's largest and most productive departments of astronomy. Each of the four other institutions operates an observatory of its own, while sharing its staff within the only community-wide department so far formally organized. In recognition of Hampshire's interest in the field, it now calls itself the Five-College Department of Astronomy. The Department's research activities in radio astronomy are growing rapidly. A meter-wave radio telescope, ultimately to be one of the largest in the world, is proposed for a site near Amherst. A less parochial justification for our support of the discipline lies in the nature of astronomy itself. Especially in its pursuit of the radio observations, astronomy is a conspicuous example of those rapidly advancing sciences which are closest to the edge of knowledge and farthest from refinement in abstract terms.

Titles of a selection of First Division courses are as follows:

A Chemical Laboratory for the City of Holyoke
Men, Microbes, and Nutrition
The Nature of the Brain
Campus Design—Problem in Applied Ecology
Why Would Any Sane Person Be A Mathematician
Calculus
Light
Game Theory
Time
The Copernican Revolution

School of Social Sciences

It has been apparent for some time that the area of the social sciences has seen extraordinarily rapid growth, both in the emergence of disciplines and in an ever-increasing reliance on its scholars for advice in dealing with social problems.

Given an appropriate choice of subject much may be gained by devising opportunities for field work and the handling of primary source materials. One important resource lies at hand in the Connecticut River Valley. All of the social science disciplines may be applied, in one combination or another, to social and ecological topics or problems that have taken shape in the surrounding area. The commitment to field work reflects the desire to see a faculty of working scholars. It is expected that a wide variety of resources in social science will be used by the faculty, and hence by the students.

It is our conviction that the frequent dissociation of the student as a person from his "studies" has its analogy in the condition of citizens who are dissociated from their responsibilities for the communities in which they live and work.

We also acknowledge a responsibility for determining the role that Hampshire College must play in its own immediate community. We have an obligation to give as well as take. We expect to create service programs in cooperation with local urban and rural school systems, to provide new organizational devices for involvement of institutions of higher learning with the community, and to commit Hampshire to a public concern for the future development of this portion of the Connecticut River Valley.

The substantive framework that guides Hampshire in its planning for the School of Social Science specifies certain disciplines or interdisciplinary configurations which best serve the central intentions of the College.

Social Organization. Man's organization of his societal units is a constantly changing and evolving pattern despite the individual's investment of personal identity in the society which nurtured him. There is the struggle to redefine community and national identity which fosters patriotism on the one hand, and defeats "The Step to Man," as John Platt would have it, on the other.

Social Innovation. Changes in social organization are frequently initiated by technological or cultural innovations. The development of new techniques of forecasting such outcomes is desperately needed, and it involves the willingness to combine the insights of history, science, psychology, and mathematics as well as the more obviously relevant disciplines of sociology and anthropology.

Cross-Cultural Perspectives. The College intends to contribute to the Five-College offerings in area studies by concentrating on Caribbean Studies. Our aim is to leaven the program in Social Sciences with the opportunity to step entirely outside one's own culture so that it may be viewed from the partially acquired perspective of another.

Language and Communication. The opportunity to use and study a language other than one's own lays down the basis for subsequent curiosity about the role of language itself as a determinant of action and phenomenal experience. At present this interest is most salient in the literature of human development, with particular interest on subcultures in our society, as well as the continuing interest in cross-cultural differences.

Methodology.   The social sciences are slowly building a unique empirical methodology which is proving its value. Issues of measurement, sampling, projection, and systems analysis have shown rapid development in the last quarter century. They now deserve understanding and comprehension by anyone with an interest in social studies.

Titles of a selection of Social Science seminars in the First Division are the following:

Cultural Deprivation and Compensatory Education
The Development of the Political Self
Due Process of Law
Man, the Adventurer: A Psychological Study of Stress-Seeking Behavior
The Outsiders
Political Justice
Psychological Conceptions of Man
Constitutional Law: The First Amendment
Anthropological Perspectives on Death and Culture
The History of the Family
Economic Theories of Imperialism
The Economics of Pollution

School of Humanities and Arts

The program of the School of Humanities and Arts is undertaken out of a principal concern to seek new ways to bring into relationship feeling, thought, and action; to arrange a productive interplay between study and performance, inquiry and expression, relating these to the shape—and the susceptibility to reshaping—of our postindustrial environment. It will be concerned with the constituents of integrity, the growth of vocation, the uses and varieties of play.

There is a need for the humanities and arts to be reborn as a central part of undergraduate education, with conscious relevance to the actual and potential circumstances of man's emerging culture and environment. The need is to find radically creative ways to bring into relationship feeling, thought, and action about human experience, to move beyond the humanities defined principally as scholarly criticism or *explication de texte.* The curriculum should make possible a productive interplay between study and performance, inquiry and expression, sense and sensibility, relating these to the quality and conditions of life in postindustrial society.

There is no need to deride the traditional view that the role of humanities courses is to initiate the student into the intellectual and artistic legacy of his civilization. The insufficiency of that view lies in its relative passivity, its conception of the college as curator, and its susceptibility to the judgment that practice and performance in the arts are not quite legitimate academic enterprises. A more productive view of learning in the humanities and arts is that meaning may best be found through combining experience and feeling with rigorous inquiry and logical explication.

The arts within the humanities are treated most frequently as objects of analytical and verbal study, not as experiences for one to enter into as a deeply engaged witness or as a human being striving to create or perform. It is unproductive to view inquiry, experience, and expression in the humanities as naturally separable modes capable of confrontation but not integration. A more fully productive view is to conceive integration in terms of collaborative projects or courses developed by practicing artists and academic scholars, to encourage individual teachers to attempt to relate experience in practice of the arts with art history and criticism, to cast the critic's role as embracing sensibility as well as intellect, and to be actively inventive about ways in which the life of learning can fuse experiencing and knowing.

The substantive framework that guides Hampshire in its planning for the School of Humanities and Arts specifies certain disciplines or interdisciplinary configurations which best can serve the central intentions of the College.

Cultural History.   Social problems and their solutions are notoriously disrespectful of the departmental boundary lines of our colleges and universities. So is a man's experience. The study of cultural history has a paradigm in the study of an individual man. A man's experience, like a man's character, has unity; his actions and his utterances are intimately related one to another, and the diverse sides of his nature must be cross-referenced.

Literature.   If historians often come short by their failure to humanize the record of man's history, teachers of literature are apt to come short in failing to locate the work of art in history. Great works of literature transcend their place and time in appealing to a humanity in us which is perennial, and at the same time are impassioned statements of men in a situation. The student's study of the worlds of others, we believe, should go hand in hand with his attempts to order them in the service of his own experience, with emphasis on language as something to be used as well as read, on language as discipline, and on language as a means of exploring and shaping his experience and environment.

Popular Culture and the Mass Media.   The history of cultures includes social history as one of its parts, and social history when it is comprehensive includes the study of "popular culture." Such studies are not only necessary to our comprehension of the past, but they can be especially valuable in making the past available to the student's understanding.

Our students are increasingly aware of the disjunction between the norms and expectations of the schools and the complexity of the real world they inhabit. We have failed to provide them with critical vocabularies for discussing and measuring the wealth of images and impressions that rain daily from a hundred sources in their technological environment. But more than that, we have let students believe that popular music, films, the entertainments of commercial television, automobile design, the institutions of spectator sports, advertising, psychedelic art, and the popular press are not the concerns of serious men, or relevant to their education. By bringing the popular arts and the media of mass communication into the college curriculum, by providing for the study of their organization, content, and methods, and by employing diverse media in the process of instruction, Hampshire approaches the student on his own ground, recognizes the importance of what has in any case (and often in spite of educators) the greatest importance as a force in his education, and makes it possible for him to react to his environment with discrimination.

The Moving Icon: Film and Video.   Hampshire College's interest in film, television, and photography reflects at least three things. First, it indicates a consciousness of how pervasive—for better and for worse—are the visual media in American culture, and a corresponding sense of the need for unusual sensitivity to their educational utility, their cultural impact, and their susceptibility to judgment, improvement, and control. Second, the College's interest reflects a belief that a growing history of extraordinary artistic achievement, and the responsiveness of students to such visual forms, demands critical attention in the curriculum to film and photography as fine arts. Finally, and most strikingly, Hampshire's interest indicates a sense of the promise of these arts when employed by the students themselves—their power as instruments of personal and social insight.

Environmental Design and the Visual Arts.   Visual awareness, the engagement of the eye, will be indispensable in the long process ahead of ordering and humanizing the American landscape. We have become strangely blind to our physical surroundings. Means must be devised to lead students to come alive to the images which constitute their world, the appliances and plumbing, pots and pans, streets and highways, buildings and bridges in the midst of which they live; to understand that the seemingly immovable objects around them were at one time lines on paper, conceptions in the minds of men sometimes inspired, often short-sighted; to see that what was once done can be done again, or done differently; to understand that the background of physical surrounding and the foreground of human activity are profoundly and intimately dependent on one another; and to realize that to make America a place of livable neighborhoods they must study neighborhood, the nature and forms of community.

Philosophy. The making of man's environment demands not only the engaged eye, but a grasp of our moral and political purposes. A comprehensive vision of the better life which can justify our works and the capacity to hold it steadily in view requires the recovery of the philosopher's commitment to questions of worth, the ends of living. Philosophy will constitute a basic part of the program.

The Arts of Play. The performing arts together offer the richest means of exploring—through study and enactment—the significance of play in personal and cultural life. In dance, drama, and music the active imagination takes form and substance. By involving the student of dramatic literature, and of dance and music as history, in the real play of drama, dance, and music; by providing within the community a vessel for passion and pity to sensitive youth of just the sort who shows the most radical tendencies to disaffiliate from the society altogether, the arts of play aspire in our community to the sort of natural centrality they had in different times.

Hampshire's music program is closely allied with the other performing arts and with the College's interest in popular culture. Excellent music resources at the neighboring institutions allow Hampshire to develop special programs congruent with our wider interests and otherwise unavailable in the Valley. Ethnomusicology, for example, is a subject where one is confronted by the meaning of music in its cultural context and sees most vividly its intimate connections with dance and drama. American popular music, folk music, and jazz is a world neglected in music curricula, rich in significance for an understanding of our culture, to which students come with a wealth of experience and commitment. Another area, electronic music, is closely and creatively engaged with modern dance and is drawing increasing interest in the Valley among those interested in exploring the connections between art and technology. The Electronic Music Studio at Hampshire College will be used in cooperation with the music faculties and students of the five colleges.

Titles of a selection of First Division seminars in the Humanities and Arts are as follows:

Alternative Environmental Structures
American Black Autobiography
Dimensions of Consciousness
The Popular Arts in America
The Making and Understanding of Human Environment
The Fiction of Contemporary Spanish America
Heroes and Anti-Heroes
Film Workshop
Illusionistic Systems
Time-Space Laboratory
Utopias: Ideal and Experimental Communities in Theory and Practice

Program in Language and Communication

The explosive growth of knowledge in this century has been, in large part, a result of men's growing understanding of the instruments of inquiry. Concepts, axioms, methods, and terms have been brought to the foreground. Their various roles in the ordering of data and their explanatory power have been examined. This growing awareness of the nature and means of our knowledge has been manifest above all in the rapid growth of language studies—in philosophy, linguistics, mathematical logic, the development of the artificial languages of the computer, and the growth of information science.

Language study has become indispensable to the understanding of concepts which a student must now have if he is to comprehend the multiplying and shifting ways in which knowledge may be organized. The encouragement of this kind of overview, the leading of students to an awareness of the nature and variety of sign systems, has yet to become an explicit objective of the liberal arts college. Hampshire is making that objective explicit and is designing a curriculum which will serve it.

Hampshire College emphasizes the study of language by means of a special experimental program under the guidance of a Committee on Language and Communication. The program focuses on four particular types of study: computer science, logic, linguistics, and communication. A College-wide course on language and communication was offered the first year.

As linguists attempt to crack the code of natural language and as mathematicians and computer scientists work on the elaboration of artificial sign systems, the flow of ideas among them has steadily increased. Their union gives promise of a steady advance in the knowledge of the fundamental structures of communication and (more than that) a greater understanding of how the mind functions. Hampshire College intends to be present at this wedding and to encourage it through the design of an experimental program of studies directed specifically to the relationships between natural and artificial languages.

Language Studies

Foreign languages will be regarded at Hampshire College as tools useful for the study of a subject and as tools indispensable for the study of many subjects when explored deeply. Hampshire does not propose to restrict its definitions of language competence to a mastery of a literature or competence in philological study. Language skills are not less useful in the study of politics, science, the economy, popular culture, or any aspect of a foreign civilization. The College will not, accordingly, make the demonstration of competence in a foreign language a requirement for graduation; the study of a language will be entirely the option of the student.

One of the prominent features of the Hampshire language program is its intention to offer intensive language training in special summer programs on the Hampshire campus. These programs will be designed to serve Hampshire's own students, those who may be interested from the other four institutions, and students from elsewhere. In the beginning the Hampshire Summer Language Institutes will be a small experimental program. In time the College intends to develop on its campus a highly active, large-scale summer program

Caribbean Studies

As already mentioned the College plans a special program of studies focussing on the Caribbean area. This will serve several of Hampshire's purposes and those of its neighbors in the Five-College group. First, the Caribbean offers a diverse laboratory for field studies of the Third World. The various states and territories of the Caribbean face acute political, economic, and social problems as developing nations.

Second, many opportunities exist in the Caribbean for the study of science and the arts in ways not easily available in the United States. Third, offerings in Caribbean Studies will be a contribution to Black Studies programs in the Valley, offering comparative studies of slavery and its consequences for cultural survival and of the cultural and political reassertion of black peoples in the Caribbean and the United States during the past quarter century.

Law

Law is part of the Hampshire curriculum for three related reasons. Particularly in this country law has been the battleground for some of man's longest-playing tensions: between stability and change, between freedom and security, between history and logic, between justice as man conceives it ideally and justice as man is able to effectuate it. In addition there is the advantage noted by Professor Lon Fuller:

> In any actual process of decision, one has to take into account not simply those considerations that should control if one were "starting from scratch," but the factor of the vested interest of the going concern. Stated negatively, one has to ask whether the disruptions of upsetting an existing and familiar pattern of relations would not outweigh any theoretical gain from a reorganization of these relations.[5]

The third advantage to the study of law is that the problems faced are so voluminously and articulately documented. Opinions, briefs, court transcripts, statutes, legislative history: all are primary source material available in the public record. The main point, however, is that the law has dealt not only with decisions, but with the reasons for them.

The intention at Hampshire is not only to create courses explicitly devoted to law topics but also to introduce law material into a wide range of college concerns, such as the psychological bases of law, the legal method, the administration of justice, law, and social change.

THE HOUSE

To encourage individual participation and growth the College is organized into college-like communities called Houses, each of 250–300 students, and each with its own living, dining, and academic facilities. Each House has in residence a Master, a senior professor on the Hampshire faculty. The Master and his family are very much a part of House affairs, academic and otherwise, residing in a home that is an integral part of the House community.

It is intended that the House government have the power to tax and spend, and that the House unit of government be the means by which all members of the House are able to participate actively in the life of the College as a whole. Each House will create its own means of developing intellectual involvement, community service, and a stimulating social life.

FIVE COLLEGES

Together with students at the other four colleges, a Hampshire student may take courses at Amherst, Mount Holyoke, and Smith Colleges, and the University of Massachusetts, and students at these other institutions may take courses at Hampshire at no cost to the students. We expect that the typical Hampshire student may take an average of four courses at the other institutions in his college career. The cooperative development of specialized areas is another attribute of Five-College cooperation which enriches the offerings in the Valley. The most successful example of this is the Five-College Astronomy Department.

A variety of other cooperative activities exists. WFCR-FM, an educational radio station, and *The Massachusetts Review*, a distinguished literary journal, have Five-College support. The Hampshire Inter-Library Center is a joint depository for relatively obscure books and periodicals, providing a research collection which supplements more frequently used holdings of the separate libraries.

Very early in the planning of Hampshire College it became obvious that, in order to succeed, it would have to be an independent and equal partner, sharing in cooperative ventures with its institutions as they do with each other. Thus Hampshire has its own land, buildings, curriculum, faculty, and students, its own finances, and its own character. It shares with them the advantages of separate existence in a greater educational environment. All of the cooperative activity can be expected to increase dramatically in the near future.

Institutional planners at each campus now, as a matter of course, are beginning to bring to their deliberations the consideration of the impact of their plans on the other four institutions. Hampshire College, serving by design as one focus for Five-College planning, has had a catalytic effect on this process, helping cooperation in the Valley to become a meaningful reality.

HAMPSHIRE COLLEGE AS A CORPORATE CITIZEN

Hampshire College is in an area of great natural beauty which has been further enhanced by the creations of man. A perimeter line drawn to connect Amherst, Smith, Mount Holyoke Colleges, and the University of Massachusetts, Hampshire's four cooperating neighbors, traces a trapezoidal shape. Over the Mt. Holyoke range to the south, and through the corridors of the highways, a wave of urbanization is coming to crest. The trapezoid itself is more a part of megalopolis than it knows, and within 15 miles of Amherst rampant urbanization is in full view, with all of the trappings: exhaust smog, traffic jams, water pollution, water shortage, racial tension, slums, tract housing, industrial blight, and the rest—a dramatic contrast to bucolic Amherst and Hadley.

In response to these problems a major aim for Hampshire College, yet largely unrealized, is to demonstrate how a new and innovative college can create deeper, and more consequential forms of engagement with the larger community, can demonstrate the social, economic, and political feasibility of such engagement, and can lead in redefining the meaning of both "education" and "college." This connotes that in addition to the traditional scholarly activities the College must explore the possibilities of action, intervention, training, dissemination, study-analysis, and funding in a context which is larger than the campus or the local community. This also assumes that the College has a primary responsibility to itself and the society whence it is derived to contribute directly and substantially now to the resolution of those problems which concern all human beings: environmental pollution; senseless exploitation of natural resources; social, political, and economic injustice; the failure of education; alienation of people from people; and disjunction of people from goals and values.

The area in which Hampshire College is located is not yet urbanized. But it is incipiently urban. There is still a chance for Hampshire College, along with the local, state, and federal government, and other responsible institutions and agencies, to demonstrate that the usual disastrous consequences of urbanization can be anticipated and avoided. Acting as a catalyst in the process, Hampshire College has noted several areas of concern:

The problems of social, economic, and political justice

- Equal employment opportunity
- Fair housing
- Equal educational opportunity
- Responsive and representative government

The problems of maintaining and restoring the human environment

- Pollution—water, air, noise
- Aesthetic qualities
- Functional effectiveness

The problems of acting effectively

- Intellectual disinterest vs. passionate concern

- Private property vs. the public good
- Planning vs. spontaneity
- Directive action vs. participatory democracy

In attempting to play out this stated definition of the relationship to the community at large Hampshire College plans to form the Hampshire Valley Center, a nonprofit corporation which would initially be virtually synonymous with Hampshire College, but which would, by its separable identity, be open to participation by members of the community and by other colleges and universities in Western Massachusetts. The Center is intended to function as a service agency, research center, and an educational laboratory relating both to the community its serves and to the colleges which are its constituent members. As a service agency and research center it will identify service opportunities, organize the talent and the other resources required to analyze the opportunity, suggest a course or courses of action, encourage action, and then evaluate and report the results of the action program.

As an educational laboratory the Hampshire Valley Center will enable faculty and undergraduate students from member colleges to participate in the resolution of real problems and to experiment in ways to make most useful the kinds of field experience available through the Center. A Hampshire Valley Center Project must always hold a significant educational opportunity for undergraduate students. Otherwise relevance to the undergraduate college's central function is lost and the service-research-educational basis for the Center is incomplete. In addition, its activities must constantly nourish and be nourished by the on-campus academic program of Hampshire and the other participating colleges.

Description of a few of the projects currently underway and planned will serve to give an idea of the range and direction of the Valley Center.

Language Training for Policemen

Through the Model Cities Program, the City of Holyoke has been able to finance 14 two-hour sessions in Spanish language training for 12 policemen.

Acting as Liaison to Model Cities Holyoke

Since August of 1969 Hampshire's Director of Field Studies has spent up to one-half of his time consulting with the Model Cities Agency of the City of Holyoke. The purpose of these discussions has been to evolve a relationship between the agency and the College which would serve the educationad needs of the College program and provide service valuable to the Agency.

Bettering the Local Environment

The presence of four colleges and a university is clearly a significant factor in any efforts to direct change in the environment of the towns where they are located. Through the Valley Center the institutions should help to define and clarify issues. As taxpayers and employers they have reason to voice their views on questions of environmental matters and should make available information which is of value to all citizens of the community.

Early Identification of Gifted Disadvantaged Children

Under a grant from the Office of Economic Opportunity Hampshire College began, in 1969, a program to identify promising but disadvantaged fourth-grade students in the city of Holyoke, and to find ways to alter the motivation pattern for these students so that their aspiration for education would not be cut off in the manner now so customary in such neighborhoods.

The Nonpolluting College Campus

Hampshire College proposes to experiment in creating, through recycling, filtering, and reuse of materials and creative use of by-products, a campus that will contribute minimally to the earth's pollution. The study projects and active involvement of students and faculty in environmental problems on the Hampshire campus grow out of the College's commitment to develop as an environmental sanctuary.

Hampshire College will produce sewage, trash, smoke, garbage, noises, exhaust fumes, and other pollutants that were not there before. An important contribution to a program in environmental sciences will be made if the College can take steps to reduce the pollution its own existence creates. Some of these steps involve changes in human behavior; others will involve wholly new applications of existing techniques or the development of new ones. Particularly important will be an exploration of ways in which the raw materials the College uses can be recycled. For the natural science building this means a long-term effort to develop ways of reducing the level of pollutants which it produces. Some of these are relatively straightforward. Others involve the use of alternative types of equipment.

REFERENCES

1. S. McCune, C. L. Barber, D. Sheehan, and S. M. Stoke, *The New College Plan: A Proposal for a Major Departure in Higher Education.* Amherst, Mass., The Four Colleges, 1958.

2. F. Patterson and C. R. Longsworth, *The Making of a College: Plans for a New Departure in Higher Education.* Cambridge, M. I. T. Press, 1966 (Hampshire College Working Paper Number One).

3. *Hampshire College 1970: A Catalog for a New College*, Amherst, Mass., Hampshire College, 1970.

4. C. R. Longsworth, *Corporate Citizenship and Urban Problems.* Amherst, Mass., Hampshire College, May 1970 (Hampshire College Planning Bulletin).

5. Quoted in H. J. Berman, *On the Teaching of Law in the Liberal Arts Curriculum.* Brooklyn, Foundation, 1956, 38–39.

Chapter Two

The Extended and Experimenting Library

In *The Making of a College* the Library is described only briefly in the following fashion:

> The Library proper is far more than the ordinary conception of a library. It is the educative aorta of the College. It should be by far, in every sense, the major building on the campus. . . . It should not be monumental, but it must be beautiful and alive, with the promise of the excitement of learning, with the civilized pleasure of being with other people who are learning, and with being in the midst of treasures of intellect and culture. The Library will house the College's main collection of books and periodicals in the usual sense. The Library will aim from the beginning to acquire materials *selectively* to avoid unnecessary duplication with the other four colleges and to support the nature and purposes of Hampshire. The Library will also strive to be *financially economical* in its selection of materials, both in acquisition of an initial collection and in seeking the best possible alternatives to standard letterpress books that present technology can provide.[1]

In speaking of the Information Transfer Center (INTRAN), *The Making of a College* was both more explicit and more open-ended.

> The spirit of INTRAN at Hampshire will be experimental and innovative; from the beginning, however, it will be a generative service to faculty and students. . . . The College will deliberately develop its technological information-transfer capability as far and as fast as economic feasibility and the criteria of liberal education established in this paper will allow. . . . This means that Hampshire College will be concerned through the instrumentality of its INTRAN Center with: (a) Open-Circuit Television . . . (b) Open-Circuit Radio . . . (c) Closed-Circuit Television . . .

It is important to emphasize that the INTRAN Center may well become the central nervous system . . . for the whole College . . . INTRAN will engage in the following things:

Conducting applied research and development to maximize the effective use of new technologies for information transfer . . . with particular attention to increasing the resources and usefulness of the Library . . . it will be essential for the INTRAN Center to concentrate its attention on finding ways . . . to achieve computer utilization in storage and retrieval.

. . . Providing a workshop where students and faculty can learn to develop and construct graphic and oral materials for communication.

. . . With the Library director, developing and helping to maintain: collections of recorded materials; special equipment for access to such materials; central rooms for individual and group viewing and listening.

. . . Collaborating actively with the other four Connecticut Valley institutions in exploring the possibilities of information transfer, and developing them on an individual basis.[2]

The differences between the Library and the INTRAN Center illustrated in these excerpts are a recurring theme in the process of developing the Hampshire Library: the image of pedestrian conventionalism and traditionalism on one side, and the new sense of communication and media on the other. The tensions generated by this division provide the context for much of the hesitation the careful reader may find in this book. On one side the division will adversely affect any attempt to change the image of the conventional library. Conversely, the continuing split poses a challenge to redefine the library by exploring some rather basic questions about its usefulness both as a symbol and as a functioning organism. Whether the College, or indeed almost any academic institution, is prepared to ask and to explore these questions is a moot point. In a review of *The Making of a College* Patricia Knapp, in 1967, had the following to say about this early approach at Hampshire to the Library:

Librarians will be disappointed at the lack of attention given to the role of the library in a curriculum whose unifying theme is the process of inquiry, in a program which calls for a great deal of independent study. The library is described as "far more than the ordinary conception of a library . . . the educative aorta of the College." But there is nothing in the report to indicate how it will differ from the familiar old "heart of the college."

This reviewer is depressed to find the library playing such a small part in this first published "organized vision" of undergraduate education in a liberal arts college which will in all likelihood join the handful which carry the standard of excellence in the academic procession.[3]

In spite of this "disappointment" and "depression," the experimenting posture and concern with communications at Hampshire seemed to provide a context for the development of a new kind of institution, a successor to the traditional book library. Indeed the very act of relegating the library to a secondary or even tertiary role may be healthy, for it forces librarians to justify the economics, and even the existence, of the systems they design, supervise, and defend.

With this caveat in mind the approaches to the library and processes of information transfer, indeed to liberal arts education, expressed in *The Making of a College* imply that within the bounds of technological feasibility and costs Hampshire College offered fertile ground to study, analyze, and test new library configurations. The advantages of starting off *de novo* to restate "the function of undergraduate education in terms of positive relevance to our time" are obvious. To be sure, experimentation is hazardous. But, within the context of the communications revolution around us, it is probably even more hazardous to seek only cut-and-dried solutions. The problem of such an unstructured situation is well stated by Kenneth Boulding:

> It is a curious paradox that the information revolution . . . so far has really failed to produce the information which is necessary to evaluate it. We may perhaps drink deeper of this particular spring before we can even know what kind of water it is.[4]

Here we are met with what might be called the parallel-system problem. The library is both a symbol and a service. We are not sure how good this service is, but we suspect that it is neither as effective as it could be, nor does it take advantage of the full range of communication media and automated systems now available. How do we design a new library without sacrificing its assumed symbolism or without diluting the functions it now accomplishes? As an institution with the stated objective of continuing innovation, Hampshire College provided an opportunity to develop a broader communication organism, one which would be cognizant of the changes both in communication technology and in the processes and content of learning.

Changes in technology, curricular design, costs, types and mobility of students, and patterns of learning are taking place so fast that a critical look at the library is imperative. It is necessary to find new library configurations—of people, space, materials, and concepts—that will break the circle of increased cost and decreased effectiveness within the institution. In the 1970's librarians will be forced, by economics and technology, to examine rather closely what the library does and what it could do to be a productive participant in the learning process and in the community.

It would be convenient to erase from the collective mind everything known or imagined about a library—to forget "heart of the university" and similar metaphoric platitudes—and, instead, to think about activities concerned with communication and community on the campus, to think about the number of messages which link a campus together, to see if somehow this structure (not necessarily a physical structure) now called "The Library" could be rebuilt around the concept of communication.

At present the college library serves five purposes. It provides (a) direct support to undergraduate instruction; that is, course reading, reserve books, and recommended peripheral reading; (b) support for independent student honors work, ranging from the term paper to the senior thesis, which may require resources sufficient for a master's program; (c) support, in many cases minimal, for faculty and graduate research; (d) space where students may study their own materials, or meet a date; and (e) a context for browsing in the literature in the expectation that, by osmosis, students will absorb the great thinking and creations of western culture.

The first three purposes are basically warehousing and materials handling functions. The fourth is concerned with square footage, so that a specific percentage of the student body can find a place to sit. These functions cannot be dismissed. They may be trivial, however.

As a result of the concern with books and people as physical objects, libraries have become static institutions, involved with the techniques of warehousing, materials handling, and seating. This is borne out by studies of the National Advisory Commission on Libraries:

> . . . Knapp indicates that 90 percent of circulation at a small Kansas college library is course-stimulated. Knapp also found that one-fourth of the courses offered by the college accounted for 90 percent of the total college library circulation. This means that a very small proportion of courses stimulated the use of most of the library's material. This coupled with the fact that over 80 percent of library use is motivated by class requirements, raises questions about the present role of libraries on college campuses.
>
> . . . the question might legitimately be asked whether or not the library really fulfills its classic role for the undergraduate public in the modern college setting.[5]

Whatever the reasons—and some are legitimate—the library has changed from a humanistic institution (which many mistakenly think it still is) to a supply depot concerned with inventory and control. This processing of packages called books also has blinded the colleges to the potentially more dynamic role the library could play as a major channel of communication and a major processor of knowledge, both factual and fanciful, in all media. This role implies a change of function as well as attitude by librarian, user, and administrator.

Modern technology and systems analysis can offer approaches to the solution of some of these problems, solutions which would enable libraries and librarians to turn their attention to those activities that are more important.

> The principal impact of technology on society is that it creates new alternatives, new possibilities that did not exist before. These are so many and so new that we must work hard to see them if we will see them at all. And we must do this work of seeing free from the constraints of past habit, and free also from the fears of the uncertain and unexpected that would, if we let them, make ostriches of us all.[6]

The fifth purpose of the college library—provision of a context for browsing—begins to hint at those important activities. Unless a conscious attempt is made to meld the library with the totality of community and institutional change, it will become an increasingly expensive and less effective appendage to the institution. The words *expensive, less effective,* and *appendage* are used purposely. Equally critical is the increasing competition the library will encounter not only for the attention of its users, but in the form of direct and personal services to users.

In order to shake loose some of our prejudices and to allow the possibility of fruitful analogs, it is worth looking at the library from several different points: size, systems, and communication. The idea of size—possibly endemic in western technological culture—is based on the assumption that the larger the library collection, the better. Sometimes we harbor the faint suspicion that quality may have nothing to do with quantity. This "cultural pathology of print" reflects the attitude that if something is written it must have value, and, therefore, must be saved. So we blithely go on adding—and not subtracting. Someone, somewhere, sometime, we say, will need this material. In the explosion of relevance of the last 50 years, with the growth of new methods of recording knowledge, and with the development of modern communications, this attitude is neither practicable, tolerable, nor economic.

The systems viewpoint is based on what might be called the grocery-store syndrome: physical objects and packages are handled, processed, massaged, stored, and loaned; and these are the only important matters. Such an approach is not necessarily bad if it is recognized as only a means, not an end. This is the key problem in a technological culture: how to use technology for basically humanistic ends. The modern systems approach does offer the opportunity to reduce repetitive library housekeeping functions that take so much time and energy. This assumes that the librarians really want to rid themselves of tedious routines and truly desire time for more critical activities—experimenting in the improvement of services, teaching and maybe even learning, developing media beyond the book, improving the art of communication, and developing a sense of community—*because this is what libraries are all about.*

The concept of communicating, the transfer of knowledge, is in the best tradition of librarianship, the humanistic tradition, to which we pay lip service but little else. If the medium is the message, as the prophet says, then the library might be looked on as the totality of all media and communication. It was suggested earlier that we try to erase from our minds everything we know or imagine about a library, to see if the library could be rebuilt within the context of the messages and communication on the campus. The problem here may well be with words and their associations. Perhaps this institution should not be called "The Library." Yet the symbolism should not be thoughtlessly discarded. A library is, in a way, a memory—society's memory. It is like many of our memories: a jumble of images, unassimilated fact, fancy, and fears, viewed, in Daniel Bell's phrase, through a variety of conceptual prisms. We must rid ourselves of some of the clutter, which the physicist so appropriately calls "noise," so we can experience the poetry a little better. Somehow we must find the mixture of tradition and technological innovation that will allow the evolution of a new type of institution. Planning in this context is not merely concerned with the structure of a physical building or the redesign of routine solutions to routine problems but rather the more fundamental rethinking of what a library should be. We must not delude ourselves, however, that new combinations of words, of descriptions, will, by some form of magic, create a new and different institution. It is extraordinarily necessary here that we understand what it is we can do, what it is we are about. Basically we are trying to create the conceptual framework, and its imperfect reflection in reality, which will provide a headstart as libraries and related activities mature and change during the next few decades. Mere adaptation is not enough, as Elting Morison implies when he asks in rhetorical fashion:

> . . . Is adaptation by itself enough without some power to select, from possible changes, the most desirable changes to adapt to? To put it another way—in seeking merely to accommodate easily to whatever turns up in the way of new machinery or new ideas, will an adaptive society lose all meaning except survival and can it, in fact, survive very long by pursuing this sole objective.[7]

How do we get from "here" to "there"? This is an especially poignant question when we cannot describe very well what "there" looks like. But, as Bertrand de Jouvenal has pointed out, "the idea of change is so germane to our time that all forms seem destined to change and are therefore objects of conjecture."[8] It is not enough, however, to assert that this is an era of change and that libraries must also change. We may not know the rate of change—that is a significant ignorance—except to say that, historically speaking, it is accelerating.

In order to know something of the rate of change, we should know where we are and where we have been. The cultural surround of libraries has been humanistic and scholarly, and conservative by necessity. This has in the past century been overlain by two attitudes: technical and democratic. The technical approach (or technician when translated to people) grew out of Melvil Dewey's efforts in the 1870's and 1880's and gave the library, as a collection of books, a more efficient set of processes, systems, and organization. Present-day efforts to automate library routines are in this tradition. The democratic approach is a reflection of mid- and late-nineteenth century culture and basically grew from the growth and influence of the public library. The development of reference services and readers' advisory services follows this line. Today's efforts, reflecting the democratization of education and the incandescence of media culture, bear the seed for major alteration of the library's goals, functions, and organization. As major molders of the academic library, the faculty, if they give any real thought to it, see the library only in context of the traditional view that the library is for scholarly purposes and wears a sort of halo, standing for humanism because somehow books and reading are humanistic. To pursue the analogy librarians, with some noble exceptions, are in the technical tradition concerned more with objects that come in the back door than with people who may or may not come in the front door. These two elements make up the conventional, and usual, image of the library. Until the third element, the users, are truly incorporated into this picture, and are not merely suppliants, the library will remain but a sophisticated and efficient warehouse.

Libraries have developed as book- and print-oriented institutions, having as users those restricted to the literate middle class, just as higher education has been designed for those with middle-class values. This attitude is an anachronism in a world of high social mobility and diversified media. It seriously undermines the library's effectiveness. This is not to denigrate the book, but rather to provide a context within which the book can be better understood and enjoyed. With this sense of detachment from the hot linearity of print, the role of the book both in the learning process and as a cultural mediator can be better understood. Within the context of higher education as envisioned at Hampshire, it is our intent to explore and test to see if the library can become something more than a sophisticated warehouse. Indeed, it may be, that recognition of the library as an active participant in education and communication, in the sense discussed here, may be a step toward a deeper and more interactive learning process in the institution.

The shift from a book- and print-oriented to a communications- or media-oriented institution is one part of the extended library concept, an attempt to make the library more central to the total educational process and to obliterate the line between what happens in the library and what happens outside. Surrounding this shift is the recognition of the library and the book as crucial cultural symbols, creations of several millenia of civilized development. This symbolic library, based on the book and tempered by the emerging media, is a place in which a person can immerse himself in the totality of recorded knowledge seeking to locate himself as a student and human being. As Franklin Patterson has pointed out,

> . . . A college library, therefore, is not just books on shelves, a display of magazine covers, the paraphernalia of a study cubicle, drawers full of annotated three-by-five cards, and a computer terminal. A library is people—people reading, talking, seeing, thinking, listening; people dreaming and growing; people creating and acting. If the library misses this point, there is nothing left but a sophisticated warehouse. When this is realized, we are taking a small step forward.
>
> The college library must not only reflect our whole culture, it must also *be* this culture. A library is not shelves of books, it is a process; it is communication in print, and today, we must add, in sound and in image. For we are no longer print-bound, and the library neglects these new media at its peril.
>
> This is not mere faddism, for we *do* live in a sea of images, and perhaps more than at any time since the High Renaissance we are visually aware and, despite the plethora and corruption of images, more discriminating. And we are learning how to live with that flow and sequence of image called television and film. These, too, are part of the culture in which the library exists and they too must be considered if the library is to be part of the revolution in communications that is sweeping the world.
>
> To view the library as bounded by print would be to restrict its response to the civilization of which it is a part. A parallel to such restriction could be seen in many libraries of the fifteenth century, which would have nothing to do with the printed book, viewing it either as the work of the devil, or as a degenerate form of the codex, and therefore irrelevant or worse.[9]

True, libraries now handle different media such as films, records, tapes, and slides. These media, however, are generally seen only as additions to the central book collection—more objects to be processed and stored. New names for the library, especially in secondary education, such as "learning materials center" or "instructional materials center," imply a place to store objects rather than a place where dynamic processes of communication take place.

One of the challenges of Hampshire College is "to reconstruct the human purposes of education, so that young men and women can find acceptable meaning in a technological social order and acceptable order in subjective cultural freedom."[10] As a critical component of this reconstruction, the Hampshire Library seeks approaches to emphasize the book and to keep it from being buried in technological and electronic trivia and technique. At the same time, it is essential for librarians to realize that technology can do much to enhance, display, and present recorded experience in ways never before available. Technology must be used to support humanistic ends, not as an end in itself. This form of obvious statement—obvious to the point of fatuity—conceals the more basic dichotomy between disciplinary specialization as represented by the scholarly book and interdisciplinary tribalism as represented by the totality of media. Yet technology bears within itself the seed to strengthen individual specialization. Ithiel de Sola Pool has described this anomaly succinctly:

> We are at the beginning of an era in which the preferred communications devices need no longer have the quality of mass communications. Increasingly, communications devices will be adapted to individualized use by the consumer where and when he wants, on his own, without the cooperation of others; he will use machines as an extension of his own capabilities and personality, picking up whatever he wants.

> The printing press made text available to the millions, while the photographic and electrostatic copiers now found everywhere enable each reader among the millions to acquire just the pages he wants when he wants them at a cost hardly greater than printing.[11]

The actual patterns of use that emerge from this technology depend in large part on the total cultural and political context: value of individual versus mass culture and standards, publishing economics and the packaging of information, the status and regulation of copyright. In the meantime, the librarian must seek answers to his immediate problems within a future that is easily predictable.

During the next decade library collections and attitudes toward collecting will be influenced by many factors. Interdependence—national, regional, and local—will affect the size and subject content of the individual library. The growth of informal agreements among smaller libraries in a particular geographical area and among research libraries on a national or even international scale will increase the requirement that colleges and universities review their commitments to faculty specialization much more carefully than they have done in the past. The tracks left on library shelves by prestigious predecessors may strengthen institutional egos, but they serve neither education nor scholarship unless the institution or its neighbors continue the commitment to that particular specialty. It may be necessary—even desirable—to keep the college library at a fixed size.

This, however, will be mitigated by the development of union catalogs, regional agreements, and the use of teletypewriters and telefacsimile transmission. Union catalogs and teletypewriters are in fairly common use now, and their application will be enhanced by the growth of automation, remote computer access, and cooperative processing. Telefacsimile will, in the late 1970's, make possible entirely new configurations of cooperative sharing and lending, if the value placed on speed of service is high. It now takes about six minutes per page for transmission through the less expensive systems. Such systems have been tested between the Reno and Las Vegas campuses of the University of Nevada and the University of California at Davis, and among 14 libraries in New York State. In the former, the time for interlibrary lending of periodical articles and similar publications was reduced from a week and a half to three hours.[12] One may question whether this reduction in time is of value; such a value, however, is cultural and may not be within the determinants for library decision.

Another form of interdependence affecting collections is cooperative processing whereby a group of libraries arrange to order and process in a central location, thus reducing duplication of effort. This, together with the growth of commercial processing, will change the nature of the staff and will require different space planning and library organization. It will also provide a base for more thorough integration of scattered library collections and for consideration of subject specialization among the several cooperating libraries.

A second major influence on collections will be the developments in microform technology, particularly with reader-printers, and in micropublishing. Economics, rather than technology, is presently delaying the introduction of acceptable reader-printers on a large scale. The reader-printer is a necessity if microforms are to be widely used. Regular readers have been common for over 20 years, but users have always been plagued by their inconvenience and awkwardness. With the reader-printer the user can scan the film, find the page or pages that interest him, punch a button, and walk off with hard copy to be used, marked, and stored when and where he wants. As a return to the noncirculating library of the nineteenth century, it means that material will always be available to the user. This does not mean the end of the book, the codex form. It does mean that long rows of periodicals on library shelves can be replaced and that the user will be able to find that article which at present always seems unavailable. It also offers to publishers the potential of combining both microprint and standard print of a single monograph. The library would circulate the latter and retain the former for permanent reference. These are important considerations for, from several studies, it appears that a library user is able to obtain only 50 percent of the materials he needs and which the library catalog tells him is in the collection.[13]

A third influence on collections—the paperback book—is pervasive, but not yet fully exploited. If we wish to speak of revolutions in media, here is one already happening. There are several ways, and innumerable variations, by which libraries can take advantage of this revolution. Several college libraries are experimenting by giving paperbacks away or trading them. The college store has a definite role to play here and librarians should investigate the possible areas of cooperation between the two.[14] Can the paperback inventory of the bookstore be integrated with the library card catalog so the user will have the option of borrowing or buying? As processes are automated such a system might become feasible. Imaginative approaches with paperback books will have a profound effect on library collections, their use, staffing, and physical planning.

There is no doubt that automation of certain library functions will proceed at an increasing rate during the next decade. By 1975, when such routines as accounting, filing, ordering, and cataloging will have standard computer programs, individual libraries will not have to bear the expense of designing and starting a new system. A cautionary word here: one should not make the mistake of thinking that money will be saved by automation, although the expense will become considerably less as programs become standardized and as the profession benefits from experience. There will be other gains, however. More time can be spent in helping students and faculty. Some professional librarians with the qualifications can teach or tutor as appropriate and thus help to bring the library more into the academic mainstream. Automation will provide the opportunity to develop union catalogs on a local basis, providing the user with a quicker way of locating materials. The extremely tedious and boring tasks of bookkeeping, filing, writing overdue notices, and checking in dozens or even hundreds of periodicals daily can be eliminated. Human talents can be used for human ends.

Most important are the future benefits that user communities will gain by routine data processing today. From such a base experiments with truly interactive systems are underway. We can expect that by the late 1970's, it will not be unusual for someone to turn to a cathode-ray tube in his office or dormitory and dial the library to learn if a certain book is in the collection *and* if it is in circulation. Further, a person will be able, within some prescribed limits, to ask the library computer to make a subject search. In a primitive fashion the computer will ask him questions by which he will be able to qualify and specify his subject search. In some systems he will be presented with tables of contents, indexes from the backs of books, abstracts, and reviews. He will be able to browse. By 1980 such systems will not be unusual, and experimentation will be moving further into the linguistic analysis of text and toward an understanding of ambiguous questions.

What does this mean in planning? It means simply this: any library, large or small, planned for the 1970's should include the physical facilities for automation: space, ease of connection, and video and audio channels. More important, it must include intelligent and knowledgeable decisions by library staff: what kinds of systems are economically feasible? What transition phases are necessary? What can be done now to prepare for these innovations? What will be their effect on staff? on function? on building design?

Computers already exist in a few large libraries, but their activities are restricted almost entirely to the automation of conventional library operations. Like the library, computer centers provide a campuswide service. They borrow library terminology. They have a tape library and a program library, library routines and program documentation, serial storage and syntax and sentences and stacks. More important than these superficial resemblances is the similarity of function: both are information processors and problem solvers. The library, of course, is far more adaptable to human needs, but far less specific in the kinds of things it can do. With the advent of third generation, time-sharing computers, however, the computing center becomes less a physical location than a central store to which anyone can have access from a remote location at anytime. This is an important difference. After libraries move, however, through the initial stages of routine data processing during the next decade, they will be in a position to do entirely new things and to respond better and more quickly to users. By 1980 libraries will be one of the major users of computer centers for routine inventory and control. They will be the major experimental users of computers in the practical application of linguistic analysis for the design of systems for browsing at a distance, in the development of networks among scattered campuses, and in the design of computer-assisted instruction.

Concerning the inclusion of nonbook media, many libraries, of course, already are servicing films, records, and tapes, but these are handled merely as additional packages, like books. If libraries are to maintain—or more properly to regain—their relevance, it will be necessary for library planners to include the totality of media in their thinking. Educational technology and the nonbook media are essential elements in the library's search for educationally relevant solutions to the problems of undergraduate education. We cannot safely predict what the library will be in 1975 or 1980, but we can prepare ourselves for change. These changes will not come as spectacular technological breakthroughs. Rather, they will come as experience, opportunity, and imagination allow experimentation with and analysis of innovative technology in the library and in the educational process. Library planners must consider the space, equipment, and staff necessary to adapt to change, as well as the opportunity to develop a posture of experimentation within the library and related communication systems and toward the learning process itself. The development of nonprint collections may cause some severe dislocations in library budgets and acquisition patterns. The use of video systems for remote scanning of images and even text will require a new look at the function of storage and collection. Change is not entirely dependent on finance. Rather, it depends more on establishing priorities, deciding what is trivial and what is important—in short, rethinking the library.

It is within this context that the Hampshire idea of the extended and experimenting college library has grown. *Extension* implies that the activities, operations, and collections must encompass more than those of the conventional book library, not as discrete clumps of materials or sets of unrelated activities, but rather as a continuum where print, sound, and image are merged. *Experimenting* implies that the library must adopt a continuing critical and innovative attitude toward both its internal processes and the interfaces with its publics.

Now knowledge is gained in any of three ways. First, by observing nature, experimenting, or testing under controls. Second, by asking someone else, presumably someone who knows more. Third, by consulting recorded knowledge, in whatever form it may be stored. The two last ways are similar except that the former deals with short-duration messages and the latter with long-duration messages. Traditionally, the library has served only long-duration messages.

The program envisaged for Hampshire College offers the chance for the library to effectively transmit knowledge in all three of these ways. For example, the idea of information-transfer experimentation centered in the library offers the opportunity to study and to experiment with the processes of communication, learning, and personal growth that take place in the library. The motto of Hampshire College—*Non Satis Scire,* To

Know Is Not Enough—provides a contextual framework for this approach to knowledge. It is through self-awareness of one's relationship to his surround that he goes beyond knowledge to understanding and wisdom.

This approach can help break down the barriers between the library and the community. As a subject for controlled experimentation and analytic observation, students and faculty will become aware not only of the problems facing libraries, but also, and more importantly, of themselves as learners and information-seekers. An effective method of learning is for both the student and the institution to learn together and to apply their findings jointly to an institution such as the library. In this sense the library itself serves as a subject of inquiry by becoming a living laboratory.

The second method of seeking information, that is, asking someone else, is a function of context. That is to say, the library becomes a place where "happenings" occur, where the community spends time because the library has vitality and meaning in life. The library communicates, which implies a centrality of purpose and function. Three major factors are relevant to such an interactive library.

1. Both college administration and faculty must share and believe in this image of the library. This requires, not mere lip service but financial, pedagogical, and intellectual support.

2. Imaginative generalists on the staff of the library must see themselves as administrators, teachers, learners, experimenters, and human beings.

3. Space allocated for the communication processes should be in the library.

The third method of gaining new knowledge, going to the record, implies, at minimum, the conventional book-oriented library. The extended library, however, should attempt not only to collect and make available, but also to exploit all storage channels and media such as (a) traditional print, including books, periodicals, and pamphlets; (b) microforms, including the ability to obtain hard copy if desired; (c) standard records and tapes—poetry, prose, music, speeches, drama, language; (d) slides and films, including single concept films; (e) open and closed circuit television; (f) television tapes of lectures, demonstrations, special subjects; (g) the computer program library, and remote access to programs and data files available in other locations and to programs for computer-assisted instruction. Some of these may be accessible from student rooms, from house libraries, and from classrooms or laboratories.

We do not yet know how to integrate these media into a cohesive and functional system. Nor do we know how to exploit the totality of these media in the context envisaged at Hampshire College. This lack of knowledge and consequent need to experiment and learn is part of the "redefinition of the purposes, structure, and operations of liberal education" expressed in *The Making of a College*. The Library Center has an important role to play in this learning process.

Earlier in this chapter the parallel system problem was briefly mentioned, and this has direct relevance to the translation of the rhetoric on the extended and experimenting library to an operating system. Much as these concepts have value for the posture of the library, it was necessary to plan an operating library for 1970. Regardless of what the future holds and of the desirability for a quantum jump in services and organization, we know the Library must serve the patterns of teaching and learning that a faculty will use in 1970. We live and work and learn in a real world. Therefore, the legitimate question becomes: given the validity of the extended library concept, what kinds of space and what range of operations should be planned in 1970 in order to support, rather than restrict, the development of this idea during the 1970's? It is worth emphasizing that the criteria enumerated and discussed below establish both the goals of the Library Center and the boundaries within which these goals will be pursued. It is worth recalling in this context the brief discussion at the beginning of this chapter on the early attempts at Hampshire to describe the Library.

1. The extended library should include, both physically and administratively, the following activities:
    (a) the conventional library including collections and systems for all media
    (b) a display gallery
    (c) a bookstore
    (d) the INTRAN Center, integrating educational technology and computer support to instruction and learning
    (e) duplication services
2. A major long-range goal is to integrate all of these activities in a functional type of organization. This is not possible at this time because people see themselves in specialized roles; for example, librarian, bookstore manager, instructional technologist, and so on.
3. Systems and procedures should be examined carefully to ascertain their usefulness and economic cost.
4. There are good book collections, totalling about 2.5 million volumes, at the four neighboring institutions. Hampshire's Library should not attempt to build research collections, except in highly limited and well-defined subjects of specific relevance to the College which supplement the holdings of the other four libraries.

5. The book collection should never exceed 150,000 volumes for approximately 1500 students. A more likely figure is 100,000.
6. Microforms should be used extensively for periodicals and serials.
7. Approximately 33 percent of the collection should be in nonprint media.
8. All materials in the collection should be accessible through one source, the Public Catalog.
9. A machine-readable base should exist for all items. If not in MARC format, the record should include an access point to available MARC records, both present and future.
10. The Library Center should participate—indeed should be a catalyst —in cooperative efforts among the five institutions relevant to communications, display, and library, information, and media networks.
11. The Library Center should develop specialized information centers in support of programs of specific concern to the College which will contribute to five-college efforts.
12. There should be an emphasis on orienting the total system toward the user:
    (a) use of commercial processing for all media (or cooperative processing if this becomes feasible),
    (b) make the library ubiquitous on the campus—by both electronic means and by personal presence,
    (c) students' participation in operational decisions and even in policy-making processes.
13. The Library Center (see No. 1) should adopt an open-ended and experimenting posture. All elements of the system should be open to scrutiny, with two principal goals in mind: economy of operation, and improvement in user services and instructional support.

These criteria, with all their possible nuances, have developed over the past several years as guides to building design, to beginning operations, and to eventual operations. They provide the context for much of the remainder of the book. We did not, in the beginning of the planning stage, realize all their implications—and we probably have not yet; for example the commitment (a) to collect in all media, and (b) to utilize outside processing, was premature. Standards for cataloging nonprint media are just aborning. In addition no commercial firms exist which can process nonbook media with the same economies available in the book processing operation. Another relationship is that our interest in the cooperative development of an educational television station for the five colleges has implications for the purchase of equipment (i.e., must be of broadcast quality) and for the design of studio and communications facilities. The simple string of words in these criteria, as we are well aware, has a complex interaction. Our hope is that they will provide us a framework within which an academic library can begin to respond dynamically rather than passively to its environment. Indeed, we have the temerity to hope that these criteria and their operational extensions will have an effect beyond the confines of the Hampshire campus.

REFERENCES

1. F. Patterson and C. R. Longsworth, *The Making of a College: Plans for a New Departure in Higher Education.* Cambridge, M. I. T. Press, 1966 (Hampshire College Working Paper Number One), 202–204.

2. *Ibid.,* 164–166, 206–207.

3. P. Knapp, Review of *The Making of a College, College & Research Libraries,* **28** (5):355 (September 1967).

4. Kenneth Boulding, Review of B. R. Seligman's *Most Notorious Victory, New York Times,* "Book Review Section" (January 1, 1967) 25.

5. Douglas M. Knight and E. Shepley Nourse, *Libraries at Large.* New York, Bowker, 1969.

6. Emmanuel Mesthene, "Values and Education" in *Cybernetics and Education: A Colloquium.* Cambridge, New England Education Data System, Spring 1968, 59.

7. Elting, Morison, *Men, Machines, and Modern Times.* Cambridge, M. I. T. Press, 1966, 219.

8. Bertrand De Jouvenal, *The Art of Conjecture.* New York, Basic Books, 1967, 153.

9. Franklin Patterson, The Library as Arbiter, *American Libraries,* **1** (3):254–255 (March 1970).

10. Patterson and Longsworth, *op. cit.,* 31.

11. Ithiel de Sola Pool, Social Trends, *International Science and Technology,* No. 76:87–88 (April 1968).

12. See, for example, William D. Scheiber and Ralph M. Shoffner, *Telefacsmilie in Libraries,* University of California, Institute of Library Research, February 1968; and Nelson Associates, *The New York State Library's Pilot Program in the Facsimile Transmission of Library Materials, A Summary Report,* June 1968.

13. Richard W. Trueswell, A Quantitative Measure of User Circulation Requirements. . . , *American Documentation,* **16** (1):20–25 (January 1965).

14. W. N. Locke, Selling Books in Libraries, *College & Research Libraries,* **30** (1):39–44 (January 1969).

Chapter Three

Translation Into Bricks and Mortar

This chapter is about translation, the translation of ideas into bricks and mortar. It is about growing and learning, for we learned with the building, in some cases early enough, in others not. At the same time we were developing and refining some of the conceptual framework discussed in Chapter 2. This also provided input to the building process. It should be realized—and this is critical—that the concepts developed in Chapter 2, and the words describing them, did not suddenly appear on an inscribed tablet. They grew and took on flesh, together with the building. Although the ideas appeared in various documents since 1967, we are only beginning to understand all the implications of the amalgamation of various elements of the Library and the INTRAN Center.

In spite of all the admonitions there was no document which could be labeled "The Program for the Hampshire College Library." There were, however, four documents which had important input, in addition of course, to *The Making of a College:*

> *Definition, Scope, and Preliminary Program for the Library and Related Activities at Hampshire College,* by R. S. Taylor (February 8, 1967).
>
> *Space Program for the Library and Related Facilities,* by Taylor, Lieberfeld, and Heldman, Inc. (March 10, 1967).
>
> *Critique* of Taylor, Lieberfeld, and Heldman *Report,* by R. S. Taylor (March 11, 1967).
>
> *Functions and Spatial Relationships of the Audiovisual/INTRAN Elements of the Library Program,* by D. P. Ely (January 1, 1968).

There were numerous other inputs, both oral and written, to what might be called "the program." It is not the intention here to reproduce, were that possible, the program for the building. Rather, we wish to illustrate the process of translation (a) by isolating and describing the kinds of input information necessary in the building of a new library in a new college; and (b) by discussing a few key and critical problems which exist in the new building.

There are four principal kinds of input information necessary in the building design. This information is augmented, massaged, and bent (even crushed) in various ways by input from the architect.

Institutional data: budget, time scale, location on campus, general style of architecture.

Image: What kind of image should this building project and what kind of architectonic space should it enclose?

Functional relationships: What are the formal functions of the building? What are the relationships between these functions? Such relationships are determined principally by the flow of messages, people, materials, and equipment, both inside and outside the building.

Operational predictions: quantification of the movement of messages, people, materials, and equipment, and the processes, including storage or space requirements, that must be performed on them or planned for them.

There are weaknesses in all the possible combinations of answers to this set of four kinds of information. In inflationary periods, such as the late 1960's, budgets have a tendency to shrink in real economic terms and buildings reflect that shrinkage. The functions of a building, which attempts to house a growing and changing organization, are not only difficult to relate to one another, but because these relationships are not yet fully defined they are likely to become part of the politics of the campus. This has some dangers, discussed later, for the integrity of the building. Such excellent and encyclopedic library planning documents as Metcalf's *Planning Academic and Research Libraries*[1] consider only the traditional library. For the kind of library at Hampshire, and we suspect for many other institutions in the next decade, this is only the beginning. One of the very real difficulties in planning the Hampshire College Library Center was the paucity of quantified data on work loads and material flow in areas other than those of the traditional library.

INSTITUTIONAL DATA

At the time of early planning Hampshire College property covered about 435 acres, which by 1970 had grown to 555 acres in the towns of Amherst and Hadley. The land varies from gently rolling farmland and orchards to the steep slopes of the Holyoke Range, with a major road (Bay Road) dividing the farmland to the north from the hills to the south. The open land north of Bay Road, approximately 120 acres, was considered the prime developable areas for the college. There are no limitations imposed by the slope. With the exception of some individual specimen trees and 20 acres of apple orchards, the tree cover was not exceptional although most of it will be maintained. The scenic value and recreation potential of the land south of Bay Road is important to the College. The steepness and irregularity of the Holyoke Range form an important part of the visual background.

The relationship of the Library to the rest of the campus can be illustrated best by the schematic drawing[2] in Figure 3-1. The functional nature of the Library and the College Center was described in *The Making of a College* in the following fashion:

> The College Center is a coherent, connected complex which in various ways would house nearly all of the central facilities and central personnel of the College. Among other things, its underlying structural coherences are intended to accomplish economies in many kinds of operations. The Library and College Center complex will house the Library proper; the College's main administrative and service offices; the headquarters and central facilities (some conference rooms, laboratories, offices, studios, workshops, etc.) of the College's four principal Schools (the School of Language Studies, the School of Humanities and Arts, the School of Natural Sciences, and the School of Social Sciences); ground level shops; coffee shop and/or coffee houses; if possible, a below-grade auditorium for college-wide activities and performances; central heating, electrical, and other services for the whole complex; malls, terraces, walkways, and the like. This is asking a lot, but it is the kind of dense, variegated "urban" mix that Hampshire College's distinctive character requires at the heart of the campus.
>
> The Library will be physically the biggest construction of the College Center, and it will have to be capable of sizable expansion and modification, as educational needs change and as the College creates additional modules.[3]

Concerning the physical aspects of the Information Transfer (INTRAN) Center, *The Making of a College* had the following to say:

> The space requirements of the Center are, at this stage, difficult to specify. They are likely to be relatively small at the beginning but to require ready access to additional space for expansion. For this reason, it would be sensible to allot to INTRAN from the beginning more space than its immediate needs require. At the least, this would mean providing the Director with an office, secretarial space, space for at least three double offices, and an engineering room which from the beginning would be interconnected with the Library, the other Schools, and the Academic and residential facilities of the four Houses. In addition, it

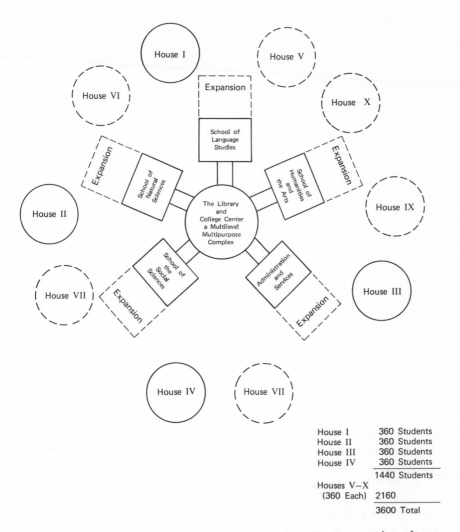

House I	360 Students
House II	360 Students
House III	360 Students
House IV	360 Students
	1440 Students
Houses V–X (360 Each)	2160
	3600 Total

Figure 3–1. This schematic framework shows a high-density complex of central functions surrounded by satellite residential-academic modules. They are not drawn either to design or scale and are oversimplified to test the concept of combining centralization and decentralization. Key: ——— immediate projection; — — — possible expansion.

would be desirable for INTRAN to have a small soundproofed television studio equipped both for two-camera, video tape recording and closed-circuit transmission. Further, as a reserve and for instructional uses in the immediate future, it would be desirable for INTRAN to have a convertible 75 capacity room useful for small, medium, and larger groups.[4]

The Making of a College also had the following space and cost estimates for the Library:[5]

Stack space	20,000 sq ft	10 vols/sq ft; 200,000 vols
Reading, browsing	10,000	500 spaces @ 20 sq ft per space
Faculty research offices	5,000	50 @ 100 sq ft
Services	6,000	20% of total stack and reading
Net	41,000 sq ft	
Gross	61,000 sq ft	
Cost at $33/sq ft		$2,029,5000

For the INTRAN Center an estimate of about 4,100 sq ft was made, including administrative areas, studio, engineering room, and computer center.[6] In the appendices of *The Making of a College* from which these estimates come the INTRAN Center was included in the School of Languages. Within the estimates for the College Center there are estimates for the Bookstore (3000 sq ft) and Gallery (3750 sq ft) both of which are part of the Library Center.

On capital outlay, besides buildings, the following relevant estimates were made:

Library books 100,000 @ $6	$600,000
Language Laboratory Equipment	100,000
Audio Visual, TV Equipment	250,000
Computer	100,000

The space and cost estimates as of the summer of 1966, when *The Making of a College* was written, can be summarized as shown in Figure 3-2.

	Space		Cost per sq ft	Total
	Net	Gross		
Library	41,000	61,500	$33	$2,029,500
INTRAN	2,750	4,100	35	143,500
Bookstore	2,000	3,000	32	96,000
Gallery	2,500	3,750	32	120,000
Total	48,250	72,350	—	$2,389,000

Figure 3-2. Library Space Cost Estimates, 1966.

IMAGE

Symbolic meaning is as much an ingredient of a library building as its qualities as an ambience, an amenity, or a communication net. The issue is not whether to include symbolism in library design, or to dispense with it, but rather what the symbolic intent of any building should be and what priority should be given to certain deliberate symbolic intentions as over against other considerations which govern the design solution.

It can be said that the very emphasis of contemporary library planners to depress what they refer to as the symbolism of past library design is itself an attitude toward architecture which is full of symbolic meaning. The point of view which says, for example, that the library can be located anywhere on the campus so long as it is conveniently situated in relation to users reflects the strong instrumental orientation which runs through the library profession today. The same orientation is expressed in the emphasis which library planners place on flexibility, on ventilation systems, on modular planning—all of which emphases indicate a conception of the library as a service facility and the librarian as a member of a service profession. Thus the new self-image and philosophy of the librarian is being symbolized in the same way that the rotunda of Low or the portico of Widener expressed a belief that the university was above all else a repository of knowledge, literally a cathedral of learning in whose glorious reading room the scholar prostrated himself to celebrate the humanistic tradition.

R. Gutman. *Library Architecture and People*[7]

Professor Gutman points to a most important self-image of libraries as a "service facility" and librarians as members of "a service profession." Such an image is strengthened by the oft-quoted admonition of Wheeler and Githens to "challenge all proposals to house a museum, art gallery, public auditorium, or any other non-library community activity in the library building."[8] This tone still echoes in most library buildings. It reflects a restricted interpretation of a library and an attitude which says "don't bother me with your paintings and films, your talking people, your music and pictures. What do they have to do with books anyway? And besides, Shhh. . ." This is an image, generated in the early decades of this century to overcome (unsuccessfully as it happened) the ascetic, genuflective, and restrictively possessive image of the library. It is not that a person should not be able to find a quiet comfortable place in which to read and to contemplate, but rather that this should not become the *only* criteria for use. We disagree with the degree of emphasis placed on the service function alone, for an image based on this appears to have several negative results. First, it makes the library a warehouse and a sort of service station: "Fill 'er up and be snappy about it." "One dollar's worth please. . . And clean the windshield too." Second, it separates the library profession from the rest of the campus and usually from the centers of activity. Third, the library becomes a mere reactive service. We wish to meld this service function with a mode of intensive interaction in which the library and the librarian not only react but initiate.

Mere juxtaposition and consideration of relationships between the various elements proposed for the building is not sufficient. Our purpose was to create a new image of the library, one in which the social functions of the architectonic space was one of the primary shapers. There are, of course, other inputs to image, equally if not more important: style of operation, personnel, and the acceptance by the academic community of a different kind of operation than they knew before. The self-conceived image of Hampshire College had to be reflected in the Library.

> Hampshire College is to be a laboratory for experimenting with ways the private liberal arts college can be a more effective intellectual and moral force in a changing culture. This role implies a redefinition of liberal education and depends upon an organized vision which can guide the process of redefinition.[9]

There are a number of criteria which help create the image of the library within this context. In all honesty, it should be understood that these criteria, at the time of building design in 1967–1968, were partially unstated rather than formalized instructions in the program. These criteria were in the process of "becoming" rather than "being," and that in itself is an important element not only in past design, but in future operations. The library is not only seeking a formalized identity, but an identity in a context of change which allows the institution itself to change.

Within this cautionary context, looking back now from the present vantage point to the early period of program definition, a number of general criteria can be stated that have to do with the image of the library and its reflection in the building.

1. The Library Center should portray the range of media from print to sound to image, without destroying the book as a crucial cultural symbol, the creation of several millenia of civilized development.
2. The Library Center should be communications-oriented rather than book object-oriented.
3. A range of environments for learning and communicating should exist within the building. Socializing among students, faculty, and staff is an important element in such environments.

4. The Library Center as a process should be ubiquitous on the campus, and the building should therefore give a sense of continuity and outward thrust on the campus, not only a sense of openness, but of opening up.
5. Control, in the conventional sense, should exist in the building but must be unobtrusive.
6. The design and structure should be as flexible and open as possible so as not to eliminate future options.
7. The Library Center should be able to merchandize itself and its "wares," and to compete for the attention of the campus community.

FUNCTIONAL RELATIONSHIPS

Naturally one of the basic inputs to building planning is the relationship of various functions. Any organization has a whole range of overlapping circles of relationships. Libraries are no exception. For building planning the question of relationship is directed toward two concerns. The first is the analysis of the movement of people, messages, and materials. The second is the concern for the organizational combinations necessary to expedite this flow and to match people with spaces, equipment, and materials.

PEOPLE. What are the traffic patterns, external to the building, which will orient it on the campus? What are the predictable internal traffic patterns of staff? of users? What are the relations of various staff functions to physical locations in the building? Where are points of contact between staff and public?

MATERIALS. At what points are materials (books, nonprint media, equipment, studio sets, gallery material, etc.) received; that is, where do they enter the building? How do they move in the building? What is the rate of flow? What are requirements for storage of materials and equipment? Are there special storage requirements, for example, for magnetic tape or film?

MESSAGES. We are primarily concerned here with the transmission and temporary storage of short-term messages necessary to perform internal administration and to assist the public. This category does not include books and other media. It should be noted that there are three message channels: oral (face-to-face), electronic, and written. Some of the written messages may be stored for future administrative purposes. What kind of messages flow between and among staff members? What is their rate of flow? If held for future consultation, what are their storage requirements? What kinds of messages move between staff and public? Are there special requirements? What kinds of equipment are necessary for the movement of messages? Do they have special requirements, for example, do they need to be close to a telephone jack? Are there noise problems, as for example with a teletype console for on-line computer access?

One of the major problems with libraries and similar kinds of communicating institutions, such as a bookstore or audiovisual center, is that the materials that are handled are also message carriers. Entirely aside from the prophet's word that the medium is the message, this is of course a peculiarity of all message-carrying objects such as books or films—the package and the message become intertwined. They change from being a physical object to be labeled, stored, and stamped, to being a message at various and unexpected points in the system. This dual nature of the objects we handle always will cause problems. This is not, however, the place to discuss this.

There is very little in any of the planning literature on the problem of relationships outside the traditional library. With little exception the literature deals with the book-oriented institution. Library planning literature is still written within the context of the Wheeler and Githens admonition quoted above. Metcalf's basic book[10] for academic library buildings has less than 10 pages (of 413 pages) on activities beyond those concerned with the traditional book.

Despite the reiterated desire for a different image, the sometimes covert assumptions behind such literature make it dangerous to use them in planning a totally integrated building. The danger lies not so much in the fact that the data and concepts are based on the traditional library, but more important, that in using the data—hard data, well thought out, thorough and useful in one context—one is apt to feel that he has similar data for other functions. A fair amount of formal data is beginning to be generated especially through the work of the Educational Facilities Laboratory and the Office of Education.[11] It is interesting to note, however, that most of the literature here relates to primary and secondary education or reflects their attitudes in higher education. This means basically that the intent and use of the collection is restricted to the teacher and that the student has very little free access to the material. This has implications for the design of space, for dissemination systems, and for equipment for the use of media. In speaking of college library planning, Ellsworth has perceptively pointed out that

> . . . Our assumptions about the amount of space needed are based on our past experience, which may or may not be valid for the future. Therefore, our buildings should be capable of major expansion or of

conversion to other uses. The days of a college library building, all four walls of which are monumental and indispensable to the aesthetic tone of the campus, are gone whether we are willing to admit it or not.

This is the theory we should follow and are following in many of our new college library buildings. Thus far no architect has been able to come up with the proper expression of a suitable skin for such a building, probably because our public isn't ready for this and still expects a library to look like a library as it used to be.[12]

The point we wish to make here is a subtle but critical one. Library planning literature reflects the highly formalized, indeed frozen, concept of what happens in book libraries. In comparison to the "softness" of the building data for other functions, the "hard data" for traditional libraries puts other functions and their relationships at what appears to be a disadvantage. One tends to find security in the definitions and positive reassurances represented in the solid and stolid row of library planning literature. The advantage is only temporary and, in fact, the days of that advantage may well be over. The hard data available to book library planners have a peculiar effect. They tend to freeze the portion of the building which has to do with conventional library functions and to loosen up those areas such as instructional technology and media-based galleries, where we cannot define the functions quite as positively. This makes the latter far more adaptable to technological change and functional alteration.

Early in the planning period, we considered a completely different type of organization for the Library Center—one based on function, cutting across all activities. This is in contrast to the usual departmental organization, in which there are a series of departments labelled book library (which in turn is divided into technical processes and public services), bookstore, display gallery, duplication center, computer center, and educational technology, and places them in one organization labeled "The Library Center" or "The Communications Center."

In order to consider the functional approach the reader must be willing to discard all previous notions about the library or about centers for educational technology or bookstores as separate little boxes. Instead, he must be willing to restructure his thinking within the context of formal messages and communications systems on the campus. This approach assumes a total integration of all communications-based activities, except formal classroom instruction, and attempts then to restructure this totality in newer and more functional ways. Similarity of function becomes paramount. We cite this approach at this point principally because it has profound implications for the design of space and for functional relationships. Hampshire's option for a departmental, rather than a functional, structure represents reality at this time rather than an ideal choice based on some future desirability. Because we discussed this at some length in the last chapter on the implications of innovation, the six functions we considered are listed here without explanation. These represent, of course, but one set of several possible functional alternatives.

- Distribution and Dissemination
- Information and Instruction
- Processing and Organization
- Educational Technology and Systems
- Institutional Research and Evaluation
- Management

Such an organizational arrangement is not, as some may suspect, an exercise in fatuity. It is an early attempt to provide a frame of reference for librarians and other communications-oriented professionals as they seek more effective organizational patterns. If such an organization is valid and acceptable, then it has some very real implications for the design of buildings, for it alters the entire pattern of relationships, of responsibilities, and of messages. It was our conclusion, however, that neither academia nor professionals in relevant activities were ready for such a drastic reorientation of internal structures. Something resembling this pattern, we predict, will come in the next two decades.

Consequently, for Hampshire College, we have thought and planned in terms of the combination of discrete departments, based on fairly standard definitions of responsibility. What is new is the act of combining these departments into a loose organization—the Library Center. As noted at the end of Chapter 2, these departments are

- the conventional library, including collections of all media, and their supporting systems
- the display gallery
- the bookstore
- the INTRAN Center, integrating educational technology and computing support to instruction and learning
- duplication services

The diagram in Figure 3-3 shows the general physical relationships among these five activities in highly schematic form. Basically the sketch illustrates the following points:

1. People should enter the building through or near the display gallery.
2. The Library Center and INTRAN Center, because of the need for security of collections and equipment, will require controlled access and exit.

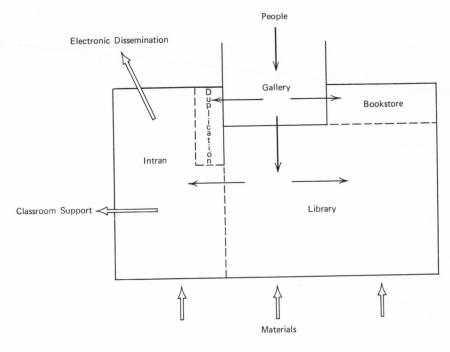

Figure 3–3. Relations among activities.

3. Users should have access to Bookstore and Duplication Services without going through possible controls for Library and INTRAN Center.
4. Materials for all elements in the Center will come through one receiving and shipping area.
5. The INTRAN Center will, at some time, disseminate materials electronically to other points on the campus and possibly beyond the campus.

Using the schematic of Figure 3-3 and expanding the section labelled the Library, we can diagrammatically represent its internal relationships as shown in Figure 3-4. Several points are worth noting in connection with this library flow diagram. It should be mentioned that the diagram makes no effort to indicate volume of traffic, but is merely an attempt to indicate the major flows of people and materials. It is also worth noting that not all of these elements and relationships were understood when the building was designed.

1. The Loan Desk would supervise and control the movement of re-

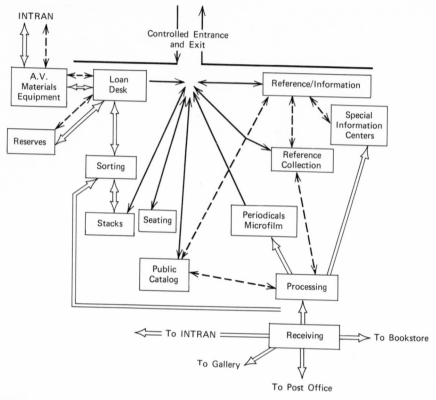

Figure 3-4. This shows internal library relations. Key:⟶ Users; --➤ Staff; ⟹ Materials.

serve books and materials, which would be a closed system; that is, shelved behind Loan Desk.

2. The Loan Desk would supervise and control the movement of audio-visual materials and related small equipment; that is, projectors, and tape recorders.

3. The shipping and receiving area would serve all elements in the building.

4. As much as possible certain operations, especially processing, would be performed outside the building, so that staff could spend maximum time and energy with faculty and students both inside and outside the building.

One of the relationships not fully understood at the time of building—indeed it is not fully understood now—was between the collection of audio-visual materials at the Loan Desk and the needs of INTRAN for materials for distribution electronically. A major problem in early design—and reflected in the building—was the ambiguity of the INTRAN operation. This problem was further compounded when it became apparent that the School of Humanities and Arts would mount a major program in film, photography, and graphics, and that probably the School would not have, in the beginning, a dedicated and permanent space for these operations. This, it must be emphasized, is not meant as criticism, but only to state that in the planning and design of a new and experimenting college there are unforeseen developments and opportunities that cannot be anticipated in the beginning. In fact, the very nature of an institution dedicated to innovation poses problems. If we waited for precise solutions to these, either no college would have been built, or the communications activities would have been completely frozen. As we said before, the conventional library suffers from too precise a definition, resulting in a fixing of functions and a loss of flexibility. Obviously, to some extent this must happen when a building is built. The very act of building induces limits and reduces options.

The general requirements resulting from the location of audio-visual services at the Loan Desk can be inferred from Figure 3-5. In addition,

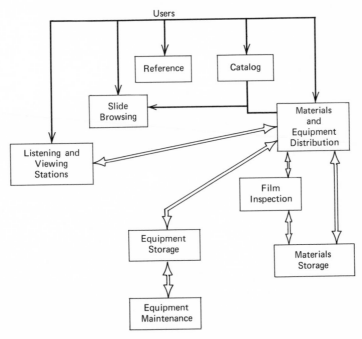

Figure 3–5. Audio-visual services provided at the loan desk. Key: ⟶ Users; ⟹ Materials and Equipment.

the intent to locate listening and viewing facilities near the Loan Desk also had several implications for planning.

1. Carrels related to this operation should be varied in function and design: open and closed; audio listening and film screening; single person and several persons.
2. Several options in listening modes should exist.

   (a) Signal controlled at the Loan Desk. This requires (*i*) a patch panel at Loan Desk, by means of which audio signals are sent to the listening stations; (*ii*) requisite turntables and tape players at Desk; (*iii*) conduit connections; (*iv*) earphones in open carrels and speakers in the closed carrels.

   (b) Material played at carrel under listener control. Material lent over Desk for use at stations. This can imply that (*i*) each station has the requisite equipment for reproducing the specific media; or (*ii*) the user may borrow the necessary equipment at the Desk.
3. Specific material and, if necessary, the requisite equipment should be lent to users for use anywhere on campus.
4. Storage facilities must provide for a variety of media packages: discs, tapes, films, slides, etc.
5. There should be no unique audio-visual catalog. The main informational access for all media, both print and nonprint, should be through the public catalog. Any special catalogs, such as film holdings, should be derived as products of a total machine-readable base.
6. If portable equipment is controlled from the Loan Desk, then maintenance nearby is necessary for small and quick repairs.

As implied earlier, there was confusion in the conception of the INTRAN operation and its functions. The division between a purely supporting activity, that is, restricted, and one that was open to the campus community was never made clear. The spaces necessary for production and related activities include

- duplication services
- graphic design
- photography, including film editing and darkroom
- storage for differing purposes
- studio and control
- experimental classroom and laboratory

In general, at the design stage, these spaces were thought of as areas dedicated to the production of instructional materials to meet the needs of specific courses and other campus functions. As we now realize this will not quite be the case. For example, this will be the only television and film studio on campus, certainly for some time to come. This could hardly be a restricted area, limited to professionals only, when one of the objectives of Hampshire College is to emphasize the creation and analysis of visual imagery.

It is worth noting, in the first rough design of the building, that the INTRAN operation was on the top floors of the building. We realized that, in all honesty, we could not predict the operational requirements or the traffic; so it was moved to the lower floors where change and alterations could be done with less disruption to other activities in the building.

Another area, representative of one of the major thrusts of the INTRAN Center, is Communications Central, concerned with the electronic distribution of messages. This area provides space for the campus telephone Centrex system, for the origination of audio and video signals to be distributed both on and off campus, for the receiving of signals from outside, and for their redistribution on campus. The requirements of this space are not many, but they are explicit.

1. Conduit connections should go from here to all points on campus determined to be suitable points of reception.
2. There must be crawl space; that is, elevated floor, for ease of wiring and maintenance.
3. Studio and experimental laboratory and classroom and originating stations should be directly connected to Communications Central.

The last major space requirement for the INTRAN operation is room for computing services. Early in our planning several things became apparent. First, Hampshire College would not acquire a large computer unless it was done jointly with other institutions. Consequently, any space planning for computing purposes should be based on such machines as the IBM 1130 or the PDP 8. Second, as a natural outgrowth of this, it was likely that Hampshire would, for educational purposes, be dependent on the time-sharing facilities of the University of Massachusetts, Dartmouth College, and/or other centers in New England.

The inputs to the building planning from this discussion of functional relationships are summarized below.

1. There will be five discrete departments in the Library Center: book/media library, bookstore, display gallery, INTRAN Center encompassing both television/film studio and computer operations, and duplication services.
2. Besides the bookstore and duplication services, where functions are fairly apparent, the range of activities of each of the other three can be briefly stated as follows:

(a) *Book/Media Library:* selection, processing, storage, and physical dissemination of all media; development of special information services

(b) *INTRAN Center:* production in a range of media of materials in support of instruction and other campus activities; selection, control, and maintenance of all relevant equipment anywhere on campus; service to classrooms and auditoria for projection, taping, video, and so on; design of campus communications systems; educational use of computers

(c) *Display Gallery:* public laboratory for students; supportive learning center in all media; exhibition space for traveling displays.

3. As much as possible, merging of overlapping functions of these departments should be encouraged.
4. The Library Center should be connected to locations across the entire campus.
5. There should be a common receiving and shipping section in the building.
6. Control of persons coming into and leaving the book/media library and the INTRAN Center is necessary.
7. Duplication services should exist both inside and outside the control.
8. Other activities of a communications nature in the building should be encouraged.

OPERATIONAL PREDICTIONS

To plan a building it is obviously necessary to go beyond mere statement of functions and their relationships. The size of its parts, indeed of the whole, must be specified. These are dependent on estimates of traffic in materials, messages, and people and the spaces necessary to accommodate them. To estimate is to predict. There are, of course, limits to the specificity of prediction, and this is particularly true in a new institution, whose primary purpose is to be open-ended and receptive to change. Without extensive discussion, for most of the points noted below are explored in more detail in later chapters, we list and comment briefly on the operational decisions and data which went into the building design, or which at least were considered early in the planning process.

Hampshire College is surrounded by four good academic libraries to which, under restricted circumstances, Hampshire students would have access. Hampshire faculty have use and borrowing privileges in all the libraries. There has been a history of interlibrary cooperation in the area based on the Hampshire Inter-Library Center (HILC) established in 1952. A daily messenger service links the libraries together for inter-library loans and the routing of HILC periodicals. The Hampshire College Library Center could make its greatest contribution to the five college libraries not with a large book collection, but by collecting, processing, making available, and possibly disseminating nonprint materials.

In 1966–1967 there were 19,000 students in the other four institutions. By 1970 this had grown to about 24,000 with all the increase from the University of Massachusetts. By 1975 it is anticipated that this will grow to nearly 32,000; the additions coming from the University of Massachusetts and Hampshire College. Because of its newness and the interest in Hampshire College, we could expect a fair amount of traffic from the other schools into the Bookstore, Gallery, Library, and INTRAN Center. It is worth noting that with the exception of the University of Massachusetts, Hampshire would have the only equipped film and television studio in the area.

Hampshire's growth rate is estimated as follows:

1970–1971	270 students	28 faculty
1971–1972	570 students	48 faculty
1972–1973	870 students	62 faculty
1973–1974	1220 students	76 faculty

Within the four institutions, there is a substantial and growing number of students who move from one campus to another to take courses. This is increasing rapidly from 782 students in 1967–1968 to an estimated 1200 in 1969–1970. Hampshire College will be part of this sharing of courses.

As much as possible processing of all materials for the collection would be contracted for outside the building. There would be a machine-readable base for all such materials. Microforms would be utlilized as is economically and practically feasible. The Gallery was not conceived of as an extensive acquisitive function. The bookstack capacity was estimated at 210,000 volumes (absolute), resulting in a working collection in the 150,000 to 170,000 range.

The book collection rate of growth was estimated in 1968, and, in the light of economic fact, its rate of growth was recomputed in 1970.

	1968 Estimates	1970 Recomputation
1970–1971	30,000	18,000
1971–1972	42,000	25,000
1972–1973	53,000	32,000
1973–1974	64,000	39,000
1974–1975	74,000	46,000

Approximately 50,000 nonprint items, (films, audio tapes, video tapes, discs, slides, and so on) should be planned for. In all likelihood the slide collection would grow extensively. In 1968 its predicted growth was not firm. Slide storage is not as much a problem of square-footage, however, as of equipment and processing. It is worth recalling here our earlier comment that there are no space estimates for the storage of non-print materials comparable to those for books.

About 340 seats should be provided in a variety of modes: reference, current periodicals, lounge, carrels, faculty studies, audio listening, film viewing, gallery, computer terminal. This is approximately 27 percent of the anticipated enrollment in 1975. This estimate was based on three assumptions.

- The College was a residential college and about 80 percent of the students would have single rooms.
- A residence house milieu would be created which would encourage study in student rooms.
- House libraries should provide seats for about 25 students in each of the four residence houses planned by 1975.

Some space in the building would be used for purposes other than those of the Library Center. The amount and type of space was unknown in 1968.

There were and still are a large number of unanswered questions. Harking back to the earlier discussion of the ambiguity of the INTRAN functions, part of the process was, and will be, to learn what kinds of questions to ask. This is not a signal of poor planning, it is the hallmark of planning in an era of rapid technological change. These questions have to do principally with (a) the variety of communication systems that may be used both in the building and throughout the campus; (b) the level and type of dissemination of nonprint media, computer configuration and use, and media production; and (c) the relationship between Library capabilities and the needs of special programs such as Summer Language Institutes and special field work planned in some of the neighboring cities.

BUILDING PLANS AND CRITIQUE

It is too bad! Always the old story! When a man has finished building his house, he finds that he has learnt unawares something which he ought absolutely to have known before he began to build. The external, fatal "Too late!" The melancholia of everything completed.

Friedrich Nietzsche, *Beyond Good and Evil,* 277

The floor plans in the following illustrations show our attempt at solutions to these criteria. They reflect the problems generated by the lack of hard data and hesitation in defining the relationships among the elements of this Library Center. These lacks, we hasten to add, are not peculiar to Hampshire alone, but result from the "softness" of the data and paucity of thinking on new library configurations. Taking a look at the total building, the following data are relevant.

Total floor space:	62,276 sq ft (includes 2344 sq ft on roof)
Total cost:	$2,494,000, including site work, architectural fees, millwork, carpeting, and stacks
Exterior:	brick veneer with exposed structural concrete
Architects:	Hugh Stubbins and Associates, Inc. Cambridge, Massachusetts
Contractor:	Fontaine Bros. Springfield, Massachusetts
Five Floors:	Basement, ground, first or main, second, and third

THE THIRD FLOOR (13,604 sq ft) includes bookstacks for 105,000 volumes and carrel seating for 128 persons, including two typing rooms. All carrels on the perimeter have capabilities of conduit connection. The Kiva and lounge areas provide seating for approximately 45 additional persons. The Kiva is a bit of play. It is a series of steps in semicircular fashion, closed off from traffic in the corridor outside by a curved screen. It is carpeted but has no furniture, except 25 cushions, and is viewed as an informal lounge. It has a bubble plastic skylight in the center of the ceiling. The solid glass window to the south looks out on the Holyoke Range. (We are aware that the true Pueblo Kiva is underground, entered through the ceiling, and completely circular, and that its use is restricted to the male elders of the tribe. We have matched none of these requirements, but we still call it "The Kiva.")

THE SECOND FLOOR (9593 sq ft) includes bookstacks for 44,000 volumes and carrel seating for 52 persons. There are six private faculty studies and a microfilm viewing area for approximately 30,000 microforms with six reading stations. The carrels on the perimeter have capability of conduit connection. There are two group study rooms, for eight persons each. The periodical reading area has seating for 20 persons in a variety of styles and opens onto a small porch over the main entrance, under the third floor visor. The Special Collections Room has about 540 feet of shelving and work space for three persons. It has separate environmental controls. The gallery at the basement level extends upward to the ceiling of this floor, just outside the faculty studies, from

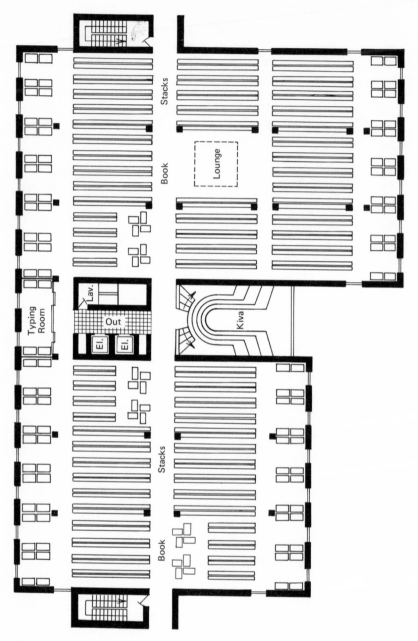

Hampshire College Library Center: Third Floor

70

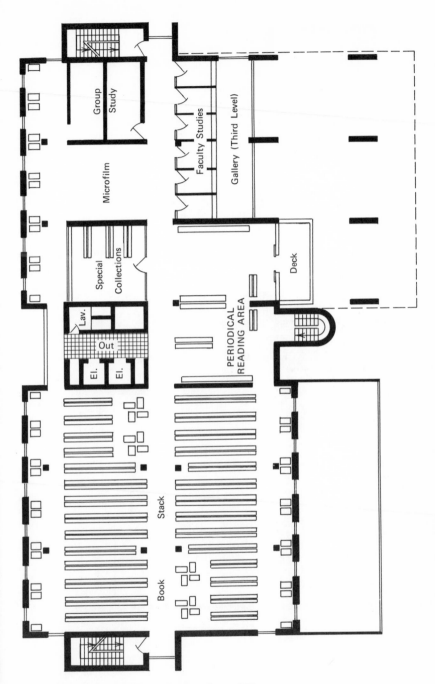

Hampshire College Library Center: Second Floor

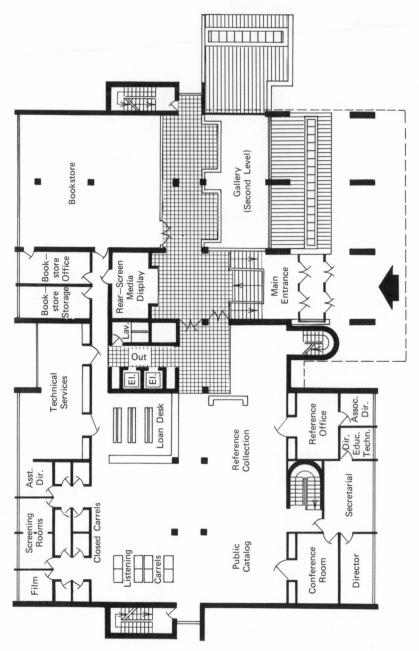

Hampshire College Library Center: First Floor

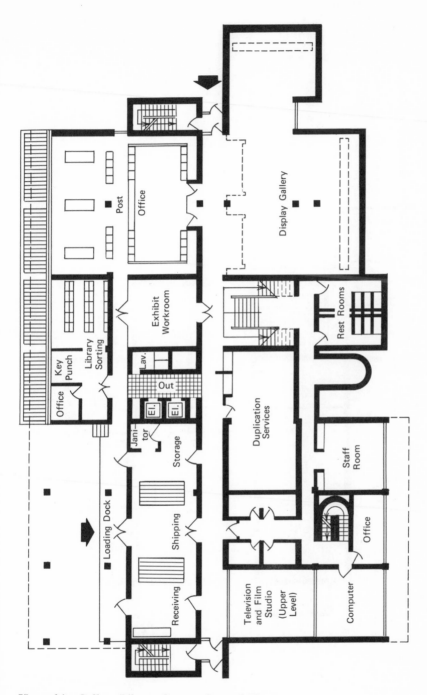

Hampshire College Library Center: Ground Floor

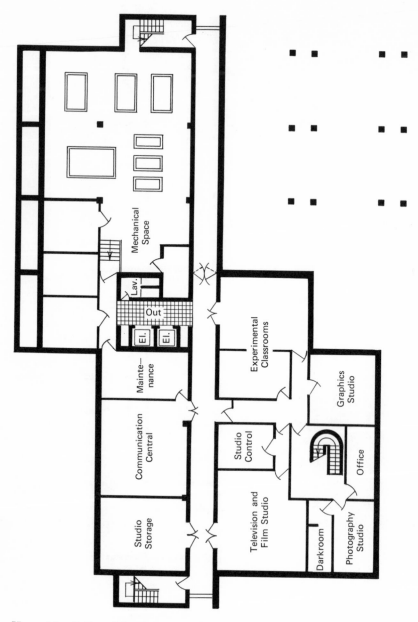

Hampshire College Library Center: Basement

which occupants can look through the upper reaches of the gallery at the Holyoke Hills.

THE FIRST OR MAIN FLOOR (13,273 sq ft) includes a wide range of activities and is intended to present a feeling of total media use from print to sound to image as well as the variety of options open to users as they enter the building. As one enters, at the split level between ground and first floors, he looks down into the gallery at the right. As he comes up a half-flight to the main floor, directly in front of him is a rear screen multimedia display. Off to his right is the bookstore and along the same corridor are balconies overlooking the gallery. To his left is the library. The bookstore sales space has some 1600 sq ft, plus 360 sq ft for office and storage.

On this floor in the library the user is also presented with a range of options in media: the reference collection, open and closed listening carrels, film screening rooms, nonprint media collections, slide browsing, and a small conference room. The reference area includes (a) a large reference and information desk directly opposite the entrance; (b) shelving for 3300 volumes, plus 200 index volumes; and (c) seating for 12 users. The public catalog units are designed to hold 500,000 cards and there are stand-up tables for eight persons. There is provision for a control desk at the exit from the library. A circular stairway at this point goes up to the Periodical area on the second floor, as does the stairway at the west end.

The Loan Desk includes reserve book shelving for 2400 volumes, as well as 210 linear feet for nonprint media shelving. The Loan Desk has provision for an automated system with conduit going to both the keypunching room and the computing center on the floor below. The Desk also has potential for patching to the 16 open and closed listening carrels nearby, and in addition is connected to Communications Central in the basement. The technical services area just behind the Loan Desk has 800 sq ft including office space for the Assistant Director for Technical Processing, and 378 linear feet of shelving. Near the Loan Desk are eight acoustic listening carrels with speakers and eight open carrels for headphone listening. There are also three film screening rooms. The administrative area in the southwest corner includes office space for the Director of the Library Center, the Director for Educational Technology, and the Associate Director for Media Resources and Services. There is secretarial space for two persons. The Reference Office has working space for three persons. The Conference Room is designed for 12–14 persons. The stairway here goes down and provides direct access to the Computing and Duplicating areas on the ground floor and to the Studio and INTRAN activities in the basement.

THE GROUND FLOOR (12,917 sq ft) also includes a wide variety of functions and activities. The most interesting is the Display Gallery (2,140 sq ft) the central portion of which rises three floors. There are one-and-a-half story alcoves off this central Gallery core. The Gallery opens onto the main lobby at this level and has a glass wall on the stairway side. There are a few conduit connections to Communications Central scattered in the floor. There is an Exhibition Workroom just down the corridor. Directly across the corridor from the Gallery is the campus Post Office (1680 sq ft). The Duplication Services (840 sq ft), with service desks both inside and outside the control, will in time provide a range of graphic duplication for the campus. The Sorting and Keypunch Area is a library receiving and holding space. The Loading Dock opens directly into a receiving and storage space for the whole building. The Computer space (380 sq ft) has raised flooring for wiring and maintenance. In this general area is an office for the Director of Computer Facilities and three small offices for programming. The adjacent Staff Room is not viewed as the private preserve of the library staff, but rather it will be used in open-house fashion for anyone who drops in—student, faculty, library staff.

THE BASEMENT LEVEL (10,545 sq ft) is divided into two parts: the mechanical space and the area devoted to INTRAN activities. The former is of no particular concern here. The INTRAN activities center around two principal areas: the Studio and the Communications Central. The Studio has 600 sq ft, of which approximately 70 percent is two stories high, and a control room. The Studio area also includes space for film editing, darkroom, graphics, and storage. Two rooms, labelled experimental classroom and experimental laboratory, provide a fair amount of flexibility and uncommitted space for future use. The Communications Central provides space for bringing signals into the campus from outside (e.g., telephone, television cable, or antennae reception) and distributing them as required. It also provides the space and equipment for initiating signals for campus distribution by cable. It is directly connected to the Studio and could therefore transmit live within whatever system we may have on the campus.

Looking back from the vantage point of the present, how well does the building match our criteria? That's not quite a fair question, of course, because at the time of design a few of the criteria discussed earlier were either unrealized or stated only in general terms. In 1970, as we begin to go into operation, we are aware that the building has some faults, stemming in part from this lack of formal criteria, criteria which in one sense were developed during the three-year project of the Office of Education reported here: to explore the concept of the extended and experimenting library. It also has many positive attributes, growing out of the exciting and challenging mission of the College and the mix of functions planned in the Library Center. Although experience cannot be transferred easily, especially when the institution is a new one such as Hampshire, candor in this discussion may assist librarians and campus planners in the future.

A brief summary of the planning history will help to isolate some of the points of major decision which had prime effect in the design process and on the eventual building. The Library Center was designed mostly in 1967 and early 1968. Three other buildings for the campus were also being designed at the same time and had a higher time-priority; that is, they had to be finished before the Library Center. They were the Academic Building, housing offices and classrooms, the Residence Houses for the first students, and the Dining Commons. Four more buildings were to follow. It must be remembered that an entire campus was in the process of being designed and built. In the summer of 1967 there were four members of the College administration and two secretaries. By the end of 1967 three more had joined the staff, and the farmhouse, which served as offices, was becoming crowded. Initial planning, discussions with the architects, and early sketching took place in late 1967. Plans were frozen early in the spring of 1968. Ground was broken in November 1968. Much of the planning and design was done in committee style with both the advantages and disadvantages inherent in such group decision. It also meant that responsibility for decision was blurred and ambiguous, and what was originally a fruitful and incredibly rich sort of interaction became difficult and tedious as campus-wide problems of faculty recruitment, student admissions, curriculum development, fund raising, and new buildings impinged on all our hours.

Early plans showed the INTRAN Center, including the distribution of audiovisual material, on the second and third floors. Also in these early plans the language study area including a language laboratory, was located in this area. The idea of a formal language laboratory was abandoned at about this time. We also realized that the location of INTRAN was a critical decision and one which would have an effect on the location of all other functions. After extensive discussion, the production facilities, electronic distribution, and computer activities of INTRAN were relocated on the basement and ground levels with a major stairway connecting it with the administrative area on the main floor. At this time it was also decided that audiovisual materials would be physically distributed through the Circulation Desk on the main floor. This move implied that the audiovisual catalog, storage, reference services, and listening and viewing stations would also be located on the main floor.

The reasons for this move are not only interesting but significant because they began to jell our inchoate ideas about the INTRAN Center. INTRAN represented the major element for which we had difficulty in predicting space and functional requirements over the next 10 years. It was felt that on the lower levels it would be easier, cheaper, and less disruptive to expand or alter space than on the upper floors. The INTRAN Center, as the major recipient and user of heavy equipment, could be serviced more easily on the lower levels. By breaking off the circulation and control of audiovisual materials and small equipment, better use could be made of space and personnel, and similar functions could be merged. The reference services could meet the public information requirements for such materials. The public catalog could reflect holdings in all media. The processing department could process materials in all media. Administrative functions for the entire Library Center could be merged. It was also felt that the new location would provide a better mixing of staff, "a necessity," as one memo stated, "if librarians are to become knowledgeable about nonprint media and their relations to the book." A most important result was that the main floor could reflect the image we wish to show—concern with all forms of communication, a continuum from print to sound to image.

This was an important step in the refinement of the INTRAN idea. It was by no means a complete solution. We still did not know just what it was that INTRAN was actually to do. Certainly, there was beautiful and necessary rhetoric, but the actual day-to-day functions and responsibilities of INTRAN were never very clear. Was it to be a service supportive of instruction, or was it itself to undertake instruction? A concomitant question: Were its spaces and equipment to be completely restricted to professional communications personnel, or were students to have access? Generally we opted for the latter; that is, student access, under controlled circumstances. A statement made in 1970 for the College handbook illustrates the result of this decision: "First priority for the use of the facilities will be given to activities supporting the academic and teaching program of the College, but there will be opportunity for a variety of personnel and informal projects. Since equipment of some sensitivity is involved, appropriate training will be required (and available) for those wishing to use the facility." This has to be this way and not entirely defined. Activities such as those included in the INTRAN operation represent the accelerating change in communications technology and are not only agents for change, but targets for change.

A second major decision in preliminary design was made early in

1968. In the initial sketches of the architects, the building was larger, and hence more costly, than we anticipated. In order to match Hampshire's budget and space constraints, it became apparent that the total space would have to be reduced. A number of alternatives were considered: eliminating the overhanging visor on the third floor, cutting off a whole series of bays at the west end, or lopping off one floor. Eventually we decided that instead of eliminating physical chunks, the building should be shrunk by making the basic bay or module smaller. Consequently, the bay size was reduced from 19.5 × 25 ft to 19.5 × 20 ft, and a few minor extensions on the building were eliminated.

This reduction in space had several results, not all beneficial. First, it did bring the bookstacks more in line with the planning and policy of collections. Less beneficial, however, was that it reduced office space and staff work space, principally on the main floor, with some claustrophobic results and some real staff crowding from the very beginning. The offices for the Director of Educational Technology and for the Associate Director for Media Resources and Services ended up small and cramped. It also reduced the space available to Technical Processes. These results will have a detrimental effect on staff and operations over the next several years. This decision came at a point in the design schedule too close in time to the deadline for finished drawings to allow the complete restructuring and replanning of the building, a process which should have been done at that time. We will find that we are trying to do too much on the main floor.

We cite this critical concern, and others to follow, in the spirit of Hampshire College, that one of its purposes is to state its plans, hopes, and ongoing evaluation as clearly and publicly as possible, both for its own benefit and as a contribution to the improvement of undergraduate education in the large. If this is not done candidly and openly, discussing failures as well as successes, then the contribution is small and meaningless. Library and campus planners will recognize, we are sure, the kind of incident described in the last paragraph, where a major decision cannot be given the time and consultation necessary because of pressures for completion within a schedule. It would have been better had we redesigned the building shell at this point, taking cognizance of both the smaller module and the emerging definition of the INTRAN operations.

There are several other physical concerns as we now plan for operation, concerns that could not be entirely foreseen. The first concerns the diversity of functions that exist in the structure, and the diversity of security requirements necessary. We knew in the beginning that certain spaces in the building would, of necessity, have to be used in the first operational years for purposes other than those for which they were designed. In contrast to the Wheeler and Githens admonition earlier in the chapter, we welcome the variety of activities. They do, however, bring in a different kind of traffic than was originally planned for.

The Gallery, again a space where function was not clearly defined early enough, now poses a security problem. A glance at the plans for the ground level will indicate that the Gallery is completely open on the side facing the Post Office, along a major traffic corridor with an outside exit. The balconies on the main floor, by the Bookstore, are open to the Gallery. This latter point has less implications for the physical security of the space, but has some effect on the acoustic and visual integrity of displays. Originally, our intent was that the Gallery would represent an educational space in the public sense, with high traffic. Little real thought was given to the kinds of exhibits that might be displayed, although we felt strongly that it should not be a traditional hanging gallery.

Several factors, too late to be considered in the basic design, affected our approach to the Gallery. It became apparent, by 1969, that this would be the only public gallery on the campus for at least the first four years. Second, we began to realize that the complete openness of the Gallery severely reduced our options for the kinds of displays we could mount. In addition, we began to develop ideas for multimedia displays in the Gallery. The openness to outside noise could seriously affect the aural impact of such shows. Student attendants in the Gallery area would be necessary in any case; but changes in the kinds of traffic and the access requirements of functions not originally planned for will pose 24-hour security problems. Some of these unforeseen functions are photographic and film instructional areas in the basement, and design studios and science laboratories on the third floor, with use demands all night and weekends. In addition, if the Bookstore becomes what we hope it will, it could bring heavy non-Hampshire traffic into the Library Center. In time we will adapt to these problems, but adaptation will mean some physical changes. Were we able to redesign the building (the luxury of *ex post facto* omniscience) we would have placed the Gallery within the controls of the book library and INTRAN Center. Though this solution would not have solved all the problems, it would have helped in the solution of some of them.

This concern with security is frequently used to chide librarians for their restrictive attitudes. Yet the custodial function of any group who has responsibility for the well-being of several hundred thousand dollars' worth of books, films, equipment, paintings, and *objets d'art* is obvious. This, however, is not the most important reason for security. The Hampshire Library Center presumably exists so that many people with diverse interests can have access to unique items in different formats, and to equipment for the creation or display of materials in a wide variety of media. This is the true custodial function of libraries. Some time in the future when images can be transmitted, displayed, and duplicated on demand, we will have eliminated many of these problems. That time is not yet here.

Another area of concern, and one inherent in the desire for flexibility and adaptability, is the need for access to a range of unforeseen communication and power facilities in a wide variety of locations. This has not been solved in the Hampshire Library Center. It represents a problem that will be of increasing concern in the design of public buildings for communications purposes in the future, and for which there is no economic and aesthetic solution at this time. The Hampshire Library Center is laced with conduits, with outlets where we do not want them, and no outlets where we need them. As we face operational systems in 1970, we realize that our options have been limited.

The tone of this critique has been, as it should be, critical. We could, like Pogo, say "We have met the enemy, and he is us." That statement is built on the tacit assumption that the building has many faults. It has not. On the contrary, the Library Center at Hampshire provides a wide variety of contexts for an exciting and effective departure in academic libraries. It will require some major physical changes over the next several years in order to make it an effective and useful building. The building, however, is but one component in this venture. As we now become operational, there are three additional factors in this equation called "success"—resources, systems, and style.

REFERENCES

1. Keyes Metcalf, *Planning Academic and Research Libraries.* New York, McGraw-Hill, 1965.

2. F. Patterson and C. R. Longsworth, *The Making of a College: Plans for a New Departure in Higher Education.* Cambridge, M. I. T. Press, 1966 (Hampshire College Working Paper Number One), 201.

3. *Ibid.,* 200–202.

4. *Ibid.,* 207.

5. *Ibid.,* 312.

6. *Ibid.,* 315.

7. Robert Gutman, *Library Architecture and People.* Rutgers University, Urban Studies Center, Built Environment Research Reports and Papers, No. 10, July 1968, 16–17.

8. Joseph L. Wheeler and Alfred M. Githens, *The American Public Library Building.* New York, Scribners, 1941, 17.

9. *Hampshire College 1970: A Catalog for a New College.* Amherst, Mass., Hampshire College, 1970, 10.

10. Metcalf, *op. cit.*

11. See for example *New Spaces for Learning,* revised 1966, Center for Architectural Research, Rensselaer Polytechnic Institute; *The Library Environment,* Chicago, American Library Association, 1965; C. W. H. Erickson, *Administering Instructional Media Programs,* New York, Macmillan, 1968; *Bricks and Mortarboard: A Report on College Planning and Building,* 1964, Educational Facilities Laboratories; R. T. Leyden and N. Balanoff, *Planning of Educational Media for a New Learning Center,* Columbia, Mo., Stephens College, 1963.

12. Ralph E. Ellsworth, *Planning the College and University Library Building.* Boulder, Col., Pruett Press, 1968, 17.

Chapter Four

Resources and Services

Although the title of this chapter is "Resources and Services," in the context of this book a preferred title could have been just "Resources." We felt obliged by the necessities of professional attitudes and the views of academia to add "and Services," a reflection of the warehouse syndrome applied by faculty and administrators and accepted by librarians. Resources are usually thought of only as "artifacts," that is, physical objects. As part of the redefinition of the college library we wish to think of resources in a human context: humanness in all its guises as reflected in the content of a book or a film, in the dynamism of a gallery exhibit, in the imaginative negotiation of a question in which a student suddenly realizes what it is to ask a question and seek an answer.

Resources are not just rows of books, drawers full of art slides, or shelves of records. Resources are also the conscious exploitation of these inanimate things to challenge, to suggest, to explicate, to guide—in short, to educate. This is what libraries are all about. As with all good and proper things compromise is required. Consequently in the sections of this chapter we discuss first the problems of defining and gathering a collection of physical objects, and then the various ways of presenting these objects to the campus communities.

COLLECTIONS

Early in our planning we had to come to some decision, or at least a direction, on the kind and size of collection, print and nonprint, Hampshire should have. The only guideline from *The Making of a College* was the following sentence:

> The Library will aim from the beginning to acquire materials selec-
> tively to avoid unnecessary duplication with the other four colleges and
> to support the nature and purposes of Hampshire.[1]

What constitutes a good undergraduate book collection when there are
over two million volumes within five miles which, with certain restrictions, would be accessible to Hampshire students? There is, of course,
a whole range of answers. One end of the spectrum was suggested by
Professor William A. Smith, Jr., of the Lehigh University Department
of Industrial Engineering in March 1968 at the Hampshire Conference
on Automation in the College Library.

> If we look at all the libraries in the area here, we would say that one
> extreme solution is that the whole traditional approach should be
> handled by the existing libraries. Hampshire's sole objective would be
> to send its students to, or to get images from these libraries for tradi-
> tional purposes. Then Hampshire College could innovate completely
> and be dependent on the other libraries for traditional services. It
> would also innovate to the degree and in a fashion so that it could
> give something to the other libraries that they do not now have. In
> other words don't look at each library independently, but look at all
> of them as a single system. And say now what Hampshire Library's
> role could be in this system. What could it innovate that would help
> the other libraries? How could they trade? In other words, put 100%
> of your money in innovation at Hampshire College. Otherwise you
> will have a very small area of innovation. And the only way you can
> avoid it is to give them in return some leverage on their problems.
> You are going to have to do some experimentation that will have a
> positive effect on their performance.[2]

The opposite end of the spectrum is complete autonomy in collecting, and obliviousness to surrounding libraries. This would mean that
Hampshire would build its collections with no regard to other libraries.
In the context of the admonition quoted above from *The Making of a
College*, this choice was excluded, an entirely justifiable exclusion, considering the four-college beginnings of Hampshire College. Generally we
believe that considerations of reality would place Hampshire's choices
somewhere between the two ends of the spectrum. Position on the spectrum, if it can be located at all, depends on several factors. It is interesting to note that, as in our discussion on building in the last chapter, the
book-based definition of the library continues to plague us. We must
constantly remind ourselves and the reader that we are discussing and
considering a media- and communications-oriented institution; and for
nonprint areas there are very few basic collection lists. Five-college cooperation, although not separately discussed here, is a thread running
through the discussions that follow.

Core Book Collections

Without doubt, the recent work stemming from the publication of *Books for College Libraries* in 1968 and the establishment of the reviewing journal *Choice* in 1964 provide valuable assistance in building a book collection for a college. One may quibble with the selections, with outdatedness, and with the judgment of reviewers, but the selection process is greatly aided by the existence of these tools. A paragraph in the Preface to *Books for College Libraries*, however, is a most necessary caution to anyone using any of these lists.

> The danger in publishing a selection list of this nature is that it may be used as a final authority rather than as a guide. This list does not claim to be a list of the best books or a basic list for any college library, for selection of books for a college library must be made in terms of the needs of that particular institution.[3]

The assumption, by college administrators and by many librarians, that all one has to do to create a library is to follow someone else's judgment is dangerous and naive. They say it is more economic to process and to place on the shelves everything on a given list. One may ask—as we must eventually—economic at what point and for whom? Is it economic to fill shelves with materials unsuited to the educational program of the institution? Or don't we care? Is it economic for the user who is faced with tier upon tier of material which does not match his needs? Or don't we care? This is admittedly an extreme position, but it is an attempt to answer the economic argument. If traditional librarianship has any meaning at all, selection of materials for the particular publics of its institution is one of the more important contents of that meaning. If librarians abrogate this responsibility they have taken a giant step toward mere warehousing. Selection, in this sense, means knowledge of present and future needs, which unfortunately most colleges are unable or unwilling to define, and knowledge of materials to match those needs. This does not imply that this is done by the librarian alone, but rather in concert with concerned faculty and with students. This is not an easy job, but true professionalism is not easy. Every time a librarian makes a decision to purchase he is anticipating a future need, he is defining a future. He has had to do this in self-protection, because faculty, with very few exceptions, have been unwilling to define the limits and needs of their courses and curricula. Yet the good and imaginative teacher should have as few constraints as possible placed on his teaching. By not defining his needs, however, he may be restricting his students and diluting his own effectiveness. The result in many cases (there are notable exceptions) has been either (a) extraordinarily poor collections, ill-balanced and ill-chosen; or (b) collections which reflect that pathological syndrome that says if something is printed it must have value (GIGO = Garbage In, Gospel Out). Program definition and informed and tough-minded selection are the only answers, if the records of our data-rich civilization are not to bury us. We could of course put these records into orbit around the earth, a temporary solution suggested by some until we find an unused planet: a sort of cosmic bookmobile.

It is at this point that well-conceived lists, such as *Books for College Libraries,* can play a valuable role in providing a guide and a reminder—but not an authority.[4] The projected successor to BCL,[5] to be compiled and published under the auspices of the Association for College and Research libraries with support from the Council on Library Resources, will follow in this tradition.

Based on our experience of the last two years, with *BCL* and other lists, there are several attributes which any good list should have for future usefulness. First, it should have a machine-readable base, and this should be in MARC II format. Such a base will allow deletion of older editions, insertion of such necessary information as "out-of-print," additions of newer editions and new books deemed worthy, and the opportunity to provide access to the material through a variety of routes. The provision of a machine-base is not cheap. Neither is it cheap that dozens or even hundreds of libraries go through the same motions, or are wasting time and energy because intellectual access is limited by the list's structure. Second, the *Core Collection for College Libraries,* as it seems to be called and abbreviated *CCCL,* should provide a series of concentric rings: the 2000 Opening-Day Collection, the 10,000 volume collection, the 25,000, and the 40,000 volume collection. Again, once a decision has been made, which is not an easy process, this can be done when there is a machine-readable base. Third, related to the concept of concentric rings, which reflect a type of absolute desirability, is the possible use of modules, based on broad interdisciplinary subject interests. The classification system does this very poorly, for it fails precisely at the point of contemporary concerns: ecology, Black studies, information sciences, environmental design. If this is a useful kind of product, a computer-based system can assist in keeping this option open. Fourth, the *CCCL* should not be a one-shot affair. It should be updated regularly, which does not mean mere addition but rather subtracting the same number added so that the list remains at approximately the same level. The process of being current can be aided by a machine-based system. Without at least some of these options, such lists are destined to lose usefulness and value very rapidly after publication. By early fall of 1970 the CCCL

Committee had considered many of these alternatives. A modified MARC format will be generated for each title. What kinds of products will be forthcoming depends in large part on costs, feasibility, and general usefulness. An attempt will be made, with the assistance of *Choice,* to issue annual supplements with possible five-year cumulations or new editions.[6]

One of our early assumptions was that a usable and publicly operable microform reader-printer would be available by 1970. Although the promise appears better at the moment of writing, there is not an economically feasible reader-printer which meets our criteria of compactness, of being operable by the public (i.e., self-service), and easy to maintain and to operate. The lack of a good reader-printer has been a serious deterrent to the use of microforms. Until a satisfactory device is economically available, and not merely promised, this form of miniaturization cannot be exploited. Both the reader and the printer must be satisfactory. A user must be able to focus easily, to have a black on white reading image, and be able to scan quickly. He should be able to do this from a comfortable reading position. The printer should be coin-operated, offering a positive print, allowing the user to walk off with hard copy when he needs it. It would of course be advantageous to have a reader-printer that would serve all formats: film (both 16 and 35 mm), fiche, and opaque card. This, with the criteria discussed above, is obviously asking too much of an industry as small and as dispersed as this one is. This unavailability of a satisfactory reader-printer has had an interesting effect on our policy toward retrospective periodical collecting. It has made us much more spare and critical in retrospective purchasing, both in microform and in hard copy. In the sciences and the quantitatively oriented social sciences, with very few exceptions, we are buying few periodicals before 1960 or even 1965. In the humanities and arts we are following much the same pattern, except for special concern for film, photography, and popular culture.

Nonprint Media

Nearly a score years ago I was present among a small circle of his friends, when Graham Bell made a rude instrument in the rooms of the American Academy in Boston give out "Home, Sweet Home," as played on a distant piano. A year or two later, after I was one of the first to put the telephone to practical use in the Boston Public Library, I recounted its possible future to a dinner party at Althorpe. The incredulous English thought my presumptuous fancies but the foolish rampage of an irrepressible Yankee. We know what has come of it.

We don't know what will yet come of the phonograph. Edison's first instrument was sent to Boston, to be shown to some gentlemen, before its character had been made known. I never expect again to see quite such awe on human faces as when Gray's "Elegy" was repeated by an insensate box to a company of unsuspecting listeners. I look to see its marvellous capacities yet utilized in the service of the librarian.

Justin Winsor, 1894[7]

Nearly 80 years later we could still "look to see" the "marvelous capacities" of the phonograph used "in the service of the librarian." The profession has not yet caught up with Justin Winsor, first president of the American Library Association and Superintendent of the Boston Public before becoming librarian of Harvard College.

Early in our attempted definitions of a collection which would make sense within the five-college context, we felt that the present state and probable future of book collections in the four neighboring institutions made it necessary that the Hampshire Library seek a new base from which to contribute. From these early discussions, from meetings with consultants, and from an analysis of local needs, a collection concept based on the future importance of nonprint media began to emerge. It was felt that Hampshire's contribution, within the library context, could best be made by concentrating our attention on film, slides, phonodiscs, and audio and video tape, together with whatever viable new formats might appear. This meant basically that we would build, over several years, a small, solid book collection, but concentrate our major efforts in nonprint media.

There are some excellent collections, particularly of art slides, photographs, and music records in the other institutions.[8] But for the most part these are departmental collections, to which physical access is difficult if not restricted and for which intellectual access is frequently haphazard or nonexistent. The principal problem from our point of view is that none of the catalogs of these nonprint collections is integrated with the catalogs of the book collections of the libraries. This means that a user interested in a particular topic, and who is aware that there are formats other than print, must go to a number of places and consult a number of catalogs, each organized in a different way.

To put it mildly, such obstacles will deter all but the most energetic and dedicated scholar, and very few students are scholars of this bent. Students live in a world of sight and sound, and to build artificial barriers is to restrict their vision and their education. A student interested, for example, in William Blake should not only be able to obtain from one source the printed text of his poems and relevant biographies and criticism, but also the poems recorded by Robert Speaight, the film "The Vision of William Blake," the slides of Blake illustrations for the Book of Job from the Pierpont Morgan Library, and even Virgil

Thompson's Songs based on Blake's poems. The mere fact that these are in different formats and therefore "belong" to different departments is an absurdity which colleges can ill afford much longer. It reflects a past in which media were carefully compartmentalized, as thought they might infect one another, with the result that total perception by all the senses was penalized.

To do these things requires an integrated collection, an integrated catalog, standard cataloging and subject heading processes, and possibly one classification system, especially if there is to be a machine-readable base for all resources. This integrated approach, and its problems, are discussed in Chapter 5. These are necessary concomitants to any total approach to the spectrum of resources.

Unfortunately there are no basic lists for nonprint media, except for some rather sketchy discographies for basic record collections. The accepted excellence of basic book lists for college libraries is based on the long tradition of print, a reflection of a culture which has defined its classics. It is worth noting that this can also be done for musical records, because of the traditions of the past three centuries. We could begin to do this for major films of the past half-century, and we could even define the architectural and artistic subjects for a basic set of slides. But note that in all of these cases the subjects are limited almost entirely to art forms. There are few, if any, classics in these media for other subjects—the sciences, government, sociology, psychology, or ecology. It may be that a few "classics" are beginning to appear, but no one has yet attempted to put these together to guide libraries in their nonprint ventures. This should be a project for the next decade, starting tentatively at first, seeking criticism and recommendations, and gradually building a solid core of basic materials. The same attributes discussed previously for basic book lists should apply.

But Hampshire's problem is that these aids do not now exist. We suspect that other libraries in the next five years will face similar problems. Our experience and advice, within the context, can only be pedestrian. We utilized all the talents of the staff and faculty to develop lists and recommendations. Of particular interest, however, may be our approach to films. Hampshire is a member of the University Film Study Center, located at Brandeis University in Waltham, Massachusetts, which eventually will give us access to the film collections in some 10 institutions. At present, and probably for some years to come, this access is principally to a few well-known major film classics. Consequently we decided that our efforts should be directed toward the short film which, because of artistic excellence, cogency of message, and subject matter, should be of interest to our publics. We developed a film information center, which in time we hope will broaden to all media, manned by a nonlibrarian who has an interest and knowledge of film. She has some student assistance. The job of the center is (a) to collect, organize, and file distributors' catalogs and special subject lists of films of potential use to the College; (b) to scan reviewing media and any other sources of critical information; (c) to order films of possible interest for preview and to maintain evaluation records; (d) to invite faculty and students to previewing sessions (sometimes running all day long); (e) to collect and organize critical comment on films previewed (see Figure 4–1 for sample format); (f) to suggest, as a result of the previews, films for possible purchase; and (g) to rent films for use in courses. It is worth noting that the reviews and critical comments are organized so that decision for short-term rental of a film also remains an option.

Although we would like to be able to formalize our criteria of choice for acquiring nonprint materials, we believe that at this moment such criteria would be premature. At this phase in our development, we depend on the educated eye and ear and an intuitive sense of program and curricular needs. As we begin to know and understand a little better what these processes are, and when we have time to stop and analyze, we will be able to state in formal strings of words our criteria of choice. It could be done now, but it would be pretentious, temporary, and of little lasting value.

The ferment now building in the film and television industry toward the prepackaged visual format will have an eventual effect on collections.[9] The Electronic Video Recording (EVR) developed by CBS Laboratories and the holographic system by RCA, as well as others both in this country and Japan, are examples of the intense competition in the field of prepackaged video. The problems of incompatability between competing systems will of course have an effect on the process of collecting; and eventually some packages will occupy the position that piano rolls, recorded cylinders, and even 78 and 45 rpm discs do in record collections today. The same process is happening with the packaged Super-8 film, except there may be a better progress toward standardization. These developments may not have an immediate effect on library collections, but during the next decade these packaged formats will become ubiquitous.[10]

Title: _____ Subject: _____

Medium: 16mm film____ Audiotape____ Videotape_____ Length_____
         8mm film____ Cassette_____ Video format____ B/W_____
         Filmstrip_____ Multimedia___ EVR _____ Color_____
         Slide_____ package_____ Other_____ Sound_____

Catalog description: _____
_____
_____
_____
_____
_____

Producer/Credits: _____ Dated:_____ Use level:_____
Distributor: Rental fee: Purchase price:
_____
_____
_____

                    Preview arrangements: _____

For use by (instructor): _____ For student activity: _____
For course(s): _____

Preview requested _____   Rental requested _____   Purchase requested ____
    Date: _____   Date: _____   Purchase fund: _____
Other action requested (specify): _____
                      Signature:

Recommended by:_____ Date:_____
Previewed by: _____ Date: _____
Review comments:_____
_____
_____
_____
_____
_____

Final action requested: Rental _____   Dates needed: _____
                    Purchase ___   (alternates): _____

Report prepared by: Approved by: Date:

Figure 4–1. Sample media report

ORIENTING THE LIBRARY TO THE USER

The basic purpose of this section is to discuss ways of orienting the academic library to the user, through better understanding and exploitation of the college environment in which the library exists and through the development of methods by which the library can respond better to the needs of that environment. Traditionally the library is looked on as a place surrounded by four walls where printed materials—sometimes nonprint materials—are stored, organized, and lent. We wish to explore the notion that the library is not a place, but a process, and that mere warehousing and servicing is only the first step in the process. The library should be a process that permeates the campus.

Underlying our concern with this is the problem of creating and maintaining a library context conducive to a truly interactive library. Now mere rhetoric or extension of the library into areas conventionally considered foreign to it do not by themselves create a new environment. They do, however, provide the context within which we can begin to orient the library toward the user. Success depends first on people—librarians, faculty, students, administrators; and secondly on our capability to present this new image to our publics as useful and meaningful responses to their total needs. Of particular note is the intent to change the image of the library from a book-oriented institution to one that is communications-oriented.

It is these responses, or at least the possibility of a range of responses, that we present here. We are aware that a change of this magnitude may well be a long hard task. Not only does it require a change in the attitude of librarians, but, probably more importantly, a change in the working habits of faculty. It is equally difficult to describe what it is we are aiming toward. Consequently we will describe means and potential activities proposed for the Hampshire Library Center rather than ends. Several interrelated activities are projected for the Library Center so that it faces its publics rather than its materials, the front door rather than the back door.

- Research on what users do and do not do in conventional libraries
- A greatly expanded orientation program utilizing all media as necessary both in and outside the library
- A program aimed at developing student reference assistants for service in and outside the library
- A gallery program designed to augment and extend the educational experiences by experimenting with all forms of expression in a public manner

- A bookstore to broaden the options open to the campus community

In order to understand how we view these proposed activities, it is worthwhile reviewing some of our assumptions concerning their context. We believe the library, as conventionally accepted and viewed, has a potential for education and learning that is largely unrealized. At least two things are necessary to help exploit this potential.

First, the image of the library as a single place or building on the campus must be changed. This implies that staff and student assistants spend as much time outside the library as inside. Questions and problems, which could be assisted if not answered, do not suddenly come into existence when a user enters the front door of the library. They start in a classroom, a laboratory, a seminar, or, most importantly, in that penumbral fringe of education, the bull session. The library should be present in some personal form at the point where these questions originate, where the need for an answer arises. This does not imply that libraries have all the answers, but they have more answers—positive and negative, factual and fanciful—than most people are inclined to give them credit for. We are suggesting then that we wish to make our publics—student, faculty member, staff, administrator—aware of the fact that the library is one major source for answers: not only answers in the conventional relationship of "1728" to "When was The Beggar's Opera first produced?", but in a deeper sense of context, analysis, and discovery.

> It may be, as someone has said of formal education, that the storage media which libraries handle are noise in the system. The real education and communication may take place outside or on the periphery of libraries and formal education. Indeed it may be that the reference interview, the negotiation of questions is the only process in libraries that is not noise. For it is through negotiation that an inquirer presumably resolves his problem, begins to understand what he means, and begins to adjust his question to both system and substantive noise in the store of recorded knowledge called the library.[11]

Secondly, we feel that much would be gained by making the library's publics part of the process of exploiting the unused potential. As a library serving an undergradute liberal arts college, students are the Hampshire Library Center's major public. It is critical that they be made part of the process, rather than mere suppliants who come in the door. The idea of experimentation centered in the library offers an opportunity to study and to experiment with the processes of communication, learning, and personal growth that take place in the library. Students should be closely involved—if not the prime movers—in the development of media presentations and orientation programs. The process of true learning is one of participation and discovery, and it is within this context that we feel students could be the beneficiaries. They probably have a better sense of the needs of their peers and of the looseness or structure necessary in, for example, an orientation film. Such an approach, we feel, will help break down some of the barriers that now exist between library and user. As a subject for controlled experimentation and communication, students will become more aware, not only of the problems facing libraries, but also of themselves as learners and information-seekers. An effective method of learning is for both student and institution to learn together and to apply their findings to an institution such as the library. In this sense the library itself serves as a subject of inquiry and, within the frame of reference of Hampshire College, something to be described and communicated about.

Another assumption is that libraries are very frustrating systems to use. This occurs principally for several related reasons. The library contains highly structured packages; that is, books and periodicals, and its accessing systems are highly formalized. Yet the inquiries that come into the library are highly unstructured; that is, loose, naive, ambiguous, because they are real questions from a real world, reflecting what Whitehead has called the "radically untidy, ill-adjusted character" of reality. Conventional library systems are of very little help here. As one special librarian pointed out,

> . . . The levels of frustration in using libraries are awfully high for most people. It's amazing, as hard as we work at making ourselves popular with these people, we still have them come in and stand diffidently at our desk and say, "Well, I don't want to interrupt, but . . ." To which I reply, "If you don't interrupt me I don't have a job." But its amazing how people can't get over this. I think it would be a study in itself, that we grow up in school libraries, public libraries, and college libraries, generally where this kind of service is not provided. Consequently you are conditioned to feeling that the library is a place you almost have to drag something out of. The library is almost the last place they want to go, because they've been conditioned.[12]

These systems; that is, catalogs, indexes, classification schemes, and form divisions, are intended to help the user. For the naive user, however, they are terribly sophisticated and much too intricate—awkward in fact. They have been designed by librarians for librarians. They are librarians' tools and seem to have little relevance for the user. Consequently we believe that the system best able to display itself in a useful functional way for the inquirer will be the most effective. One of our concerns will be to see if there are ways of improving the "merchandising" of the content of the college library.

This brief discussion should not imply that the Hampshire Library

Center will solve all of these problems. Our intent is only to describe the context from which our concerns spring. The activities we anticipate undertaking are essentially loose and open-ended (not ambiguous, however) because we feel that style and ability to respond are as important as program. What we are basically trying to do is to create an environment, an environment which encourages both a change in library style and, concomitantly, a change in the patterns of library use. This is *the* long-range program in orienting the library to the user, rather than insisting that the user adapt wholly to an "unnatural" system.

Exploratory Probes—Research and Experiment

The word "research" has been used to describe the first group of activities. This rubric perhaps dignifies activities which are highly subjective and empirical. Possibly they should be called "exploratory probes," for our purposes are (a) to begin to understand a little better what it is a library does do and what it could do, and (b) to create an environment, through student participation, which will enhance the Library Center's effectiveness. As professional librarians we know very little about the interface between a user and whatever face the library turns toward him—catalog, index, reference librarian, rows of books or other media. We need to know more about the successes and the lack of success in libraries.[13]

For this purpose we will develop a very small group of students who are willing to observe themselves critically over a period of several years. Some of these students will work for the Library Center, some will not. We are concerned with two major facets here. First, how they as individuals attempt to answer questions of relevance to themselves. If they use the Library, how they use it. Why they do not use the Library under certain circumstances. What other sources and channels of information they use. What kinds of decisions they make in accepting or discarding information. The second role of this small group is to become aware of and describe some of the informal substantive information networks that exist on the campus and between the campus and the outside.

We are quite aware that knowledge cannot be distributed in packages, although at times we may behave as though it could be. Rather, knowledge is a state of mind to be created. It is our purpose here to develop insights into three general problems, both for our own benefit and hopefully for the benefit of the small group of students involved.

> The describable elements of an informal nature that affect the flow of messages in a small institution

- The form these messages take and what role they play in the "life" of the institution
- The possible roles for the library, in all its guises, within this context

We will not derive answers to these questions. Rather we will be creating an environment within which the librarian and the student together can examine some of the ways a library can become a more responsive institution, responsive in the total sense.

Though there will be only a very small group of students in this group, we see them as a sort of leaven in the loaf. During the first year we would expect to select two students for this effort (from a total population of 250). These students would be selected, with possible assistance from the Social Science faculty, because of their potential interest in social institutions and social communication. An interesting sidelight on this selection process surfaced when we asked the opinion of several future Hampshire students and they insisted that it would be best to let these students be self-selected and not to ask the opinion of the faculty. Informal seminar sessions would be held as needed to exchange ideas and information. We can anticipate some difficulty in explaining our ideas, consequently we plan a two-month series of meetings (one hour a week) to probe some of the limits of this work. Other faculty members might be invited when we felt their participation was relevant. This group of two students would grow to about four students in five years. Along the road we expect that we would develop empirical insights affecting our total operation and activities. The participating students, after we have been assured of their interest and ability with these problems, would be paid a small stipend.

Instruction and Orientation

We believe that present library instruction is sterile and self-defeating.[14] There are, of course, some noble exceptions: Stephens College, [15] Earlham College,[16] and Mount San Antonio College[17] are examples. We wish, however, to approach this problem from a slightly different point. First, we view instruction and orientation in a wider perspective and not as ends in themselves. Library instruction is presumably directed toward showing students (and other users) one of the ways of defining and seeking possible answers to problems in which they are interested. It is their interests which must be tapped, *not* the library's. In general, we feel that present library instruction and the standard library handbook exist in a vacuum because they bear no relation to any particular problem the student has. We are aware that this is probably true of a good deal of college instruction. But the lack of relevance forms part of present student dissatisfaction with higher education. The small step we propose here is directed toward meeting the user with some form of assistance at the time he has a problem; that is, to make the Library more relevant to him. This is a problem-oriented approach. Available tools—at least those that are economically feasible—are primitive. We will limit ourselves almost exclusively to those devices, displays, and systems which could be used within the Library Center. Over a period of several years, particularly when the communications system for the College becomes reality, use of the programs would be available anywhere on the campus.

With these goals in mind, our purpose here is principally to design, develop, and test small programs for orientation in whatever medium appears to be best adapted to the particular concern. Librarians have hardly begun to make effective use of simple print and graphic design to display to users the richness, organization, and usefulness of resources. In addition, video, film, and computer media offer a tremendous array of possibilities, hardly touched for interactive systems at the user's level.

We believe it very important that students themselves should be intimately concerned with the design and development of these systems. A sensitive student will have a better feel for the kinds of information his peers need to know, and for the best formats to use to get a message across. Learning how to organize a message to communicate to others and then translating it to a form of media display may well be an important part of the educative process. In a sense this is a bootstrap operation in which the students are helping to pull the straps, and in which both student and the Library Center are beneficiaries.

During the first several years of operation we anticipate that our attention will be directed toward three general areas of concern. First, we wish to develop one large multi-media presentation to introduce students to the idea of information overload, to the multiplicity of media, and to the potential roles the Library Center can play. By this presentation we hope the student is confused, bewildered, even antagonized, because we want to shake up his image of the Library, to make the familiar strange. We want him to see the Library upside down, cross-eyed, inside out, so that he can begin to create a new relationship to the Library. We expect, as we grow and learn and develop our own perceptions, that the program itself will change. This is proposed as the only large audience presentation of this type, although we may experiment with other goals—pure entertainment, for example—as a way of opening up the public's image of the Library.

We suspect that success with this program may be a more difficult task than the rhetoric indicates. The image of the static library is burned deeply in the cultural consciousness. Mere multimedia shows without a concomitant growth in response and systems vigor may tend to deepen the chasm between image and reality. This is a difficult but important problem, one which underlies much of the orchestration of this book. But a start must be made.

Second, we expect to develop media—both print and nonprint—presentations at points in the Library where a student may have problems in using the indexes and catalogs; for example, we might develop a three- to five-minute film or slide program on indexes, on the public catalogs, and on the disc and tape collection. The key is that such presentations must be directed toward self-help, at the point where they would be useful to the user; that is, when he has a problem.

Third, video, film, and slide presentations will be developed to explore and to instruct in the information resources and systems of a single subject. Thus a student interested in child psychology, materials science, architectural design, ecology, Caribbean studies, or the history of art could watch at his convenience—and repeat if he so desired—a video tape or film which illustrates the peculiarities of information and knowledge in that particular subject: the indexes, handbooks, films, newsletters, the major centers or laboratories, and the informal communication structure of the subject. This is seen as a sort of brief overview of the sociology of a subject: the peculiarities of communication in that particular field, the ways information is collected and disseminated, the role of nonprint media, and the informal sources available.[18] The resources of the Library Center would be noted only where they are relevant and applicable, for these resources represent only a few of the many sources that users can and do tap. Libraries must be understood in this larger context, as a switching center to all relevant information, not restricted to its own resources. The user should also be able to walk away with a brief and concise document, somewhat similar to the Library Pathfinder developed by Project Intrex at M.I.T.[19] The point here is that the Pathfinder, or its equavalent, can be reinforced by visual display in film or video. They may also reflect the breadth of approach we wish to introduce.

A number of devices and media lend themselves to these kinds of display: small rear screen units for short films or filmstrips; carrels with rear screen projection for slides and cued audio tapes. In the beginning, film would be largely excluded because of the necessity to experiment with and adapt the programs as we grow and learn. Video or slide presentations appear best at this moment. Though limited, one of the more interesting devices we have seen recently is the Medical Juke Box developed by the Albany Medical College.[20] This unit contains 160 audio programs, indexed and available by a simple alphanumeric code, with randomly accessed slides for illustration cued to the audio portion of the program. At the present time, however, there is a limit of 160 slides in the system, and this poses a real physical constraint on the program.

We hope that experimentation with these various approaches to library instruction, and with active student participation, will help to make the utilization of the resources of the Library Center a richer and more effective experience. More important in this context is the understanding, for both librarian and student, that the Library represents but one of a number of resources. The critical point is to be able to inform the user of the range of resources from which he can choose, inside and outside the Library. For those critics who might say that we are slighting or undermining the library, they are quite right—we are undermining the conventional library. The user has already recognized the limits of conventional libraries, and consequently he makes use of a variety of resources and develops his own sources. We wish merely to make him more aware of the options he has and consequently to make his choices better informed and more rational.

Reference and Information Services

One of the major keys to orienting the Library to the user is the reference and information services. In the conventional sense of a passive service which responds when asked, libraries, particularly special libraries, have performed this service well. We believe that the "respond-when-asked" approach is highly restrictive, however, and limits the full utilization of good librarians. We hope to explore several alternatives in the Hampshire College Library Center.

As anyone who has served at a reference desk can attest, a fairly large proportion of the questions are at a simple level, frequently directional only, and could be answered by a nonprofessional. Such a person—and we are suggesting students for this role—would act as a sort of filter, answering questions where he had some competence, and as a switching center, referring questions to others on the staff. We do not always know, of course, when a "simple" question really is simple, or when it begins to lead to something larger and more complex.[21] A key condition is that the student assistant recognize what he does not know, and that he have a flair for interviewing and counseling. Question negotiation and reference interviewing, given a small group of interested and sensitive students, could be taught by simulation and role-playing situations. An example of this can be seen in the Inner-City Simulation films and film strips, produced by Science Research Associates, for training students who tutor in ghetto schools.[22]

We expect to make intensive use of students in reference situations. This will take comprehensive planning and training, but it will have several beneficial effects. We believe that students, especially the so-called nonuser of libraries, will go to their peers to discuss their problems with more ease and rapport than they would with professional personnel. Imaginative use of student reference assistants will also allow the professional librarian more time to get out of the building and talk to students and faculty on their own "turf." It will make the Library and librarians more visible and hence, we believe, the Library Center more effective.

A second approach, related to the one just described, is our expectation of training a few students who will be reference advisers in the residence houses. Again our purpose is to make the Library Center available and visible outside the physical building labeled "Library." Such students will serve a few hours each week at standard in-house reference service. Their principal responsibility will be, however, to be known and available as reference assistants in the residence houses. We would back them up with announcements and "advertising," providing status and reputation so that other students will recognize them as information resources and advisers. These student advisers would be thoroughly instructed in reference interviewing, in sources and resources, and in the variety and forms of media available in the Library. They may be given a very small set of reference materials and any other forms of support (e.g., films and subject guides) we feel would help them. We would expect to develop a series of small training manuals, possibly modelled on the recent work of the School of Library Science at the University of California at Berkeley.[23]

To accomplish this we would train several such reference assistants the first year, in the hope that one or two would become Reference Advisers in Merrill House, the first residence unit, in 1971. They would receive a small stipend, plus any hourly wages for work in the Library Center itself, including training. The others would serve chiefly in the Library Center. We do not believe this should be a highly formalized and structured program. That is to say, it must be formal enough so that the student assistants have developed sufficient reference knowledge to be useful, but informal enough so that we can respond to specific situations as they arise. The danger in all such proposed programs is locking oneself in, so that we become sterile and eventually nonresponsive to new situations. We must remain open-ended.

There are many problems with such an approach. How to select such student advisers is the first one. What background and personal traits can be used to predict the responsible dedication and common sense attitude necessary for such advising? How can we be assured that there will be some continuity of available service without restricting the student to specific hours and duties? We cannot know if the potential we think exists here really has validity unless we try it. It is another attempt to break down the walls and make the Library Center present in some form across the campus.

In addition to this approach to reference services, we expect to develop, as feasible, information centers supporting special interests of the College, and which we hope eventually will serve the wider interests in the five local institutions. An information center is a combination of knowledgeable persons; a collection of materials, including ephemera such as newsletters, clippings, and so on; a file organization, manual or automated as feasible; knowledge of who knows what; and a sense of mission. Even before Hampshire College was in operation we had established one such service: the film information center discussed above.

We anticipate the development of several other information centers during the next few years. We foresee particular interest in two areas: the collection of local government information on the cities and towns of the Connecticut Valley in Western Massachusetts, and data concerning environment, pollution, and local ecology in the same area. Both of these topics will be of concern to the College. As with other efforts this approach is directed toward making the Library more visible, more useful, and more intimately affiliated with the total concerns of the College.

DISPLAY GALLERY[24]

> . . . This discovery indeed is almost that kind which I call *serendipity,* a very expressive word, which as I have nothing better to tell you, I shall endeavour to explain to you; you will understand it better by the derivation than by the definition. I once read a silly fairytale, called *The Three Princes of Serendip*: As their highnesses travelled, they were always making discoveries, by accident and sagacity, of things they were not in quest of: for instance, one of these discovered that a mule blind of the right eye had travelled the same road lately, because the grass was only eaten in the left side, where it was worse than on the right— now do you understand *serendipity?*
>
> Horace Walpole to Sir Horace Mann, 28 January 1754[25]

The encouragement of serendipitous discovery is one of the most important and creative activities any institution can undertake. In their systematic tools, such as a priori classifications, formats, alphabets, and subject-finding systems, libraries have generally tended to stifle chance encounter. While these formalized systems have played an important role in the ordering and development of knowledge, their very use has, of course, frozen the ways we as individuals look at the world. That librarians were not satisfied with this ordering is illustrated by the growth of reference services—in the best sense a sort of midwifery—in the last half-century. We believe that there are at present largely untapped and exciting approaches to extend and to amplify both the concept of reference and the continuity and breadth of the traditional library. The idea of display, enhanced by the potential of computers and nonprint media systems, offers ways to unfreeze the formal ordering of library content, without destroying the usefulness of knowledge classification schemes.

As early as February 1967 one of the first documents on the Hampshire College Library contained this preliminary assessment of the potential of the gallery as a public face of the Library.

> *A display area* is more than an art gallery or the standard case type of exhibit. Its basic purpose is to provide space and facilities for experimenting with all forms of expression and technologies in a public manner. The display is a communication channel often relegated to a minor role in libraries. Its function is well understood by advertising agencies. There is no reason why Hampshire College, with its experimental posture, should not exploit this channel creatively to tempt, to challenge, to suggest, and to communicate.[26]

In this context we view the Display Gallery in the Library Center as the antithesis of the traditional college gallery, usually a passive receptacle for travelling exhibits of minor art objects, unused by the natural or social sciences, and frequently unavailable to the humanities and arts departments as creative arenas. Hampshire believes that the Display Gallery and other exhibit areas provide unique resources which can be used to further significant educational and community purposes.

Within the building the gallery is the focal point for exhibit and display, but it is not the only such area. The rear projection screen at the top of the main entrance stairs is an important display space which we expect to utilize in several ways: (a) as a bulletin board or student classified ad display at specified times of the day; (b) as a display space to promote bookstore sales, new library materials, and new or old services; (c) as an extension of gallery displays; and (d) just for pure entertainment. The glass windows of the Bookstore along the main corridor become a visual wall for display. In a sense the total building becomes, as necessary, an extension of the Gallery. This is part of our attempt to temper the artificial divisions, to truly make the Library Center, in Norman Cousins' words, "a headquarters for the cross-fertilization of ideas."[27] In a more subtle sense the building, especially its contents, its activities, its interactions, may itself be an object of display. This is entirely in keeping with the discussion in the previous sections on the development of a critical awareness in students of themselves as question askers and information seekers. We see the Gallery as a way of loosening up the formalisms, of encouraging the chance encounter through imaginative use of visual, aural, and tactile means. There are generally three ways the Gallery can be used to accomplish these objectives.

The Gallery as a Laboratory for Design and Communication

In Hampshire's view one of the essential functions of the Display Gallery is to serve as a laboratory for students, where projects can be developed within the full gamut of Gallery organization, three-dimensional communication, and creative production. Students should be offered the opportunity to solve problems in the visualization of verbal concepts, in the construction of large space displays and models, in the articulation of felt needs for expositional explication of interdisciplinary concepts. The Gallery, and the ancillary spaces throughout the Center, become not only areas for public display, but more importantly laboratories where students can find out what it means to organize an idea visually and to test themselves publicly. We believe that student participation in the Gallery may provide a base for future professional interest in museums, galleries, and visual communication not ordinarily available to the undergraduate.

The Gallery as a Supporting Learning Center

There should be some way to make museums a wholly natural, delightful part of all our society, as natural, easy, and everyday as breathing in and out.

Eric Larrabee[28]

Museum—a dead circus.

The Left-Handed Dictionary[29]

The flexibility of gallery space permits the viewer (listener, feeler, taster, smeller) to explore the natural sciences, technology, social organization, human development, social conditions, cultural history, and the design-and-motion arts in a setting outside the usual classroom or course boundaries. At a time when students must become more involved with depth analysis of printed materials, the Display Gallery can offer a three-dimensional or moving counterpart to verbal ideas. We envision in time the Gallery alive with coordinated exhibits, exploiting both new and old media for the explication of concepts. Thus the book, film loops, sound sequences, animated films, cassette recordings, audio booths, photo enlargements, video screens, and computer terminals can all be coordinated to enhance exposure to the varied sides of a single idea. As examples of this kind of exhibit, we cite the following possibilities:

> *The Man-Made Environment:* The whole roster of man's impact on his environment: architecture, urban design, popular culture artifacts, the verbal environment; all forms of art as the man-made environment, from music to computers
> *Mind and Men: The Social Environment:* Inscape and social landscape; the mind as the inner environment; institutions and social conflict; problems in communication; the individual in the community; local political forms and customs
> *Man in the Natural World:* Man as a biological organism; man's relationship to the totality of living forms; his descriptions of the natural world, the "laws of nature" as interpreted by man.

We cite these merely as subjects of interest at the time of writing, all grouped around the theme "Man and His Environment."

The Gallery as a Community Service Resource

The third area of Gallery concern parallels Hampshire's commitment to community service, working with the cities and towns of the Connecticut Valley to assist them as they attempt to meet various social, political, educational, and environmental problems. For example, the Early Identification Program, mentioned earlier, is presently underway at Hampshire. The personnel in this program work with selected schools in the City of Holyoke on the problem of motivating disadvantaged fifth grade children to recognize their own potential for the opportunities of higher education. The Gallery could be an important public podium and display for them.

The Gallery could provide both physical space, public display, and an experimenting posture seeking creative and useful methods for improving communication on a variety of levels. We are considering, for example, the development of simple portable displays to illustrate local government structure, tax problems, or environmental pollution. They would be tested first in the Gallery, either in preliminary or finished form, and then made available to communities or groups who might find them useful. College and university galleries have not even touched these problems yet. We see the Gallery eventually as a significant link between Hampshire College and the community, with Hampshire students performing a catalytic function, combining their talents and energies with those of the community to the benefit of both.

Within these different gallery contexts, we hope to be able to explore a series of critical questions. Is the gallery, for example, a legitimate (and what does that mean?) extension of the Library? Are exhibition and display galleries capable of an expanded role in formal education? How best can aural and visual and tactile experience be integrated into the gallery setting? What are the physical elements and the staff requirements necessary to enable an institution to make maximum use of a gallery? What role can such a gallery play within the larger community, urban or rural? What kinds of messages seem "best" for what kinds of people? for what kinds of subjects?

THE BOOKSTORE

[The Bookstore] should, in short, augment and complete the material of the library itself. Like the library, it should serve the surrounding community as well as the campus.
Like the library, too, the bookstore should organize special promotions serving timely or relevant subjects of inquiry, or building sales around series of lectures, dramatic productions, or musical presentations. A bookstore so operated comes alive as an educational collaborator and an essential partner to the library . . . . Indeed, so closely related are the functions of these two facilities that it may well be advisable for the Advisory Committee on the Library to serve as the advisory committee on the Bookstore.

Swarthmore College,
Critique of a College[30]

The quotation from the Swarthmore College self-evaluation of 1967 is an excellent summary of the relationship of library and bookstore. But it is curious that, having pointed out all the similarities, the report did not recommend some form of managerial combination of the two functions. The cue to this failure to take the next obvious step may be in the observation of Russell L. Reynolds, General Manager of the National Association of College Stores, who pointed out[31] that the college store is concerned with merchandising and selling, in contrast to the library's concern with acquiring and holding. Whether or not this is strictly true is not the point. It is part of current myth and prevailing assumption. The whole context of the Hampshire Library Center is to alter the usual posture of the library and to make these two functions complement one another.

The Bookstore should be an exciting place—a place where students, faculty, and others come because they know they will see interesting books, records, films, tapes, and artifacts, and will meet friends. It should have a sort of "general store" atmosphere, and must not fall in the pattern of supply bureau or fusty bookstore. As Hampshire College is a model for undergraduate education, the Bookstore should be a model for the college bookstore of the future. The store comes under the management of the Library and is an extension of the Library—one side sells, the other lends or transmits via cable. Means must be explored and developed to encourage an active relationship between the two in support of the program and community of the College.

Starting from this as context, we had several basic questions to be faced and decided upon.

1. *Should the store be profit or nonprofit directed?*

Actually this question is not a real one—but is the one usually asked. The real question is how large and what should be the nature of the subsidy to the Bookstore. When we do not take account of maintenance, heat, power, building amortization, and general related back-up services, we are in reality no longer talking of profit in a true business context. These questions exist, but cannot be locally ascertained until Hampshire College has had operating experience.

The original question, therefore, has to do with an attitude toward the store and the accountability of funds which could be labelled "profit," but not including the basic subsidies noted above. One of the basic propositions of Hampshire College is "that an academic program of good quality can be organized . . . so that its costs can be met principally out of tuition income."[32]

Conventionally college stores owned and operated by the college, and which are profit-directed, put their profits into the general fund of the institution, into such activities as the student union, or into the development of new services. Among "nonprofit" stores the most common form is the cooperative which usually takes one of two forms. In one, the cooperative pays dividends on stock owned by members of the campus community. Very few of the smaller cooperatives pay dividends primarily because the "profits" are ploughed back into capital expenditures or into the development of new services. A second kind of cooperative are those which, at the end of the year, give a percentage rebate (cash or merchandise) on sales slips turned in by their customers. It appears that no new cooperative stores have been established since the early 1950's.[33]

Within this area of profit or nonprofit our general assumption is

(a) that the Hampshire Store should be profit-directed; and (b) that the "profits," when and if they are realized, should be earmarked for student activities or some similar campus-wide activity, or reflected in a discount system for the entire campus community.

2. *Should the store be internally managed or should it be leased to an outside store operator?*

Colleges in general are finding that a number of services, previously assumed as part of the institution, can in reality be more easily and less expensively performed by outside concessions. Examples of this can be seen in food services, building maintenance, computer use, and store operations. Librarians have seen this happen in book binding and book processing. We will undoubtedly see the rise of more such commercial services or state dormitory authorities as academic institutions become more aware of hidden operational and capital costs. Such a shift of course means certain subtle losses to the smaller institution: loss of autonomy and control over operations; loss of a feeling of personal service which may or may not exist in reality; and loss of a sense of wholeness of operation. As commercial companies develop a sense of academic needs and environments, however, such leasing arrangements will allow an institution to concentrate its administrative energies toward its prime responsibility of education and learning.

In a study made in 1962 for the National Association of College Stores, of stores with gross annual sales of \$30,000 to \$100,000, 11 percent were not owned by the college; of those whose sales ranged from \$100,000 to \$300,000 annually, 8 percent were not college-owned.[34] By 1970 these figures had probably doubled, and in New England alone, 19 college stores have shifted to a lease arrangement in the last five years.[35]

Hampshire has tentatively opted for a commercial lease arrangement for several reasons.

1. The difficulty of finding the right kind of bookstore manager is severe—one who knows student cultures, merchandising, accounting and business systems, and sources of supply.
2. A leased operation, particularly a firm specializing in college stores, can obtain better purchasing terms because of centralized buying. In addition, with several stores such an operation, using a centralized inventory, can move items as necessary from one store to another, thus giving better and faster service.
3. The College did not wish to subsidize a store operation beyond the overhead costs involved. It is doubtful that an internally managed store can begin to cover its own costs before 6 to 10 years of operation, especially in as small an operation as Hampshire College.

Any form of contractual arrangement with an outside leasor for store operation should spell out carefully and completely the responsibilities on both sides of the contract, with special attention given to the kind of service the store should provide and the image it should project.

3. *What types of merchandise should the Bookstore carry?*

Please stop nagging us about puppy dogs and toothpaste. Last year (1964) they produced thirty per cent of our sales, took sixteen per cent of our space and less than twenty per cent of our investment while earning fifty-five of our gross profit.[36]

It is worth noting that one of the major factors in considering this question was the location of Hampshire College. It is situated nearly four miles from the nearest bookstore. There are no other stores, except fruit stands, within easy reach. It is possible that, within five years, a small shopping center might develop within walking distance of the College. However, this does not yet exist. In early planning it was assumed the store should cover a wide range of merchandise and services. Readjustments during the fall of 1970 and an active student-faculty advisory committee have convinced us that the store should limit its scope to the following:

- Text books and other media required in courses
- Nonrequired books, especially paperbacks, related to the general milieu of the institution
- A limited amount of audio-visual materials; discs, tapes, posters related to the general milieu
- Supplies: general supplies in support of instruction, including tape cassettes
- Magazines and newspapers
- Services: fulfilling personal requests for specific books and other media not carried by store; sale of student crafts

The few academic libraries which have or have had bookstores associated with them such as the University of California at Santa Cruz, the University of Kansas,[37] and the University of North Carolina, for the most part limit themselves to nonrequired books, attempting to serve neither the class needs nor the broader interests of the campus. As we said at the beginning of this section, our objective is to bring the two operations—the Library Center and the Bookstore—into close association, providing a base for the exploration of ways each could enhance the operations of the other, and thereby providing a more effective instrument in support of the College and its community.

A scanning of *The College Store Journal,* the official publication of the National Association of College Stores, indicates that the college store is also caught up in period of change. The importance of the paperback and the gradual change in teaching styles from text book to open-ended reading list are of course reflected on the shelves of the store. The consequence of this is that the college store now has a different kind of sales probability. The assigned hard-cover text with a fairly specific number of predictable sales is quite different from the open-ended reading list of several hundred paperbacks and article reprints. Returns to publishers of unsold stock is an expensive process.[38] Problems of vandalism and theft are rising. Like the library, however the context and potential for service are present.

REFERENCES

1. F. Patterson and C. R. Longsworth, *The Making of a College: Plans for a New Departure in Higher Education.* Cambridge, M. I. T. Press, 1966 (Hampshire College Working Paper Number One), 202–203.

2. *Planning for Automated Systems in the College Library,* Report of a Conference held at Hampshire College, March 14–15, 1968, R. S. Taylor (ed). Amherst, Mass., April 1969, **23** (also issued as Appendix No. 3 to the *Interim Report* on USOE Project-OEG-1-7-071180-4351).

3. M. J. Voigt and J. H. Treyz, *Books for College Libraries.* Chicago, American Library Association, 1967, v.

4. James O. Lehman, Professional Developments Reviewed: *Choice* as a Selection Tool, *Wilson Library Bulletin,* **44** (9)L957-961 (May 1970).

5. CCCL, *Choice,* 7:359 (May 1970).

6. Personal communication with Philip McNiff, October 9, 1970.

7. Justin Winsor, The Development of the Library, *Library Journal,* **19** (11):372–373 (Nov. 1894).

8. Susan Severtson, "Valley Survey of Media Resources," January 1969 (typescript).

9. R. Kahlenberg and C. Aaron, The Cartridges are Coming, *Cinema Journal,* **9** (2): 2–12 (Spring 1970). This is a good review of the present status, plans, and problems in the development of packaged video and film. The article is a digest of a special report originally prepared for the board of trustees of the American Film Institute.

10. A news release from CBS Electronic Video Recording, dated November 16, 1970, announced an interesting program whereby 100 public libraries in New York State will install small collections of EVR casettes, with the adapter necessary for showing them on a regular television set.

11. R. S. Taylor, Question Negotiation and Information-seeking in Libraries, *College and Research Libraries,* **29**:194 (May 1968).

12. *Ibid.,* 180.

13. See, for example, R. S. Taylor, The Process of Asking Questions, *American Docu-*

mentation, **13**: 391–396 (October 1962) and the work cited immediately above which grew out of a longer report of the same title, published as Report No. 3 in the series: Lehigh University, Center for the Information Sciences, *Studies in the Man-System Interface in Libraries.* Also other relevant reports in this series: No. 1—C. E. Hieber, *An Analysis of Questions and Answers in Libraries;* No. 2-V. Rosenberg, *The Application of Psychometric Techniques to Determine the Attitudes of Individuals Toward Information Seeking;* No. 4—J. S. Green, *GRINS, An On-line Structure for the Negotiation of Inquiries.* In addition, the M. S. thesis by M. B. Leibowitz. *A Proposed System for Displaying Accessing Techniques to Library Users in the Field of Metallurgy,* Lehigh University, 1967. See also R. Tagliacozzo and M. Kochen, *Information Seeking Behavior of Catalog Users,* University of Michigan, Mental Health Research Institute, Communication 272, June 1970.

14. B. H. Phipps, Library Instruction for the Undergraduate, *College and Research Libraries,* **24**:411–423 (September 1968).

15. B. C. Bartlett, Stephens College Library Instruction Program, *American Library Association Bulletin,* **58**:311–314 (April 1964).

16. J. R. Kennedy, Jr., Integrated Library Instruction, *Library Journal,* **95** (8): 1450–1453 (April 15, 1970).

17. Harriett Genung, Can Machines Teach the Use of the Library? *College and Research Libraries,* **28**:25–30 (January 1967).

18. See, for example, American Psychological Association, Project on Scientific Information Exchange in Psychology, *Reports* 1–17, Washington, D. C., 1963–1967; S. D. Garvey et al, Communication in the Physical and the Social Sciences, *Science,* **170**:1166–1173 (December 11, 1970); H. Menzel, Information Needs and Uses in Science and Technology, in *Annual Review of Information Science and Technology,* Interscience, 1966, 1:441–458; and similar reviews, *ibid.,* 1968, 3:1–30, by W. J. Paisley; *ibid.,* 1969, 4:1–29, by T. J. Allen; *ibid.,* 5:1–32, by B. Lipetz; and National Research Council, Committee on Information in the Behavioral Sciences, *Communication Systems and Resources in the Behavioral Sciences.* Washington, D. C., National Academy of Sciences, 1967.

19. Massachusetts Institute of Technology. Project Intrex. *Semiannual Activity Report,* PR-9, Cambridge, Mass., March 1970, 55–59; also PR-10, September 1970, 84–92.

20. Brochure from Albany Medical College, 1970.

21. For discussions of these problems see R. S. Taylor, Question Negotiation . . . , *op. cit.*

22. D. R. Cruickshank, The Use of Simulation in Teacher Education: a Developing Phenomenon, *Journal of Teacher Education,* **20**:23–26 (Spring 1969): and D. R. Cruickshank, *Inner-City Simulation Laboratory: Director's Guide,* Chicago, Science Research Associates, 1969.

23. See especially *Interim Report* (Project No. 7-1085, Grant No. OEG-1-7-071085-4286): M. E. Maron, A. J. Humphrey, and J. C. Meridith, An Information Processing Laboratory for Education and Research in Library Science: Phase I, Institute of Library Research, University of California, Berkeley, July 1970.

24. This section on the Display Gallery is derived in part from two proposals, "To Create a Display Gallery as an Interdisciplinary Learning Environment," by Estelle Jussim, December 27, 1969, and January 9, 1970, Hampshire College.

25. Horace Walpole, *Correspondence with Sir Horace Mann*, W. S. Lewis et al, (Eds,). New Haven, Yale University Press, 1960, *IV*, 407–408.

26. R. S. Taylor, *Definition, Scope, and Preliminary Program for the Library and Related Activities at Hampshire College*. (February 8, 1967), 14.

27. Norman Cousins, *Present Tense, An American Editor's Odyssey*. New York, McGraw-Hill, 1967, 159.

28. Eric Larrabee (Ed.), *Museums and Education*, papers of the Smithsonian Institution Conference held at the University of Vermont, August 21–26, 1966. Washington, Smithsonian Institution Press, 1968, 8.

29. L. L. Levinson, *The Left Handed Dictionary*. New York, Collier Books, 1963, 152.

30. Swarthmore College, *Critique of a College*. Swarthmore, Pa., November 1967, 380–381.

31. Personal communication with Russell L. Reynolds, September 1969.

32. Patterson and Longsworth, *op. cit.*, 65.

33. Personal communication with George E. Piper, June 1970.

34. National Association of College Stores, Inc., *College Stores Survey*. Oberlin, Ohio, September 1966, 1, 19.

35. Personal communication with George E. Piper, August 1970.

36. The College Store is at the Crossroad . . . ,*The College Store Journal*, August-September 1965.

37. Thomas R. Buckman, Students, Books, and Libraries at the University of Kansas, in *The Library Reaches Out*, compiled and edited by Kate Coplan and Edwin Castagna. Dobbs Ferry, N.Y., Oceana Publications, 1965, 267–296.

38. Book Returns Can be Costly to the College Store, *The College Store Journal*, **35**: 19–22 (June-July 1969).

Chapter Five

Planning, Systems and Processes

Modern systems, in addition to being all-encompassing, on-going processes, are information-based. . . . The important aspect of the information base is not the information in process in the system, however, but rather information about what is in process. It is the use of this information, about the form of information in process, to control the system, that distinguishes the modern system from a collection of procedures.

Frederick G. Kilgour[1]

Mr. Kilgour's excellent short article from which this quotation is taken uses several key words and phrases, within which important ideas and rationalizations are hidden: *information-based; information about what is in process; users as part of the system; all-encompassing; on-going processes.*

The word "system" has acquired many meanings. This chapter is concerned principally with two aspects of a system: (a) the movement, organization, marking, and dissemination of physical objects; and (b) the processing of information about the status of those objects. There is a larger meaning which, in a very real sense, is the substance of this total report, and the systems discussed in this chapter are set in that larger context; that is, the library as a social system. Our intent in this chapter is to describe the other side of the equation: the planning and processes necessary to handle packages and messages; the provision of information about the status of those materials; and the generation of data which tells us how the system is performing.

Generally librarians have been concerned only with the procedures for handling physical objects, overlooking the problems of messages, status reporting, and data for managerial decision-making. Together with the restricted vision of what libraries could do, this neglect adds to the basic frustration of the library user. Kilgour's phrase "information about what is in process" is of critical importance when we look on the internal systems of the library as dynamic processes. The relative status of the physical objects, both those to be added and those already in the library, is constantly changing. A book, film, or set of slides coming in the back door, and a user searching the catalog or asking for information about the status of an item, alter the relationships within the collection. It is this sense of dynamism which is unreflected in conventional library practice. Systems planning, though primitive at this time, is directed toward overcoming some of these problems. It is principally through the intelligent use of computers that the diversity of such data requirements can be satisfied.

Although the chapter is divided into separate parts, these parts are intertwined because they have to do with planning and prediction, goals, and paths from "here" to "there." They also have to do with obstacles, with compromise, and with the fact that neither the profession nor academia, nor in fact the structure of the marketplace, support a total approach to problems. They also have to do with assumptions about the behavior of users and about administrative questions that must be answered daily, whether there is hard data to support an answer or not. Harsh as these remarks may seem, they are not meant to be negative. They are meant to emphasize both the necessity for systems planning and the limits of such planning. It is something of a defeat, for example, that we must discuss the processing of nonprint media separately from commercial processing, but the latter, at present, is limited to the processing of books. The planning of operating systems must take cognizance of these realities.

There are many techniques and variations on techniques that are useful in planning. It is necessary to be quite clear what the planning process is and what it is not. Within our context here planning is directed toward a process which is nonrepetitive. We will not, certainly not in the near future, design another Hampshire College Library Center building or system. This is a one-time-through project. The planning process itself, however, can be moved from project to project, applicable, with variations, to any specific future systems objective. Different data and different constraints will change according to local conditions, but the way of organizing remains the same.

PERT PLANNING

The Program Evaluation and Review Technique (PERT) is the most current and the most generally useful approach. PERT was introduced in 1958 as a result of government requirements in planning very large nonrepetitive programs. In the early 1960's the basically time-oriented characteristic of PERT was extended to include manpower, costs, and systems engineering. Thus the combination of these four elements brought together an integrated set of performance, cost, and scheduling procedures which provided a frame of reference for planning and control.[2] Its usefulness in overall library planning is apparent, with certain cautions to be discussed in this section. In undertaking this kind of structured action for planning, however, one must understand the requirements, limits, and burden of PERT systems.

PERT planning rests basically on the charting of activities and events along a time dimension. What one ends up with is basically a network with events as nodes, and activities as connectors as shown in Figure 5-1. An event is a point in time. There are a number of different kinds of events: decisions based on previously gathered data; judgmental decisions; budget decisions; receipt of material or equipment necessary for the next set of activities; the conclusion of an activity or set of activities. An event is especially important as a point at which something is completed, something is started, or a decision is made. Particular points in the process where the lines of several tasks or subsystems converge provide "bench-marks" at key points to ascertain progress, scheduling, manpower requirements, and delays—in short to identify problems. If the planning network is to have usefulness there are certain basic general rules in making the charts.[3]

1. Each activity must have a predecessor and successor event; and each event at least one preceding and one succeeding activity, except at the beginning and end.
2. No activity may start until its predecessor event is completed; and no event is completed until its preceding activities are completed.
3. There can be concurrent or parallel activities between two events, caused by technical uncertainty or need for redundancy.
4. No event can be followed by an activity which leads back to that same event.

Although these ground rules have been developed principally to aid in the computerization of the planning process, they are necessary concomitants to any graphic planning scheme. This process of planning

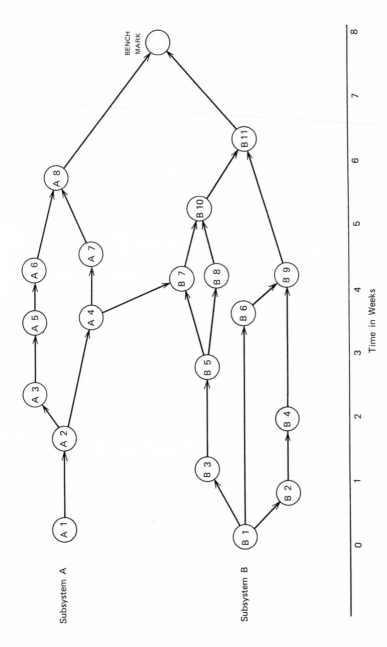

Figure 5–1. This is a sample PERT chart. Key: ○ Event; → Activity

along a time scale is important in order (a) to provide time estimates for the completion of each activity, and (b) to see relationships between and among the activities and events of different subsystems. This requires both optimistic and pessimistic time estimates for the completion of certain activities. If the planning process has been complete and the "elapsed time" estimates, including potential delays in work and delivery schedules, are accurate; then the chart can inform the librarian of the "critical path," that sequence of events that represents the longest delay in the project schedule. Such intelligence is basic to the planning process so one can say that, in order to accomplish a given project, *x* time is necessary. The total elapsed time may be too great, in which case it will be necessary to review the schedule and identify possible activities that can be eliminated or compromised to meet the required time schedule. This, of course, has dangers built into it because if the planning process has been carefully thought through, elimination or hedging on certain subtasks will raise the probability of failure or insufficient preparation. Such decisions can be made only in the context of a specific situation.

In planning the Hampshire College Library Center we thought in terms of a generalized PERT approach. By "generalized" we mean a rather loose approach, adapted to our situation, yet giving us sufficient scheduling and decision structure to allow us to view it as a process. We decided on this generalized approach when we found that the preparation of PERT charts was requiring so much time that there was little time left to perform the activities and gather the data required. PERT charting had become an end in itself. At that point we decided it was appropriate to abandon the preparation of the minute charts for most tasks unless there was specific need. We also found that it was necessary to stay loose because many of the decisions had to be made outside the Library organization. Sometimes those decisions were not made, or could not be made because of circumstances entirely outside the Library's purview. However, the planning process proceeded inexorably. This is an extremely important point and its effect can best be illustrated by a poster hanging on one of our office walls (a memento of the planning process):

> No
> Decision
> is a
> Decision

Something has happened and those caught in the middle of the process often do not realize what it is. They have made some tacit—and frequently unknown—assumptions to cover the void. The inability to recognize that such assumptions have been made may lead later to larger problems. Having said that, we have also underlined the importance of the formal planning process. At minimum a generalized PERT system should inform the planner that at some point a decision had been made, either consciously or unconsciously.

However, to assume that planning for an open-ended library in a college "in the making" can be controlled as rigidly and as elegantly as an Apollo mission is naive. Money, time, talent, simulation, and computer capabilities just do not exist for a college library at the level necessary to carry through real PERT programming. In addition, much of the data necessary to make decisions is not only unavailable, but, as we will discuss later, we do not yet know what questions to ask, especially in the nonprint and communications areas. As Hayes and Becker point out in their perspicacious *Handbook of Data Processing for Libraries,*

> . . . By its very nature, dealing with the substance of human communication as it does, the library involves a high proportion of essentially judgmental issues. It acquires material whose value is unknown; it attempts to describe it for future uses which must be unknown; it must find it when the relevance of the content was 'til then unknown. It must do this for a great variety of materials and users, and within a limited budget.[4]

A conventional library, let alone an experimenting and extended library, is an extraordinarily complex organism. The analysis and automation of library clerical processes are not trivial problems, though superficially they seem analogous to routine business data-processing. There are vitally significant differences, as Hayes and Becker state[5] which must be recognized in management planning. First, libraries are concerned with files of enormous magnitude: in the largest libraries, possibly as much as 10,000 times greater than the inventory files of a very large company. Secondly, the daily activity per item in a library file may be very low, less than 1% of the equivalent business file record. Thirdly, as a service operation the files of a library "are comparable to the manufacturing plant of a company and not to its bookkeeping records." Finally, library operations and their costs "are relatively ill-defined, at least in the form required for mechanization." The mere fact that these differences are recognized is a major step, because much library automation in the past has been based on a similarity of operations with business data-processing, with consequent compromise of service.

To return to an earlier point, it is important that any systems planning such as PERT be recognized for what it is—a powerful tool for structuring the planning process. At this level of the process at Hampshire College it is really no longer strictly a PERT approach, but rather a loose structure which informs us that certain decisions were made or must be made in order to proceed. Its efficacy in planning the Hampshire Library was constrained because we worked in situations which lacked structure or definition, and because we lacked the time and personnel necessary to isolate and to analyze the necessary minutae at various stages of the process. Hampshire College is basically an unsystematic environment. Original planning goals were affected by changing political and economic elements which conspired to alter, postpone, or deny decisions already made. There was no faculty to define curricula or teaching style. Subsequent faculty additions with consequent changes in curricula and teaching style, levels of local interlibrary cooperation, and changes in communication systems have had, will have, and must have an effect on planning. This does not imply that no planning can take place, rather that planning must be flexible enough to absorb these changes without basic shock to the system. The irony of course is that planning proceeded, decisions were made, system were developed, and the College is operating.

A second negative factor to formal planning arises from the larger context of national developments. The understandable slowness in the development of MARC systems causes a tentativeness in local decisions. Our desire to be compatible with national systems and our need to be in operation in 1970 made for an unstable situation. In addition our desire to have *all* media processed outside the library has proved, with the exception of books, to be unattainable at the present time.

The chart shown in Figure 5-2 illustrates the overall context of the Library Center planning from 1967 to 1970. The time schedule shown is only approximate. Institutional and library objectives, the general constraints, and the physical building have been discussed in previous chapters. It is worth noting that constraints, that is, limitations on planned operations, collections, staff, and systems, could and did appear anywhere along the schedule. Decision delays, changes in costs and predictable income, a building strike, new information, some misjudgments, and some lucky breaks all contributed to alterations in the process. The fork on the right-hand end of the chart is illustrative of our determination not only to provide conventional library service but also to allocate part of our time and energy toward the development of new systems, new services, and new configurations.

The diagrams in Figures 5-3 and 5-4 show some of the preliminary planning, especially the kinds of information (or noninformation) and decisions, and estimates of traffic and operations that were isolated at

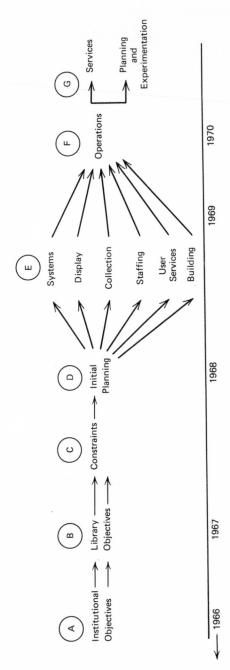

Figure 5–2. Overall planning context

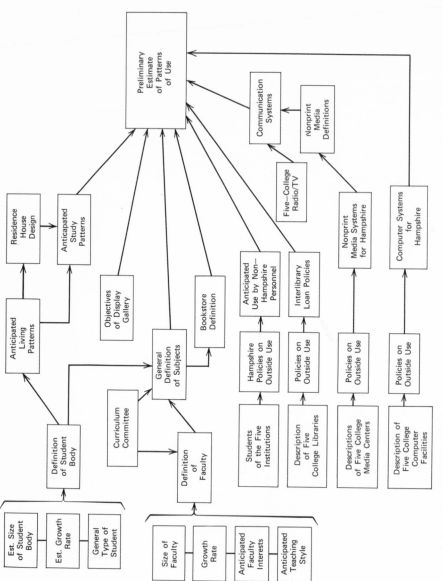

Figure 5–3. Generalized PERT planning (1)

120

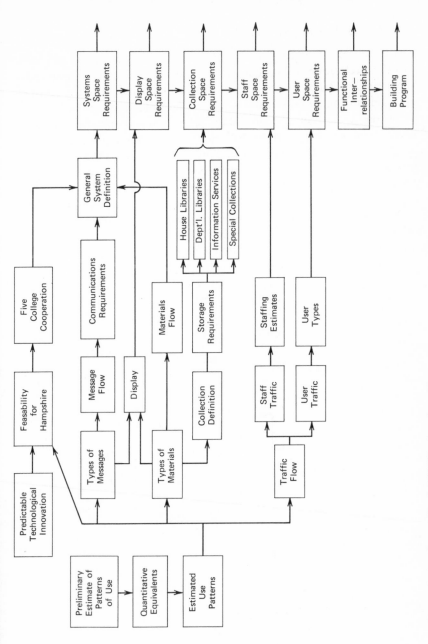

Figure 5-4. Generalized PERT planning (2)

121

point D (initial planning) in Figure 5-2. It is worth noting that, although most of the preliminary planning was directed toward establishing space requirements and relationships for the physical building, at the same time we were generating preliminary policies, definitions, and operating patterns for the design of systems. Many of the boxes on the diagrams required data-gathering, analysis, and, to be candid, pure guesswork (some times hidden under the euphemism "judgment"). In PERT terms the boxes represent both a culmination of a specific set of activities and a framework for the next set of activities. In many cases, they were complete planning subsystems in themselves. They are that complex. The major node in Figure 5-3 (Preliminary Estimates of Patterns of Use) is basically summarized in Chapters 1, 2, 6, and 7. The activities in Figure 5-4, a continuation of the diagram, are discussed principally in Chapter 3, although bits and pieces emerge in all the chapters.

Figure 5-5 starts from this point and begins to expand some of the sets of activities, events, and decisions necessary to arrive at an operating sys-

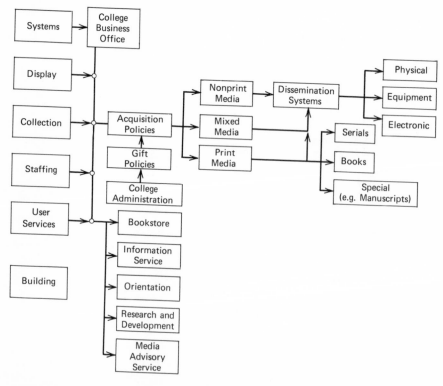

Figure 5-5. Generalized PERT planning (3)

tem. The PERT diagramming of this stage became so complex and time-consuming that it was dropped for reasons discussed earlier. In many cases definitive statements of policy, for example acquisitions policy and dissemination systems for nonprint media, had to be deferred until we had more input from the College itself and more experience in observing the needs and constrains of faculty and students. For illustration Figures 5-6 and 5-7 show a detailed PERT plan for the development of a periodical ordering, check-in, and accounting system. Even here not all the detail is shown. However, this appears to be about the finest level of detail that is still practicable. One may find it necessary, in carrying out a specific task, to outline, even schedule, the steps necessary to reach a conclusion.

Although some readers may find this description of planning tentative, or even, Heaven forbid, negative, it is not meant that way. We believe it of extraordinary importance to talk about real things in real time with real constraints, rather than imaginary systems in a make-believe world, and to share both progress and stasis with those who will design library and communication systems during the next decade. The act of defining and developing PERT (or other) diagrams is a significant exercise in the discovery of the patterns of decision, work, and accomplishment. There are parts of the PERT process which must be rigid and inexorable, especially when there is a fixed deadline for a highly complicated end product. There are also parts of the process which are basically political or judgmental in nature. The true art of planning is the ability to differentiate between these two. It may be precisely at this point that the conventional expert fails, for, in his inability to distinguish between systems decisions and political decisions, he relies too much on the formal systems decision. The intelligent use of a generalized systems approach, being specific where necessary and general when expedient, is a necessity if libraries are to be moved from their present cul-de-sac to a new level of operation and service.

INTEGRATION OF MEDIA

One of our major objectives is to be able to deal with all media formats through the same systems of ordering, processing, storing, lending, accessing, and disseminating. The user should be able to approach all media packages through similar routes. The interface between user and library should be the same whether he wants a film, a recording, or a book; that is, he should be presented with one catalog for all media, one reference librarian for all media, one storage scheme for all media. On the library side of this interface, the systems and processes side, everything

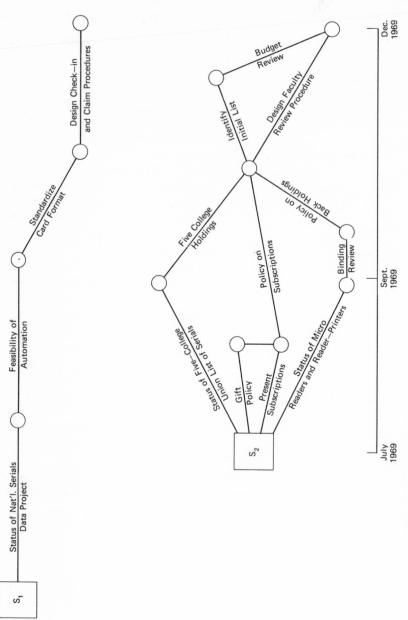

Figure 5-6. PERT planning for periodical ordering (1)

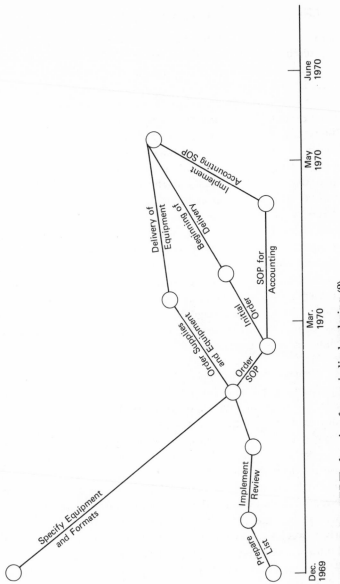

Figure 5-7. PERT planning for periodical ordering (2)

125

militates against such integration. The reviewing and listing sources are entirely separated; there are book reviews, film reviews, record reviews. Single sources of purchase for all media are nonexistent. Worth noting, however, is that librarians have been dealing with different jobbers for different formats (books, periodicals, government documents) for years. With the exception of sound recordings, there are no good single sources for different nonprint formats. Film, video, and slide sources in particular are highly dispersed. We would like to believe that single jobbers could cover the entire field from print to sound to image. This may happen in the next decade for materials at the elementary and secondary school levels. The difficulty comes at the college and university level, because of the diversity of objectives, levels of sophistication, specializations, and teaching styles. However, this may come sooner (a) if real standardization comes about with cartridges, cassettes, and similar packages, and (b) if a visually and aurally sophisticated audience of significant size develops.

Both the dispersed market situation and the use problems of different media formats have implications for the design of systems and processes. There are six stages in the total system where similarity of process ideally should be sought, whether the format is book, film, slide, recording, or video tape.

1. *Review, selection and initial purchase decision* should follow the same pattern regardless of format. Books and recordings have good reviewing sources. Slides, or more appropriately slide packages, have no reviewing sources. Film has limited but generally good reviewing mechanisms. Film poses peculiar problems, however, principally, one may suspect, because the unit cost makes it appear so much more expensive, and because faculties do not yet know how to relate film holdings to educational and learning needs. Though thousands of books and even recordings are purchased from advertisements, author's reputation, or short reviews, we hesitate when it comes to films costing $200 to $500. Consequently a previewing system has to be established.

Unfortunately for the college library most of the work and "how-to-do-it" references on selection of nonprint media have been directed toward the precollege level; for example, Hicks and Tillin in their *Developing Multi-Media Libraries*[6] imply that their book is applicable to all kinds of libraries. Would this were so! The examples and the references in the book reveal that school libraries are really the beneficiaries of work thus far. This is of course to be expected for the school libraries are already making the shift from a print base to a total media base. Hicks and Tillin also call attention to an interesting shift in the approach to use of media.[7] Audiovisual centers have in the past existed almost exclusively for the use of teachers in developing their courses of instruction. The selection, organization, and access to materials were limited to the teacher. Students were excluded, mere recipients of visual or aural messages in the classroom. This was true also—and still is in many cases—of audiovisual centers in support of Schools of Education, thus strengthening and perpetuating this restrictive attitude among young teachers. This attitude is now changing, especially as materials and equipment are developed for individual use, to one directed toward open-use and self-instruction. It is revealing that the book-based college library went through this same change at the end of the last century, from restrictive and exclusive practices to the highly open practices of today.

We wish to see if this change can be translated into feasible and useful systems for the college library, embracing the total spectrum of media. In the initial selection phase one of the major needs is a standard pattern of reviews for nonprint media, similar to the role played for books by *Choice*. In fact we hope that, congruent to our concern with media integration, a reviewing journal might make the same approach. An integrated public catalog attempts to do just that for the user. Why should not the same integration exist for those who determine and select the input to these systems?

2. At the second stage of systems—*ordering, accounting, and report status*—the same forms should be used for administrative records and should follow similar routes. This is of course an ideal, which, for several reasons, must be compromised.

First, the market is not structured to serve multimedia interests. Book jobbers, periodical dealers, record dealers, film distributors, slide producers—they each have a separate corner of the market. To this list should be added the nonprint media produced by noncommercial outlets: college departments, special nonprofit organizations, government agencies at all levels, industrial concerns unassociated with media, and individual artists. This dispersion requires a good deal of ingenuity, not only to maintain awareness, but to regulate purchasing and accounts so as to minimize expenditure of time and energy. It will take a considerable amount of time before a single company or group of cooperating commercial interests will be able to integrate these diversities into a viable and economically feasible venture.

A second reason for compromise here is discussed in more detail later. It concerns our desire to move processing operations out of the Library Center to commercial firms. At present only book and record processing on a commercial scale is economically feasible. There does not appear to be any possible processing of other nonprint media in the near future. Such diversity causes different order and status report requirements and internal routines.

A third form of compromise arises from our own hesitation in combining print and nonprint accounting systems until we know something more of their effect on one another. At present the Hampshire Library Center's materials purchasing accounts are internally divided into some 13 subject categories. Since there are no departments we feel we must have some assurance that we are building a balanced collection. An ironic point of this account division, however, is that we have a separate account labelled "nonprint media"; that is, print is separated from nonprint in our internal accounts. In a sense this is an attempt to assure balance in another direction, between print and nonprint. We justify this division because we find nonprint media particularly difficult to divide into these kinds of subjects. This may in fact be a euphemism for a general lack of experience, because books themselves are frequently multidisciplinary and we pop them into different accounts with little hesitation. This kind of decision is minor, but the cumulation of such decisions tends to erect walls and strengthen prejudices. In time this particular division of internal accounting will be overcome.

3. *Receipt and check-in* of the physical object should follow the same pattern for all formats, with invoices following the same routes. A minor point, but another brick in the wall: film, for example, has three possible forms of receipt and destination—as rental film, as preview film, as purchased film. Because of the frequent time pressures for showing rental films, this means that all films are filtered first through that office which arranges rentals, the Film Information Center.

4. One of our objectives is to have all *material processed outside the Library Center.* We are not concerned here with the reasons why this is not possible for all media, rather with the effect this fact has on the integration of media and systems in support of that objective. Because commercial operations for book processing are easily available and apparent, printed materials tend to structure their own systems, and, in a way, to set the standard. This essentially means that if we take media integration seriously, other media must adapt to book processing systems. Since this is not possible, for reasons already discussed, separate systems tend to establish themselves. Different formats then travel different routes through the technical processing department and individuals become specialized in the kinds of media formats they handle and the kinds of operations they perform. Specialization of function can of course raise efficiency if the narrow view is taken. Specialization also tends to restrict

and limit integration, if we truly want this to occur throughout the organization, both vertically and horizontally.

We suspect, however, that the forces against integration run somewhat deeper than mere functional operations, and have something to do with a cultural commitment to print vis-à-vis the newness of nonprint materials. After all, libraries have separate personnel, even separate departments, for serials and for monographs, for Arabic or Chinese materials and for English language materials. Yet somehow these various formats and languages are viewed and treated as compatible systems, certainly in college libraries and, for the most part, in university libraries. As libraries become more adept and acclimated to media variety, we think integration can be accepted as we now live comfortably with the various print formats. Such acceptance can be encouraged by the growth of commercial media processing and by a program of in-house staff education.

5. One of the primary methods of integration is *to group physical objects together*, which requires a single classification scheme, and/or *to interfile their tokens* (catalog cards) in one array, presumably alphabetical. The grouping of physical objects ideally means that all material on a single topic should be in one location, so that the user, in browsing, will find books, periodicals, films, slides, recordings, microfilms, prints, and so forth, stored together, all specific to the topic. There are at least four factors that militate against such a utopian solution, which, though obvious, are worth stating here.

a. A single physical item can be placed in only one location. The intellectual vagaries of any classification scheme are such that many browsers will complain that "their" materials are located in the wrong place.

b. The physical problems of integrated shelving of all media are deterred by several problems of design.[8] Varying sizes and shapes do not mix well physically and the problems of reading-shelves in a collection of any size; for example, 20,000 items and up, would be very difficult. Media producers and distributors could help if they would standardize packaging, particularly packages of sufficient physical size to be marked, shelved, scanned, arranged, and browsed easily. In addition, descriptive information on the outside of the package, as is now done on record jackets, would enhance the potential of mixed storage. Shelving manufacturers are beginning to provide a variety of choices for storing materials, satisfying both the need for efficient space utilization as well as aesthetic and design criteria.

c. A classified mixed media storage arrangement also poses difficulty because the random access portability of printed forms requires nothing more than the human eye for scanning and browsing. All other formats require the interposition of a device in order to hear or see the item. This does not preclude the possibility that record players, tape players, slide and film projectors, self-controlled video monitors, and microform readers could be scattered through the storage areas. Today it would be something of an absurdity to attempt to satisfy the requirements of all formats until manufacturers and producers arrive at compatible standards, and until equipment is designed for public use. There may be, however, some immediate possibilities; for example, 35mm microfilm mixed with print on the shelves might be possible, if we required only reading and not printing capability. However, we believe that one of the major deterrents to effective and widespread use of microfilm is the lack of an inexpensive, easily operated reader-printer. In addition the growth of microfiche poses an additional problem of compatibility. Audio tape, especially in cassette form, discs, and slides in sealed unit also provide possibilities.

The Hampshire College Library Center in the beginning will not make any attempt to integrate physically a mix of media formats. We may over the next several years experiment with a few formats, however, if we can meet the requirements for browsability and for on-the-spot use. For this reason, and others to be explicated, all media will be classified, using the Library of Congress classification. Even though at present we store each kind of medium uniquely according to its format, by classifying we leave the option open for integrated shelving in the future. In addition, classification provides, through a machine-readable shelf-list card, the basis for a classified catalog of all media, with a number of possible by-products. By using designators for each media format or special location, a separate print-out can be made for films, slides, discs, or for the reference collection. The standard catalog cards are interfiled in the public catalog.

There are, as one might suspect, some difficulties in using the Library of Congress classification system. It was designed for the classification of books, and there are certain anomalies when different media formats are shoehorned in. Just how does one classify a recording of the sounds of a cocktail party? or a computer-generated film such as *Permutations?*[9] Fortunately L. C. classification has been used effectively for musical recordings.[10] Special classifications such as ANSCR,[11] although more adapted to contemporary recordings, merely add one more classification for a special format. Even with the admitted, or as yet undiscovered, difficulties of using the L. C. classification schedule for all media, we feel the long-term gains outweigh the problems.

A minor but nagging problem is that of media designators, which act as format codes at the beginning of the call number. There are about 30 different kinds of audio-visual formats at present.[12] Undoubtedly these will expand and change. It appears at this point best to limit strictly the number of designator codes and utilize the text of the card itself to expand or qualify.

By classifying, one major criterion for integration then has been at least partially met. We can opt at some time in the future for integrated shelving. With a simple machine-readable base we can produce an integrated classified catalog (see Figure 5-8 for sample page) and, if necessary, an alphabetical main entry catalog. The public catalog, on cards, represents all media. An interesting and critical point here is that, notwithstanding the variety of system requirements dictated by media marketing and formats, the user is presented through the catalogs with some sense of a unified spectrum of formal communication from print to sound to image. He is the beneficiary, as he should be, of a mixture of systems and procedures which go on behind the scenes. Knowing of the existence of an item, however, and having that item in hand are two different things. The real test of the system comes at the point where the user wants to obtain and make use of the physical item.

6. The systems then for the *dissemination,* both physically and electronically, are the most critical, for it is here that the back-up systems either succeed or fail. If the user cannot obtain something the catalog informs him the Library has, easily and without excessive bureaucracy and dispersion, then the Library has failed in one of its major public interfaces. Studies of information-seeking behavior indicate that "ease of access" to an information system is more significant than "amount or quality" of information obtained.[13] Ease of access pertains to the storage and dissemination systems. The desire for quality in the information retrieved is a function of personal motivation, an institutional environment that supports critical awareness and successful interfaces with reference and media personnel discussed in the last chapter. At the same time, if the library is concerned, as it should be, that the user be able to obtain "quality" then it must provide easy access to that quality.

We are at this point principally concerned with the physical dissemination of packages. We expect that, as time and funding allow, electronic dissemination of image and sound from the Library Center to various points on the campus will begin to alleviate some of the problems of physical movement, and, we are sure, will pose some new problems. Electronic distribution will be discussed in the next chapter.

Complete accessibility and availability of all media in a collection will not be completely solved until we are able to duplicate everything on demand, retaining master copies as the collection base. At present this is

AUTHOR   TITLE   YEAR   VOLS   PREFIX   CALL NUMBER

N   FINE ARTS

		1898	1	R*	N 50.
AMERICAN ART DIRECTORY					A54
EHRENZWEIG, A		1967	1		N 71.
HIDDEN ORDER OF ART					E5 1967
RAPHAEL, M		1968	1		N 71.
DEMANDS OF ART					R34
EVERSOLE, F		1962	1		N 72.
CHRISTIAN FAITH AND THE CONTEMPORARY ARTS					E9
HUBERT, J		1969	1		N 5970.
EUROPE OF THE INVASIONS					H8
RUBIN, W		1968	1		N 6494.
DADA AND SURREALIST ART					S8R8
PIERSON, W		1960	1	S*	N 6505.
ARTS OF THE UNITED STATES					P55 1960A
		1970	1	R*	N 6536.
WHOS WHO IN AMERICAN ART					W5 1970
HARTT, F		1969	1		N 6915.
HISTORY OF ITALIAN RENAISSANCE ART PAINTING, SCUL					H37
GABO, N		1962	1		N 7445.
OF DIVERS ARTS					G19
GILL, E		1966	1		N 7445.
BEAUTY LOOKS AFTER HERSELF, ESSAYS					G47 1966
GRABAR, A		1968	1		N 7832.
CHRISTIAN ICONOGRAPHY					G6613
MAURY, C		1969	1		N 8195.
FOLK ORIGINS OF INDIAN ART					A5M3
VON ECKARDT, W	1967		1		NA 680.
PLACE TO LIVE					V6
GOODY, J		1965	1		NA 735.
NEW ARCHITECTURE IN BOSTON					B7G6
KIRKER, H		1969	1		NA 737.
ARCHITECTURE OF CHARLES BULFINCH					B8K5
		1968	1		NA 2560.
CONCERNING ARCHITECTURE ESSAYS ON					C6 1968A
ARCHITECTURAL W					
		1956	1	F*	NA 3750.
WORLD OF MOSAIC COL 16					W927

Figure 5-8. Sample page shelf list: R = Reference; S = Slides; F = Film.

obviously impossible, not only for financial and technical reasons, but also because of the legal constraints of copyright. We suspect that the latter may be the greatest obstacle to the development of such a system. In addition the cost of maintaining master copies, and duplicating from them, for infrequently used items would be grossly uneconomic. Over the last decade several interesting Operations Research approaches have been developed and tested in limited fashion[14] which begin to explore the magnitude and complexity of defining a high-use core book collection, a necessity if a noncirculating book library is to become reality in the future. A corresponding effort for nonprint media is undoubtedly a long time away. Because of the ease with which standard nonprint media can be electronically disseminated, however, the potential for deriving a definition of a core collection in these formats does exist.

Consequently our problem at this time is one of designing and operating a dissemination system built on a series of compromises, leaving as many options open as possible for future alterations. There are several criteria basic to this design.

1. All media and necessary small portable equipment (projectors, players, etc.) should be controlled from one point in the Library: the Circulation Desk.
2. A control card (circulation or book card) should exist for each item of material and for each piece of equipment. Control cards should be of the same size and similarly formatted for all material and equipment, varying only in printed statements or description and in color as necessary.
3. Control cards should be in machine-readable form or the option for key punching be kept open. This essentially means that the physical size and card stock of control cards be based on the standard data card.

Based on these criteria a series of dissemination systems was designed, which if not completely compatible were directed toward compatability. Chronologically speaking the book system came first, because as we have implied before, it was available and standard. The book control card is illustrated in Figure 5-9. With the exception of slides all media cards are at present based on this model. Records and tapes are shelved near the Loan Desk for public access. Films are shelved behind the Loan Desk and their use is controlled directly. Small equipment for loan is also controlled directly across the Desk. Some of the carrels in the vicinity of the Loan Desk are equipped, some are not. Slides, because of their size and portability, and equipment, because of unique considerations concerning utility and maintenance, pose special problems. With the exception of

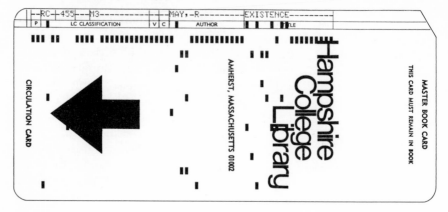

Figure 5–9. Book control card

these two, all media use basically the same control card as that used for books. The equipment control card is shown in Figure 5-10.

Although we have a machine-readable control card for all items, during the first year of operation we are using the Systac System of Bro-Dart Industries for circulation purposes. We expect to shift to a batch-process automated circulation system in the second or third year of operation. The Systac System can be used without damage to the punched card. We made this choice at this time for two reasons. First, Hampshire College has no computer of its own, instead we use the system at the University of Massachusetts remotely. A four-college computer center was just beginning to take form. Computing problems are discussed in

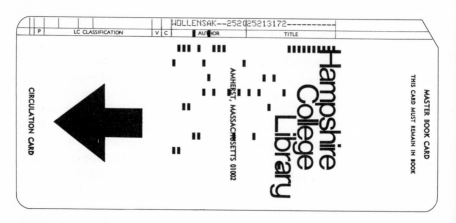

Figure 5–10. Equipment control card

Chapter 6. Second, with only 270 students, an automated circulation system is grossly uneconomic. It will still be uneconomic with the 600 students anticipated in 1971. However, the system can be designed, tested, and debugged at that time without gross inefficiency in service and operation.

As mentioned previously, the slide collection—small now but destined to grow rapidly—requires a special kind of treatment. Several criteria formed the basis for our system decisions here. First, slides should be browsable. Second, a user should be able, from his browsing, to request a single slide or a set of slides for showing or study that match his need. Third, there should be an approach to slides through the public catalog: at first as small collections, eventually with an entry for every slide. To match these criteria the slide system has a series of elements and processes.

1. Slides are grouped in general, or specific if required, subject categories. These categories are derived either (1) from the title of the package as sold by the distributor if this seems appropriate; or (2) from our knowledge of appropriate groupings for Hampshire College.
2. Each such collection receives a Library of Congress classification number, and each slide in the collection is numbered from 1 to 300. If a collection is larger than 300, it is by definition too large and should be broken up. If that is impossible, then by adding an extra symbol to the Cutter Number, the cycle from 1 to 300 is started again. Duplicate slides are acquired in most cases, one for browsing, one for circulation and use.
3. The browsing slides are placed in racks of 100 slides each and stored in an Abodia Visual-5000 Slide Cabinet. This cabinet has the following features:

   (a) The 100-slide racks can be labelled and moved in and out of storage easily for viewing, with a light source in the back of the viewing area.
   (b) The slides in the racks cannot be touched by the user, but call number and title are visible for each one.
   (c) Duplicate slides for circulation are stored by call number in locked drawers below the viewing unit.

4. The user requests on a slide control card (Figure 5-11) those slides he wishes to borrow, and a desk attendant obtains them for him and puts them in a carousel, if desired or appropriate.

This system meets our criteria. There are, however, several anticipated problems, some of which may prove the undoing of the system.

Sli

Write all but last part of call number above.

Circle numbers corresponding to the last element of the call number for those slides desired.

Slide Circulation Card

Hampshire College Library

DD M-13465

1	2	3	4	5	51	52	53	54	55	101	102	103	104	105
6	7	8	9	10	56	57	58	59	60	106	107	108	109	110
11	12	13	14	15	61	62	63	64	65	111	112	113	114	115
16	17	18	19	20	66	67	68	69	70	116	117	118	119	120
21	22	23	24	25	71	72	73	74	75	121	122	123	124	125
26	27	28	29	30	76	77	78	79	80	126	127	128	129	130
31	32	33	34	35	81	82	83	84	85	131	132	133	134	135
36	37	38	39	40	86	87	88	89	90	136	137	138	139	140
41	42	43	44	45	91	92	93	94	95	141	142	143	144	145
46	47	48	49	50	96	97	98	99	100	146	147	148	149	150
151	152	153	154	155	201	202	203	204	205	251	252	253	254	255
156	157	158	159	160	206	207	208	209	210	256	257	258	259	260
161	162	163	164	165	211	212	213	214	215	261	262	263	264	265
166	167	168	169	170	216	217	218	219	220	266	267	268	269	270
171	172	173	174	175	221	222	223	224	225	271	272	273	274	275
176	177	178	179	180	226	227	228	229	230	276	277	278	279	280
181	182	183	184	185	231	232	233	234	235	281	282	283	284	285
186	187	188	189	190	236	237	238	239	240	286	287	288	289	290
191	192	193	194	195	241	242	243	244	245	291	292	293	294	295
196	197	198	199	200	246	247	248	249	250	296	297	298	299	300

Figure 5–11. Slide control card

Their importance is something we cannot know until we have had sufficient experience for judgment. The purchase of duplicate slides, of course, reduces the potential size of the collection. We justify this decision on the basis that size is of less importance than both browsability and usability. Classified storage is inherently wasteful of space and a large collection of slides may require an inordinate number of cabinets. It may eventually be necessary to design larger racks and cabinets based on the desirable design criteria of the present cabinets. A potential solution exists in the use of microfiche with color images of the slides. The microfiche could then be used as the basic scanning and browsing medium at a much lower expense. Subject categorization may be difficult and, though we speak of generating a card set for each slide, this is a task where we have no measurable set of work standards and consequently can only guess that the magnitude of the process is large. It is possible that it might be simpler to maintain the subject grouping, with many additional subject entries per collection, in the main catalog, and generate a computer listing of individual slides. Such a listing could be adapted from the Santa Cruz Slide Classification Project[15] in particular as it has been adapted by the California Institute of the Arts.[16] But we still do not know the costs of such a task. As Simons and Tansey point out in the preliminary draft of their final report (curiously this statement does not appear in the final report):

> Most librarians know the rule of thumb that it costs as much to catalog a book as it does to buy it. The same amount of cataloging effort for a single slide costing perhaps a tenth or a twentieth as much as the average book is clearly out of scale. The paucity of fully cataloged slide

collections (or even partially cataloged slide collections) stands as testimony to this fact.[17]

In summary, whether or not the Hampshire Library will be able to meet the diverse, and sometimes contradictory, requirements of media integration is a moot question at this point. We have attempted here to understand and to describe the problems and to design processes and systems to meet some of those problems. We know there are certain trouble points: some within our control, some inherent in the explosive growth of nonprint media, and some in the structure of the marketplace and in the system incompatibility generated by a highly competitive market. The problems, however, are so important to the future usefulness and significance of libraries and related communications-oriented institutions that serious, continuing, and expensive study must be undertaken.[18]

COMMERCIAL PROCESSING

Early in planning the Hampshire College Library the decision was made that, whenever possible, processing of materials would take place outside the Library. This was reflected in building design, discussed in Chapter 3, and in staffing a technical processing operation. There was one basic and immediate goal: that by September 1970 an ongoing operation exist and a basic collection of materials in support of instruction be available. In 1967–1968 when planning was started, the goal was of the order of 35,000 volumes and an undetermined number of nonprint items. The size of the book collection was gradually scaled down, for both economic and operational reasons, to about 20,000 volumes, and some 5000 items of nonprint materials. Operationally in building the collection we intended to place a great deal of dependence on those faculty who were on the planning staff in 1969 and early 1970. We found, with some notable exceptions, that faculty members were either not interested or not able to define and recommend a basic book collection in their field. We cite this phenomenon principally to alert librarians who may find themselves in a similar situation and to urge that librarians take a much more active role in collection building.[19] This lack of response was even more true for nonprint materials and, in fact, the Library Center staff itself was ill prepared to develop a basic nonprint collection until we had established the Film Information Center and were able to concentrate and organize information on these media. An additional delay resulted from our unsuccessful efforts to find a commercial processor for any of the nonprint media and consequently in the time necessary to establish our own internal systems.

In seeking to remove processing operations from the Library Center, there were two possible options. The first was to seek some form of co-operative processing system among the five institutional libraries of the area. Although such a cooperative effort is a possibility sometime in the future, the politics (in a nonpejorative sense) of cooperation and the necessary planning and start-up effort, together with our requirement for an operating system in 1970, essentially eliminated this choice. The experience of The Colorado Academic Libraries Book Processing Center is indicative of the planning, fiscal, and operational problems involved.[20]

The second option was to go to a commercial book processor, the road we have chosen at this time. Commercial processing is a relatively recent phenomenon as Barbara Westby points out in her description of the problems and listing of processing firms.

> Commercial cataloging in its modern connotation is ten years old. Yet the concept is not new. It was proposed as early as 1872. The Library of Congress offered copies of its catalog cards for sale in 1901 and the H. W. Wilson Company began its card service in 1938. However, its modern development, combining both catalog cards and book preparation, dates from 1958. The expansion from one firm in that year to over fifty in 1968 indicates the phenomenal growth of the commercial cataloging industry during the past ten years.[21]

Whether or not a processor is to be used will nearly always hinge on costs and manpower. Cataloging manpower is especially in short supply, even if we limit ourselves only to the book operation. Audio-visual cataloging, at the level required by colleges, is almost nonexistent. Costs are difficult to determine and, in choosing a processor, they must be considered in two categories:

1. *Internal costs*

- Availability and salary scale of library staff
- Library routines added, eliminated, or revised as a result of outside processing
- Rate of tolerable error and the cost of rectifying such errors

2. *External costs*

- Basic processor's rate per item
- Added charges for special cases
- Transportation and other handling charges

One-to-one comparison of costs between in-house processing and commercial processing is made extraordinarily difficult by the paucity of standard and justifiable figures for in-house processing. The same problem is reflected in that portion of the commercial processing operation which the library itself handles. It is most important to understand that commercial or outside processing does not eliminate all in-house operations; rather it eliminates some and changes others.

In their brief listing of unpublished cost and time studies, Tesovnik and DeHart[22] state that "lack of uniform methods for gathering statistics and the complexity of technical service operations are factors that militate against conducting time and cost studies." When one scans and attempts to compare the studies they review, it is painfully apparent that the variety of local salary scales, procedures, special arrangements, and inflation undermine any useful results. This can of course be overcome by developing a set of standard times and using them for comparison. These do not exist; hence we must use cost-based studies.

Edward Turner of Washington and Lee University, in his recent study of technology and small college libraries, has possibly the best summary of recent cost studies.[23] It is worth noting that "recent" means "since 1960." The figures that Turner cites range from $3.75 (1966) to $4.50 (1968), but one of the higher figures, $4.33, dates from 1960. It is safe to say that these figures in 1970 would be closer to $5.50 per item, even in a highly efficient processing department. An approximately comparable figure for commercial processing experience in 1969–1970 at Hampshire is $4.37. This includes average cost per processed volume, very rough estimates for labor and related costs, and overhead at 20 percent. All of these figures must be treated with extreme caution, especially when used on a comparative basis.

The choice for commercial processing sets in motion a long train of new decision-making situations for the librarian. Books as physical objects follow entirely different routes in the receiving and check-in process. Different patterns of verification and spot check are required than with in-house cataloging. Different files and data forms have to be established. Processors will not, for example, provide cross references for the catalog. What routines, if any, have to be established to take care of this feature of the public catalog? These internal variables must be considered in addition to the rates quoted by the commercial firm. A reputable processor should inform a prospective client of this fact and should indicate where in the total system these costs or changes will occur.

Once agreement has been made to utilize a commercial processor, a number of specific decisions regarding processing are immediately required. These should be included in detailed specifications to the processor. How is the book to be processed? What sort of labels are required? Where should they appear? What kind of pockets and book cards are needed? Are book jackets to be removed? How are reference books to be labeled? How should paperbacks be treated? What about treatment of oversized books?

Specifications should be worked out in collaboration with the processor. Unless the library is prepared to pay high unit cost for special formats, the librarian must be willing to question his own demands and to compromise so that unit costs can be maintained at the lowest possible level. A commercial processor bases his operation on high volume, assembly line techniques, and a high degree of standardization. Variations will, of course, drive costs up.

New libraries have an advantage when these decisions are made. Unless biases for specific and intricate detail are held by the librarian, he has no operating routines and procedures which must be met and is therefore free to use the standard processing systems which the processor has to offer and on which his costs are based.

Despite careful planning and succinct specifications certain problems will inevitably arise. Concentration on these problems, by the way, does not mean that they exist only with commercial processors. As Anne Peters of Library Processing System Inc., has pointed out,

> . . . One cannot get certain things from commercial processing which are likewise impossible in the best organized cataloging department, namely, complete elimination of human error and an absolute time between ordering a book and placing it on the library shelves.[24]

Libraries themselves tend to gloss over many of these problems, or to consider them in the normal range of operations. They are heightened here because the library-processor relationship is new and all the nagging and persistent problems, plus new ones, seem to surface because the total situation has been altered. In addition, physical distance between library and processor adds to the communication problems.

Acquisition Problems

The first question is to decide which books to order from the processor. In some cases the processor acts as a book jobber. In others, the company has an arrangement with a separate jobber or depends on transshipment from a jobber used by the library. In the former, because he is dependent on a high turnover of stock, he deals mostly in easily available, in-print items. Out-of-print, foreign, small-press, and hard-to-obtain items become a problem. They are, however, also a problem for the library doing its own processing. If the order is placed through the processor, unnecessary delays or even failure to fill the order may result. If the library orders those items elsewhere, then commercial processing is not eliminating the multiple dealer files, or separate ordering and invoicing procedures as it ideally should. In practice, these files and procedures probably will be significantly reduced, but not eliminated, by using a commercial processor. The problem comes in deciding how large those files can become before they negate the advantages of outside processing.

Certain accepted ordering procedures must be altered. Special files must be maintained. Procedures must be set up to handle confirmation reports and cancellation notices. What kinds of reports, how frequent and in what form, are required? How should orders be submitted? In the preoperational period we have found that batch orders submitted every two weeks have been satisfactory, both in internal processes and in receipt. As we go into operation we anticipate a different scheduling of orders. How are shipments made and who covers the cost? In our case the processor pays shipping costs. What kinds of invoicing procedures will be followed? Internal routines must be established to handle invoices expeditiously, without eliminating necessary check routines. How are corrections and cancellations to be handled? This is a key problem, as it is in any library, but exaggerated here by physical distance; because, though corrections and cancellations represent only a small portion of the total, they consume a fairly large proportion of time and energy.

Cataloging Problems

First questions, of course, concern the general context of the cataloging operation; for example, what classification scheme is to be followed and how is it to be used? We have opted for the Library of Congress classification number as it appears on the L. C. card. Special problems, however, occur in using the Library of Congress classification scheme in the areas of fiction and in law. The PZ3 and PZ4 schedules have proven unsatisfactory to many libraries. Most prefer to classify these works in the P (literature) schedules. This decision should be made early and included in specifications to the processor. The L. C. schedules for law are, at the time of writing, just being completed. Special arrangements must be made for dealing with books in such subjects.

It is not economically feasible for the processor to check and update a catalog card revised by the Library of Congress. This may cause problems in establishing consistency in the public catalog and may require special procedures. The question of subject heading changes, and *see* and *see also* references also exist.

Cataloging problems may be the most difficult to anticipate in specifications. They are difficult for the processor to deal with since they can often be decided only by the librarian familiar with the collection and the use to which a specific title may be put. Are special variations to be required in cataloging series? How, for example, should sets be cataloged? As a set or by individual title? Will a general rule be adequate in the specifications to deal with the majority of cases? This decision, again, will affect costs, since multiple-volume sets are processed less expensively than separately cataloged monographs. Can the extra title cards be supplied for those not included on original tracings and for series?

Check-in procedures also must vary from those of normal operations. Each book must be carefully revised. Titles must be reviewed for cataloging and processing errors as well as for bibliographic errors. The rate of tolerable error must be decided by each library. Particular problems arise in partial shipments of multivolume sets. It is important to see that correct processing charges are applied in these cases.

In the areas of automation, no processor is yet able to provide a MARC II record at a reasonable cost, and as part of the standard package, including the book itself. As MARC records expand in the future, and hopefully retrospectively, there is the eventuality that the processor can provide this standard record. In the meantime, however, any library contemplating a machine base should insist that the L. C. card number be included in the record, for it provides an access hook to the MARC tapes. At the present time the processor can provide, at minimal cost, a machine-readable record, which may serve as a basis for a book catalog and related products, and possible input to a national or regional network. A point frequently overlooked is that if a punched card is generated for circulation, the card must be scored so that it can be folded to fit in the book pocket of smaller books.

If there is to be a complete machine cataloging record on tape or disc, it is important to determine early in the process to whom that record belongs—the processor or the library—and in what form it is to be maintained. It is a valuable record for, once made, it can be used repeatedly by the company in future processing.

In September 1969 Hampshire College convened a small one-day conference on commercial processing, including representatives from two processing firms and a group of librarians, some with experience and some without experience but interested in the possibilities.[25] The conference came to several conclusions, which emphasized the interdependence of library and processor, the dependence of the processor on the Library of Congress, and the increasing necessity for interlibrary systems cooperation.

1.   From the standpoint of the library, the most important evaluative criteria were (a) speed of service, and (b) number of unfilled orders or cancellations.

Comment: It is worth noting that, in the Colorado study on academic library processing, the mean time to process a book from time of order placement to time book was cataloged, in the nine libraries under study, was 151 days.[26] In a small sample of our orders in 1969 we found an approximately equivalent time to be 112 days with a commercial processor. These figures may not be comparable. For example, the Colorado figure includes the processing of foreign titles, the Hampshire figures none. There were probably cancellations in the latter case, thus filtering out certain problem titles. The question of unfilled orders and cancellations is still a serious one and should represent a major area for improvement.

2. On the question of costs, it is extremely important that the librarian understand the hidden costs involved, both for his library and for the user. Such an understanding, based on a solid systems (manual or automated) knowledge, would go far in assuring a fruitful and useful contractual relationship. The processor is not a substitute for the complete catalog operation and librarians must be aware of this. It becomes a different operation, and new systems and routines must evolve.

3. The speed of the service becomes important if the library attempts to meet pressing current needs of its patrons. The library, under such circumstances, either must mount its own operation or hope that the processor can provide quick service through temporary cataloging. There was a difference of opinion here between the processors on whether they could provide temporary cataloging and still maintain the same pricing schedule.

4. Besides the usual vagaries of publishers, service from the Library of Congress for basic cataloging and card availability appears to be a major obstacle to speedy service. The conference group went on record in deploring the recent personnel and budget cuts for the Library of Congress and its consequent effect on libraries. Because a whole national system has been built around the L. C. card service, it is imperative that some solution to the vagaries of national budgeting be found. The effect is not limited to processor and client, but to the whole system of libraries serving millions of people.

5. One possible and attractive long-term solution to the cataloging problem was put forward by Vincent Piccolo of the Worcester (Mass.) State College Library.

> . . . there is a need for cataloging brokerage houses to supply individual libraries with a standardized cataloging product in whatever quantity, form, or schedule it is demanded; and that the source of this standardized product should be a combination of the Library of Con-

gress and an independent authority to extend and complement the Library of Congress's total output.

This independent authority should be a non-profit entity designed and governed by a board appointed by professional library associations. Support for the authority would come from a portion of the institutional membership fees of libraries in associations and from direct subscriptions by commercial processing services . . .

Ideally commercial processing services could purchase materials for a client from many sources, process these materials according to a client's specifications, and supply cataloging from a complete bank of cataloging information. We know that the chief lack at this time is the cataloging bank. Before the incentives of business create too many diffuse sources of cataloging information, I think the profession should take the initiative and create its own authorized and authoritative source to complement the Library of Congress. Then commercial services would be responsible for procuring and processing only. Cataloging policy and production would remain the responsibility of the profession where it belongs philosophically.[27]

6.   There is a strong and definite need for standardization of services. Libraries must develop a sense of what is feasible in a commerical operation and not require trivial exceptions, several of which were described at the meeting. There is a danger today, as many new companies come in the field, that librarians will be attracted by low prices and promises of service that are unreal. Too many commercial newcomers to the field have an inadequate understanding of the complexities of the business and of its real costs. Undercapitalization and an overabundance of contracts with a consequent abuse of credit by some firms has led to disastrous entanglements and much bitterness.

7.   In the area of nonprint media commercial processors, for a variety of reasons, are ill prepared to provide much service. The diffuseness of media producers, the lack of centralized jobbing channels, the lack of standardization in cataloging, and the inapplicability of such standards as the Anglo-American rules all conspire to work against any current solution. It appears that at the present time only *ad hoc* and temporary systems can be devised. This is particularly true where there is a desire for automation and a combining of all media forms in one catalog.

8.   Commercial processors, for the most part, have dealt with small public, junior college, and school libraries. In moving to the four-year college library, processors are frequently not prepared for the problems of out-of-print materials, foreign books, and foreign languages common to the college library. They are also ill prepared for systems automation.

Much of what was discussed at the Conference could, with little change, be applied to cooperative processing arrangements. We think it is significant that this is so, and may have implications in the design and development of a commercial operation essentially functioning as a processing base for a group of cooperating libraries. This is an area that should be explored.

In summary it is necessary to repeat our previous cautionary comment. The problems reviewed here are not especially new to library operations. They are emphasized in this context because, as it has been said, if you wish to find out how something works try to change it. There is no doubt that commercial (or cooperative) processing will become a major factor for both new and old libraries. However, such a move requires a thorough analysis of procedures, staff use, and traditional library requirements for the present information contained in the card format.[28] Such an analysis is healthy and it should establish much more flexible systems, able to react to new problems as they appear. At this time commercial processing, especially for academic libraries, is too new and too untested to provide a fixed response to old systems. It is in this very flexibility that a new and more efficient set of alternatives can be derived, fruitful to the library and profitable for the industry.

AUTOMATION

In March 1968 Hampshire College convened a small conference to define a general frame of reference in planning for automation in the college library.[29] Our purpose at that time was to explore the feasibility of automation for any new college library, and the degree to which such a library could and should automate. Some of what follows is derived from that report. Consideration of three areas of concern are basic to decision in library automation: system and user economics, alteration of staff, and management requirements.

First, the systems should be economic. That is, they should not cost appreciably more than conventional systems, after the initial investment in start-up costs. The question of costs is a very difficult one, especially if we take account, as we should, of the user's costs. For sake of illustration of user-systems costs, let us look at the spectrum of systems and services the library might provide. At one end—the chaotic or absurd end, if you will—all materials are dumped, like coal in a coal bin, into a huge box labeled "Library." Every time a user wants something he has to go through the pile until he finds it, if he ever does. At the other end of the spectrum—call it Utopia—all materials are so organized that a user can always find what he wants, when he wants it, in the kind of package he wants it in, and delivered where he can use it. Now somewhere between these two extremes a library must find a point on the spectrum where both its internal costs and the user's costs reach a workable equilibrium.

Librarians have tended to concentrate too much on the control of their internal costs, almost always at the expense of the user. Although the tone of the discussion here may imply much the same, the user is very much the cornerstone of our planning. The danger is in the form of our rationalizations. As a reflection of western technocratic values justification is usually made on the basis of internal systems cost savings. After a while this form of savings becomes the only real justification, and blatant advertising is used to convince the user he is getting what he wants or deserves, which, if one is a cynic, may strike the latter as true. The point here—and indeed of this entire report—is that, even though we have difficulty measuring user "economics," it must become a real part of the costing of any systems concept.

Second, these systems should free professional and administrative staff from routines so that they can dedicate a substantial portion of their time to students and to faculty. At the same time staff must be assured that the system in back of them is capable of generating useful responses to users. This is especially necessary as the library staff becomes more visible and as they attempt to stimulate potential use. It may seem that these first two criteria are contradictory. They are contradictory only if the sole purpose of the system is to raise and to measure productivity by the speed of handling materials and by the performance of certain kinds of nonintellectual processes on those materials. If these are the limits of cost economics, then there is indeed contradiction. If, however, the tenor of the previous chapter is accepted, then the importance of matching user and material is controlling. The point here is that automation of library processes, seen in the context of a social rather than an engineering problem, will provide a new base for the enhancement of user-system interface. The danger of course is that, like the engineers and managers in Kurt Vonnegut's *Player Piano,* we will talk in social terms but we will mean mechanical efficiency.

Third, these systems or their feasible extensions should generate management and administrative data not available from conventional library systems. Management and administrative data—a bland sort of phrase. Do we, does the library profession really know what kind of data it needs in order to make realistic appraisals of ongoing operations? The American Library Association manual on library statistics,[30] specifically the second chapter on "College and University Libraries," has nothing to say about this. It is principally concerned with uniformity in gathering statistics for national and comparative purposes. The care and argument that surround the publication of these kinds of statistics betray a professional narrowness that refuses to ask real questions. The tables as they appear in similar gatherings of the U. S. Office of Education[31] cover four areas: size of collection, operating expenditures, staffing, and salaries. These data are a good illustration of what is known as the "Biderman concept" of "administratively convenient data" as distinct from true data.[32] All sorts of data collected and published by federal agencies are administratively convenient to define, to obtain, and to structure; but they may or may not have much resemblance to the phenomena which presumably they represent. Library statistics fall in this category. They have little relation to operational realities. They tell us how much institution x is spending compared to y and what the comparative salary ranges are for middle and lower staff. Except for the data on expenditure per student and faculty member, they contain very little significant social or systems information. They represent a sort of counting syndrome, which the profession accepts but never really questions.

We need operational data, at the national and local level, that will enable both the profession as a whole and the individual librarian to measure performance (not size) against some standard and to predict tomorrow's operations for planning and budgetary purposes. The computer offers the profession, as libraries are automated, an opportunity to redefine the kinds of questions to which we need answers. This is a hard problem indeed—to frame the questions—for, in a way, the questions a profession deems important define that profession. This probably will not happen soon, and automation will overlay what is basically a nineteenth century institution. However, the mere application of such a basic tool as the computer will force change and demand answers to questions that have not been formulated yet. The elements of a systems study are beginning to appear, both in texts and studies such as those by Hayes and Becker,[33] Morse,[34] Chapman,[35] Burkhalter, [36] and Raffel and Shishko,[37] and in the emergence of systems staffs in libraries. But, despite the desires to implement a different kind of system, professional, social, and academic frames of reference require that libraries not become too unfamiliar with established patterns of work, study, and scholarship. This caution is not, as some may suspect, merely a form of copping out. The library as an institution, despite brave prose, has not yet reached the position of power or prestige to initiate fundamental change. In addition the inertia built into both academia and libraries, combined with the institutional conservatism of the faculty, does not provide a context conducive to change.

It is quite apparent that, despite all our rationalization, a good portion of basic decision-making in the library—as indeed it is elsewhere—is an act of faith. A danger exists principally in the form the rationalizations take and the way they are believed. It is easier to coat with words than to be skeptical. A second danger is the tendency to underestimate seriously the amount of time and the development costs required to bring a system to the point where it produces the records and services wanted, in the form they are wanted. Such underestimation, whether the result of self-delusion or overt overselling, frequently affects the usefulness of the systems and their products.

It is within this context that the Hampshire Library Center, as a result of the March 1968 conference, developed a framework within which we can evolve our systems. To some extent it has been a source of anxiety, for the following statements represent positions and financial commitments beyond the economic capabilities of a new private college. It must be recognized that these statements were developed in 1968 and early 1969, at a time when the MARC development was undergoing great changes. But they do represent the frame of reference within which our initial decisions were made.

1. The MARC system is basic for any future national or regional capability.[38]
2. The MARC system at this time only has meaning if it can be used to generate order information and catalog products, and as a sort of investment for the future.
3. Retrospective MARC data is of major importance to a new college library.[39]
4. There is no "clean" system without a tremendous financial commitment by the library. (Clean = total system, automated or not, representing precisely, and with minimal error, the exact holdings of a library.)
5. MARC formats for nonprint materials (phonorecordings, films, etc.) are several years away; and retrospective MARC listings for these items 5 to 10 years away. Such items as slides may never receive coverage.
6. A new library must at minimum develop a machine-readable base for its holdings which is easily convertible to MARC formats, or which provides access points to individual MARC records; for example, the Library of Congress card number.
7. Commercial processors and data generating firms, in 1968–1969, were not yet prepared to provide retrospective MARC data except at very high costs, if at all. The situation is gradually improving.
8. Workable and economically feasible remote access on-line systems are at least five years away, especially for the college library, and then only in the larger context of regional cooperation.
9. Any design of systems should take into consideration eventual conversion to an on-line mode.

10. Library automation for the Hampshire College Library, in any depth, only has meaning when developed in the context of neighboring institutions, or in a larger configuration. For economic and efficient reasons it is necessary to think in terms of a cooperative system, either of the five institutions or of a larger complex such as the New England Library Information Network (NELINET) might become.[40]

In evaluating options for the Hampshire Library it became apparent that there were three possible positions relative to automation. These positions are not necessarily opposed to each other, but they are sufficiently different in approach to indicate separate notice.

The first is what might be called the experimental and cooperative approach. Those who espoused this position basically say that the Hampshire Library should be as experimental and innovative as possible, and should depend on the other four institutional libraries for conventional services. Such an approach obviously requires commitments by the other institutions which they are not, at this time, willing or able to undertake. However attractive the idea is to an experimenting institution such as Hampshire, it would require that the Library gamble with its basic responsibility—providing conventional service to its publics.

The second position is basically a systems approach based on certain fundamental assumptions concerning the function and objectives of libraries. Those who hold this position say that the primary function of a library system is to provide data for users on the position and status of packages called books, periodicals, and so on, within the system. Adherents of such an approach insist that it is necessary not to confuse the data *in* the book with the data *about* the book. It is the latter kind of data with which they are concerned. Products of such data, particularly when in machine-readable form, are (a) catalog cards, book catalog, or on-line access to bibliographic file; (b) order data and status of orders; (c) circulation cards and systems; and (d) a serial control system. Such a system depends on one of two things: either a huge retrospective bibliographic data base in the MARC II format, or the development by the Hampshire Library Center of a machine-readable file in MARC II format of its acquisitions. The huge data base does not exist. The cost to the Hampshire College Library Center of keying the record of its own acquisitions, including nonprint materials, for its own purposes only is too high a price to pay for an automated system.

The third position basically states that the Hampshire Library Center must provide conventional services in 1970. It should at this time concentrate on building this core collection and on establishing highly efficient routines. At the same time it should have a parallel program which explores, defines, and designs new configurations of space, people, and systems, and isolates feasible areas for experimentation in automation and cooperation.

These three positions are not incompatible, given money, time, and imagination. With the Hampshire bias toward extension, cooperation, and experimentation, the Library Center would like to break completely with the traditional warehouse image. Financial constraints pose of course one major problem. Perhaps more important, however, are the factors of planning time, the politics of cooperation, and, despite the many systems described in the literature, the paucity of hard data on costs and explicit systems design. Another important constraint is the unreadiness of the library profession to make the necessary decisions on standardization and systems. Such a state of affairs also affects the ability and willingness of commercial or governmental services to provide economic packages and systems for library automation. The library market for automation is still too unpredictable, which militates against any real investment in research and development. It will come; but a library designed for operation in 1970 is caught in a betwixt-between land where landmarks are not yet plotted and compasses are erratic.

As a result of the Conference in 1968, and of advice from other consultants, as well as a thorough analysis of the Hampshire College Library environment, the following policy framework was developed for planning and action:

1. The Library Center will generally espouse the third approach discussed above, with as much of a commitment to experimentation and automation as is economic and practicable. This is not, as it might be assumed from superficial reading, a bland and fatuous statement. It is a positive statement designed to generate a long hard look at what college libraries should and could do in an academic context.

2. The approach of the Hampshire Library Center toward automation is somewhat at variance with the second position described above— the systems approach. Although data processing is an extremely important first step in maintaining control of and in providing information about the status of packages in the system, it is *only* a first step. There are two further goals which must dictate the objectives of automation. The first is to provide access to the contents of the material in the system. This is to say the system must be able to respond positively to real questions in the real world. Secondly, library systems must work toward a repackaging of the material provided its users, in whatever media, in whatever format. Automated library systems, especially those which will manipulate linguistic, aural, and visual data, will have much to offer in this repackaging process.

3. A core collection of books (25,000 to 35,000) would be processed by a commercial processor, to include a machine-readable shelf-list-card and a circulation card. In spite of the advice of consultants this record is not in MARC format, but accessibility is maintained through the L. C. card number.

4. As soon as feasible the record of nonprint items should be added to the system. This requires an equivalent machine-readable base so that the products (book catalogs, special listings, etc.) would include all media.

5. We will maintain a standard public catalog for all media based on the 3 x 5 card, augmented by whatever products can be generated by the machine-readable shelf list.

6. It appears probable that the automation of library routines—at the college level—will be most effective and economic when it can be accomplished within the context of cooperation. The potential for cooperation is high among the five institutions of the Connecticut Valley. Such cooperation, however, cannot be accomplished overnight.

It is necessary to take a hard look at the implications of these framework statements. They represent, in some cases, financial commitments beyond the economic capabilities of a new private college, such as the development *and effective utilization* of retrospective data in MARC format. These requirements almost say that a small college library cannot automate without exorbitant costs—exorbitant relative to the institutional budget. There is another question of course—whether it can afford not to automate—but this, because it is truly unanswerable except as an act of faith, must be considered moot at this point.

We do not believe the book catalog, or a derivative microfiche catalog, is a feasible answer at this time as a substitute for the conventional card catalog. The costs of updating a book catalog are high compared to what appear to be the equivalent costs of updating a card catalog. The latter can be updated daily in a small library. The queuing problems with a microfiche catalog are apt to be extreme when compared with similar queues at a card catalog. In addition the labor costs of maintaining currency in a microfiche catalog would appear to be high and onerous.

The economic use of MARC tapes requires total use from order generation to card production to serials control to circulation procedures to management data generation. It also requires, at this point in time, extensive development of software packages to translate the storage format of MARC into useful configurations for internal and external library use. Only the largest and most well-off libraries can afford this. Smaller libraries such as Hampshire's must wait until this software is available, in the meantime specifying and analyzing the problems as it sees them. It is worth noting that this discussion has encompassed only print; automated control of nonprint media as a national standard is nowhere near the level of development of that of books.[41] However, past and future experience with the MARC format for printed materials will undoubtedy speed up the development of suitable and compatible systems for other media.

REFERENCES

1. F. G. Kilgour, Systems Concepts and Libraries, *College and Research Libraries,* **28** (3):167–170 (May 1967).

2. Robert W. Miller, *Schedule, Cost, and Profit Control with PERT: A Comprehensive Guide for Program Management.* New York, McGraw-Hill, 1963.

3. *Ibid.,* 29–38.

4. R. M. Hayes and J. Becker, *Handbook of Data Processing for Libraries.* New York, Wiley, 1970.

5. *Ibid.*

6. Warren B. Hicks and Alma M. Tillin, *Developing Multi-Media Libraries.* New York, Bowker, 1970.

7. *Ibid.,* 4.

8. Robert Muller, Multi-Media Shelving, *Library Journal,* **95**:750 (February 15, 1970).

9. *Permutations* (motion picture) IBM. Made by John H. Whitney, released by Museum of Modern Art, 1968.

10. Ruth Hilton, "Classification and Cataloging of Phonorecords: A Practical Guide for Librarians," September 1969 (not published).

11. C. Saheb-Ettaba and R. B. McFarland, *ANSCR, The Alpha-Numeric System for Classification of Recordings.* Williamsport, Pa., Bro-Dart Publishing, 1969.

12. Jean Riddle et al., *Non-Book Materials, the Organization of Integrated Collections* (Preliminary Edition). Ottawa, Canadian Library Association, 1970.

13. Victor Rosenberg, *The Application of Psychometric Techniques to Determine the Attitudes of Individuals toward Information Seeking.* (Report No. 2, Studies in the Man-System Interface in Libraries) Bethlehem, Pa., Center for the Information Sciences, Lehigh University, July 1967.

14. See for example P. M. Morse, *Library Effectiveness, A Systems Approach,* Cambridge, M. I. T. Press, 1968; R. W. Trueswell, Determining the Optimal Number of Volumes for a Library's Core Collection, *Libri,* **16** (1):49–60 (1966); E. F. Turner, *A Study of the Implications of Modern Technology for Small College Libraries.* Lexington, Va., Washington and Lee University, March 1969. (Final Report, OEG Project No. 7-0910).

15. Wesley Simons and L. Tansey, *A Slide Classification System for the Organization and Automatic Indexing of Interdisciplinary Collections of Slides and Pictures.* Santa Cruz, University of California, August 1970.

16. As reported by representatives from the California Institute of the Arts at the meeting of the College Art Association, January 1970, Washington, D.C.

17. Simons and Tansey, *A Universal Slide Classification Scheme with Automatic Indexing* (preliminary edition). Santa Cruz, University of California, 1969.

18. For a good review of the current status of efforts toward the solution of some of these problems see Pearce S. Grove and Herman L. Totten, Bibliographic Control of Media: The Librarian's Excedrin Headache, *Wilson Library Bulletin,* **44** (3):299–311 (November 1969).

19. David O. Lane, The Selection of Academic Library Materials, A Literature Survey, *College and Research Libraries,* **29** (5):364–372 (September 1968).

20. R. M. Dougherty and J. M. Maier, *Colorado Academic Libraries Book Processing Center: First Six Months Operation,* Boulder, University of Colorado Libraries, June 1970. See particularly Chapter 5: "Some problems to be anticipated by others. . .".

21. B. M. Westby, Commercial Processing Firms: A Directory, *Library Resources and Technical Processes,* **13** (2):209 (Spring 1969).

22. M. E. Tesovnik and F. E. DeHart, Unpublished Studies of Technical Service Time and Costs: A Selected Bibliography, *Library Resources & Technical Services,* **14** (1):56–67 (Winter 1970).

23. Turner, *op. cit.,* 53–55.

24. Personal communication from Anne Peters, November 10, 1969.

25. Commercial Processing Conference, September 8, 1969. Attendees: W. D. Joyce and V. Piccolo of Worcester State College; Barbara Westby of the Library of Congress; David Remington of Bro-Dart Industries; Anne Peters of Library Processing Systems, Inc.; James Kennedy and Merle Boylan of the University of Massachusetts; Anne C. Edmonds of Mount Holyoke College; C. T. Laugher of Amherst College; Richard Harwell of Smith College; Estelle Jussim, Judith Watts and R. S. Taylor of Hampshire College.

26. Lawrence E. Leonard et al., *Colorado Academic Libraries Book Processing Center Study,* Boulder, University of Colorado, June 1968, 21–25.

27. Correspondence with Vincent Piccolo, October 1969.

28. Ben-Ami Lipetz, *User Requirements in Identifying Desired Works in a Large Library.* New Haven, Conn., Yale University Library, June 1970 (Final Report, Grant No. SAR/OEG-1-7-071140-4427).

29. R. S. Taylor, Ed., *Planning for Automated Systems in the College Library,* Report of a Conference held at Hampshire College, March 14–15, 1968. Amherst, Mass., Hampshire College, April 1969.

30. Library Statistics: *A Handbook of Concepts, Definitions, and Terminology,* prepared by the Staff of the Statistics Coordinating Project. Chicago, American Library Association, 1966.

31. *Library Statistics of Colleges and Universities, Fall 1969, Data for Individual Institutions.* Washington, June 1970.

32. Noted by Wilbert Moore in *Daedalus* (Summer 1967) Toward the Year 2000: Work in Progress, 942.

33. Hayes and Becker, *op. cit.* (Published in late 1970 by Wiley, too late for extensive use in this study.)

34. Morse, *op. cit.*

35. Edward Chapman et al., *Library Systems Analysis Guidelines.* New York, Wiley, 1970.

36. Barton R. Burkhalter, *Case Studies in Systems Analysis in a University Library.* Hamden, Conn., Scarecrow, 1968.

37. J. A. Raffel and R. Shishko, *Systematic Analysis of University Libraries: An Application of Cost-Benefit Analysis to the M. I. T. Libraries.* Cambridge, M. I. T. Press, 1969.

38. Library of Congress. *The MARC Pilot Project: Final Report on a Project Sponsored by the Council on Library Resources, Inc.,* Prepared by Henriette D. Avram, Washington, 1969. Also *MARC Manuals Used by the Library of Congress.* Chicago, American Library Association, 1969.

39. Library of Congress. *Conversion of Retrospective Catalog Records to Machine-Readable Form: A Study of the Feasibility of a National Bibliographic Service.* Washington, 1969. See also H. D. Avram, The RECON Pilot Project: A Progress Report, *Journal of Library Automation,* 3:102–114 (1970).

40. See reports of Inforonics, Inc., Maynard, Mass., 1967–1969 on systems design, catalog data file creation, MARC II conversion. See also Goldstein, Samuel et al., *Development of a Machine Form Union Catalog for the New England Library Information Network.* Wellesley, Mass., New England Board of Higher Education, September 1970.

41. Grove and Totten, *op. cit.*

Chapter Six

Educational Technology and Information Transfer

. . . we are fools to use radio and television in the modern world. . . .
Only madmen would use radio and television if they knew the consequences.

Marshall McLuhan[1]

Professor McLuhan has caught the right flavor of subversion which is inherent in the communications revolution surrounding us. It is changing industrial society and it will drastically affect the processes of education. It is the speed of this change which essentially concerns us here, because planning for transition and for the future requires that we make certain general assumptions about the processes of education, the degree of control that we are able to exercise, and the rate of usable and financially feasible innovation.

The term "educational technology" is usually accepted as meaning free-standing devices (hardware) such as projectors or tape recorders, and the packages (software) necessary for the storage of audio signals and visual images. Such interpretations are especially acceptable when thought of in the context of the traditional library. Such hardware and software can be absorbed into the library system with hardly a burp. Libraries and audio-visual centers have operated on this view, but it is far too restrictive a view because the mixture is too volatile and because the effective use of these media requires some basic changes in their educational surround.

There are several major elements, some cultural and some technological, some mythological and some real, which we should understand in order to make decisions concerning this technology. Perhaps the most difficult to consider rationally is the dichotomy between promise and performance, or more realistically, between aspiration and disillusionment. As Anthony Oettinger has pointed out,

> . . . The introduction of technology into education is an age-old process alternately exhilarating and depressing. The vastness of prevailing ignorance about both education and technology is matched only by the acrimony of debate about the value of educational technology, debate highlighted by a persistent confusion of ultimate promise with immediate possibility. . . . That is one reason why it is vital to distinguish carefully between the long-range promise of educational technology and the technology that is ready for immediate delivery.[2]

Professor Oettinger is quite correct in questioning the myths of educational technology. In a basically unplanned society, especially one in which superficial is confused with fundamental change, the technology and the attendant myths take on a life of their own. The existence of this mythology becomes an integral part of the process of adaptation and change, with consequent effect on the planning system.

All of these are new systems or new approaches concerned with old problems of teaching, learning, and communication. We must of course be sure that we are not attracted by mere gimmickry. An easy sentence to write; but when does "gimmickry" become an accepted part of the system? Basically this means that, though in part commitment to educational technology is an act of faith, it must be viewed skeptically. We must continually ask if the steps we are taking are real or imaginary, if they lead us somewhere.

A second major consideration is the potential for new approaches that have occurred in the last decade in the feasible applications of communications technology. We can now seriously plan for a communications network within an institution, among a group of cooperating institutions, or within the larger context of a "wired city."[3] The range of options that are now apparent offers a veritable feast of possibilities, but at the same time poses problems in anticipating with certainty even short-term developments. Two elements of these possible systems are critical: the rapid growth of cable television and the increasing use of remotely accessed, time-sharing computer systems.

The usefulness of television has in part been limited by the highly structured and monopolistic growth of commercial television and the low-level utilization of the potential of CATV systems.

The phenomenon of a thick strand of tensiled copper wire encased in plastic may change television as much as television changed wireless radio, for the miracle of the wireless is about to be replaced by the practical necessity of the wired city.[4]

The possible applications of such systems to the College are discussed in the second section of this chapter.

Present trends toward the installation of dial access systems in libraries, especially random-access systems, are proving useful for structured and scheduled modes of instruction. For the most part, however, the actual channels to the store are highly limited thus restricting the user in his choices.[5] In addition, dial access systems for the most part are limited to audio signals, which closes out much of the most exciting potential. However, the experiences of Ohio State University, Oklahoma Christian College, and Oral Roberts University imply that straight audio facilities can and do have a high level of use. The Dial Access Study carried out at Catholic University in 1968 indicated that 45 percent of usage is for teacher-mediated instruction; about the same for enrichment; and the remaining 10 percent is for use in review, remedial teaching, and primary presentation of course content.[6] Audio alone is undoubtedly useful in certain situations—and it is likely that we have not yet fully explored this potential—but designing solely for audio limits future options. Early expectations for the random accessing of moving video images has been disillusioning, for as it turned out only still images could be accessed, duplicated, and transmitted automatically.[7] The potential of coaxial cable systems as an internal network within an institution, the "wired city" of Fred Friendly mentioned before, seems to offer a much broader range of present capabilities and future options, even though the programs cannot be randomly accessed. The recent example of cooperative development with a CATV system between Indiana University and the City of Vincennes is a case in point and one to be watched and evaluated.[8]

It seems most likely that effective development of these systems for undergraduate education will come through small systems—"small" in a geographic sense—with considerable intertwining of television and telephone systems. For a campus such as Hampshire's a cable network with a "community antennae" or a working agreement with local CATV interests, for example, would serve both for off-the-air reception and transmission and for live or stored programs on nonbroadcast television channels which can be used either on demand or by schedule.

But all of these systems await testing and evaluation and this cannot be done without long-term actual "hands-on" experience by the total institution—students, faculty, librarians, educational technologists, and administrators. This means that instead of justifying the potential use of a system on the basis of rhetoric that is transparently wishful thinking or worse, dishonest, it will be justified in hard-headed experimental terms.

> My aim in analyzing the myths, the institutional failures, the brazen exploitations, the oppressive self-delusions that make a mockery of technological change in education is not to deny the promise, but to rescue it from unmerited disillusionment. I say there are no easy victories, no quick answers, no panaceas. If we are to realize the promise, we must not allow our human and material resources to be diverted into showy changes in form that will continue to block changes in substance. Fundamental ignorance remains to be overcome in many realms that bear on the successful application of modern technology to education and we must therefore be prepared to encourage long-term investment in the exploration of diverse paths.[9]

So writes Professor Oettinger in words that will hardly reassure those who require the rhetoric of structure and a comfortable pathway of change.

A third major consideration in the use of technology for education is that it asks new sets of questions about the processes and objectives of education. It tends to put into question traditional teaching practices. Like the present automation of nineteenth century library processes, educational technology will enhance, protect, and embalm conventional formats such as the lecture, because this is what we are accustomed to. At the same time the use of technology will place in question the use of the lecture in many circumstances and, because communications technology offers so many alternatives, it hopefully will encourage more effective utilization of teaching talent, and this is the key goal: better education. As historian William H. McNeill pointed out at a 1967 Toronto meeting of the American Historical Association:

> Some academic historians seem to fear any change in familiar routines of the classroom, perhaps because they feel that if the communications industry really gets its camel nose into our lecture halls, their grasp upon the lectern will be loosed and their lecture notes become suddenly obsolete.[10]

Such systems also have the tendency to view teacher, student, message, and medium as one system and consequently to provide the impetus for new formats for learning. The audio-tutorial course in biology developed by Samuel Postlethwait at Purdue is a case in point.[11] It appears to be eminently successful, though very likely nontransferable as a package to other institutions, because, as Oettinger points out,

> . . . the keystone is Postlethwait and his enthusiastic crew. Where comparable talents can be mustered, comparable results can be expected. Where not, the results might well be inferior to those obtainable

through conscientious teacher-proofing. In this respect, therefore, higher education, like military or industrial training programs, provides a better laboratory for educational technology than lower schools.[12]

Given the tools and capabilities of educational technology then, the talented instructor will be supported and encouraged to experiment with modifications of his courses. Depending on the priorities the academic community really assigns to education and learning, this talent will be either rewarded and encouraged or neglected and thwarted. Poor teaching does not suddenly become good because it appears on a television monitor, or because there is a mix of various media in the course. In fact its poorness may be compounded, with a consequent growth of cynicism among students.

If we view educational technology in a cost-benefit frame of reference, there will undoubtedly be high start-up costs per unit (however the unit is defined). But the demands of new media will force better definition of both long and short-term objectives. They may, in the beginning especially, place constraints on open-endedness; and the desire to ascertain a cost-benefit figure may destroy the real values of creativity and motivation existing in the use of educational technology. Richard Hooper, Harkness Fellow studying educational technology in the United States, has pointed out that education is essentially a human process and will always defy exact measurement.

> If analytical techniques (similar to those used in industry which deals with definable products and profit objectives) are applied uncreatively, they might drive out the moments of spontaneity, the intuitive idea, and the unpredictability of human relationships. The benefits of education which can be given a dollar value (for example, students' earning power in later life) should not be overemphasized at the expense of benefits which resist economic analysis.[13]

In using any cost-benefit basis of judgment, these are elements which must enter into our consideration.

From its beginning Hampshire College has maintained a lively interest in the technologies of communication, data storage and retrieval, information transfer—in short, of those technologies which show promise of encouraging and assisting valid educational change and improvement.[14] The planning staff of the College has watched with interest developments in open- and closed-circuit radio and television, large-group "multimedia" instruction, computer-assisted instruction, independent and individualized instruction, dial-access retrieval systems for audio-visual materials, technologically supported simulation games, and programmed instruction. We have been encouraged by the imaginative and exciting uses to which some of these tools have been put. At the same time we are aware that many of the programs have had far less impact than their designers and proponents thought they should have. We will later explore some of the reasons for this failure, not to celebrate those lapses, but rather to understand them because they are the key to the changes that have not—or have not yet—taken place. We do feel that an institution, such as Hampshire College which is based on critical reevaluation of teaching in higher education, can provide the context for creative and effective developments in educational technology. As Hampshire's planners have long believed, these technologies can

> . . . provide students with greater access to material and experiences
> . . . enable teachers to demonstrate and display material to large groups
> . . . make the educational process more flexible by making access to material easier and by making it duplicate or repeatable on command, and relieve teaching of repetitive time-consuming tasks. . . .[15]

PLANNING FOR EDUCATIONAL TECHNOLOGY[16]

To accomplish these altogether laudable ends there are four general directions and concerns. First, we must acquire and make available teaching and resource materials in optical and electronic, as well as print, media. This has been extensively discussed in the last several chapters. Second, such materials must be produced when the need is apparent and in a format that can be used. Third, it is necessary to assist the faculty in defining and developing teaching contexts within which a range of media and instructional formats can be creatively designed and used. Fourth, these resources should be as easily and ubiquitously available to students and faculty as paperback books or television network newscasts.

Each of these goals is important. They require energy, tact, imagination, and, for some, considerable monetary investment. They are above all interdependent. The most vital teaching demonstration, recorded on videotape by a master teacher, is useless if students cannot get at it or if faculty are unaware of its existence, or its power, or its place in the curriculum. We also felt it necessary that this enterprise begin as early in the life of the College as possible. When the number of students and faculty is small and the impetus and pioneering energy exists, the potential is highest for establishing a pattern and tradition of use necessary for Hampshire's future usefulness as a model for undergraduate liberal education.

The production and switching facilities of the Information Transfer Center (INTRAN) within the Library Center are an essential element in Hampshire's search for economic and educationally relevant solutions to the problems of undergraduate education. Hampshire cannot today reliably predict the applicability of technology to education for 1975 or 1985. Hampshire can, however, prepare itself for change. Response to change will come as experience, opportunity, and imagination allow us to experiment with the effects of technology on education. The INTRAN Center represents the space, leadership, equipment, and commitment necessary to adapt to change, as well as the opportunity to develop experimentation with the learning process and with the Library. The Center is the most visible evidence of a college-wide concern to use the new media in all relevant aspects of education. Within this context, the INTRAN Center has a number of functions.

1. As a base for experimentation with communication technology, the INTRAN Center will confront the issue which Jerome Wiesner, Provost of the Massachusetts Institute of Technology and a member of the Hampshire National Advisory Council, has suggested is central to the application of technology to education: the man-machine interface. Clearly, as Wilbert McKeachie, Chairman of the Department of Psychology at the University of Michigan, has observed, faculty criticism and hostility toward machines exists most often in the case of faculty members who have not seriously tried to use the new media.[17] Thus it is the responsibility of those affiliated with planning and operating the Library Center and the INTRAN Center to devise means of introducing it to the uninitiated, demonstrating its potential, and training those who are interested in the necessary skills.

2. The primary switching function of the Center will be to act as a central nervous system eventually linking the Library Center to each student's room in the residence halls, and to classrooms, faculty offices, and administrative facilities. Buildings presently completed have conduits running to each of these locations. The INTRAN Center will act as a switching point to coordinate the campus use of closed- and open-circuit television and radio, and for access to resident and remote computer programs.

3. In its efforts to make both rational and economic the administration of a college, Hampshire will use the facilities of the Center to experiment with the collection and retrieval of much more information about the entire life of the College than is now generally available. Such information will provide the means to improve administrative effectiveness and to support research in the operation of a college. These can include, for example, detailed data on patterns of student applications and acceptances, financial management, or faculty interest profiles.

4. The Center will develop means and materials to encourage students and faculty to be more efficient and self-sufficient in the use of

library facilities, thus relieving librarians of routine question answering. Aspects of this program were discussed in Chapter 4.

5.   The INTRAN Center, fully integrated with the Library Center, will also serve as a place for making, storing and distributing the technological components of modern teaching. These include 8 and 16 mm films, slides, CBS Laboratories' Electronic Video Recordings, RCA's Selecta-Vision, cassette videotape when it is available, conventional videotapes, transparencies, audiotapes, and records. In this area the key words are imagination and accessibility. It will be necessary, of course, that the staff have a thorough awareness of such holdings and of the production capabilities, as well as an ability to relate a faculty or student request to them.

6.   The INTRAN Center will provide opportunities for students to learn skills necessary to use the various technologies and to become intern staff members in the Center. The students will be encouraged to produce curricular and other materials in various media for themselves. It should, moreover, be possible to offer students at the other four colleges the opportunity to gain a working familiarity with several dimensions of the field of information transfer and educational communication. More generally the INTRAN Center will collaborate actively with the other four institutions in exploring communication possibilities. The aim is economy and avoidance of duplication, moving toward a sharing—via various communication modes—of Valley resources so that they may be made more accessible to all members of the interinstitutional community.

Communication Systems

In planning for a communication system for the Hampshire campus our purpose was to facilitate and promote the sending of messages in the following formats within the community:

- Television, live and recorded
- Film and video recordings of film
- Voice recordings and live events
- Musical recordings and live events
- Telephonic conversations

By the end of the first academic year, in Spring 1971, an operating pilot model of a campus communication system was functioning. We believe we can involve teaching faculty in its exploitation and in the establishment of a valid pattern for future development. The basic criteria for an adequate system are fairly extensive and quite explicit.

1. *It must be ubiquitous.* That is, information held by the Library Center should be accessible not only in the Library Center, but in seminar rooms, faculty tutorial offices, and student rooms.
2. *Many kinds of information media must be accommodated.* Information in formats ranging from print to videotape to digital data is of importance to modern scholarship and teaching; the communication system must store it, retrieve it, and disseminate it on demand.
3. *The system must be responsive.* Users must be able to control the schedule and rate of information transmission, and to request repeat transmission if necessary.
4. *The system must allow for expansion and accommodation of technological innovations.* The possibility of expansion within the campus should not be constrained by any particular philosophy or implementation of machine systems; nor should the system implemented preclude the use of new techniques for information storage and transmission as they are developed. It must be as open-ended as current knowledge and funding will allow.
5. *The system must be simple and reliable in operation.* Even at a greater initial capital cost, the system must approach the reliability of commercial communication systems: telephones, telegraph, community antennae television.
6. *The system should serve as a model.* Other institutions of comparable size and with comparable aims should be able to make use of our experimentation in their planning.
7. *The system should permit two-way communication when appropriate.* We are sensible to the dangers of making students passive vessels for information. This can happen all too easily with media which do not encourage and permit user involvement. A frequent form for this involvement could be, for example, two-way voice communication.

Systems Design Outline

The outline of a system which meets some of these criteria and shows promise of expansion in the near future into a configuration meeting all of them, in whole or in part, is described below.

1. *Coaxial cable interconnection* of the Library Center with student rooms and faculty tutorial offices. In the first phase of the College development plan, this is about 600 locations. Coaxial cable can carry a wide variety of signals, from audio, to data in digital form, to video.
2. *Television receivers at each location.* The choice of television does

not necessarily imply that conventional forms of instructional television will be the sole means of communication. On the contrary, we think of television primarily because of its proven efficiency as a distribution medium for a whole continuum of informational media. These range from computer output to presentations using sound and still pictures to full television productions. In addition, recent developments, such as CBS Laboratories' Electronic Video Recording (EVR), RCA's Selecta-Vision, Panasonic's videotape cassette, and others, make use of a television set as the display device for stored information. By equipping each location with a television set, we feel prepared for the possible future widespread use of such packages.

3. *A multichannel electronic distribution network.* Clearly, even at a small college, more than one presentation must be carried over such a system. The system we envisage for Hampshire College will have the ability to transmit simultaneously several different programs at the same time. These may be for individuals or groups, and may be films, live or recorded television, or several other information media.

4. *Telephone Instruments at each location.* Present plans call for each office, student room, and classroom to have Touch Tone telephones.[18] These instruments will be used for inter-communication, to request transmission of materials from the Library to the user's location, and to control (in some cases) the functions of the transmission device.

5. *Wide circulation of individual audiotapes and players.* Many instructional processes do not require electronic visual components, and do not need to be transmitted simultaneously to each user. For these cases, we expect to distribute individual copies of audiotape recordings, probably in cassette form. Tape players are now available at very reasonable cost; it seems likely that through rental, sale, or loan each Hampshire student will have his own tape player.

6. *Provision of high quality visual viewing spaces.* We believe that an electronic image distribution system, even one based on color television, would not provide sufficiently high visual fidelity for the more exacting requirements of students of art, film, photography, and (possibly) the biological sciences. Thus we are providing facilities for viewing projected films and slides in each classroom and lecture hall and in individual locations in the Library Center. We do not yet see a practical way to distribute these high-quality images into student rooms. We hope that recent developments in portable film projectors and the growing use of independent study at all levels of education will spur manufacturers in the design of new hardware in this area.

7. *A switching and storage area in the Library Center.* This is one of the

prime functions of the Library, and space, power and conduit connections have been provided in the INTRAN Center. A television/film studio, storage, control room, graphic and photographic facilities, technical and master control spaces are located in the Basement of the Library Center. These are fully interconnected by conduit to other spaces in the Library, and to other buildings on the campus.

8. *Production facilities in television and still and motion picture film.* These spaces have been provided for in the INTRAN Center, as outlined above. We are developing production facilities in these spaces which can be easily used by people—faculty, staff, and students—who have a minimum of "production" training.

There are several reasons for choosing a system of this type as a basis for our experimentation with instructional communication. It may be asked why we have not chosen to use a dial-access system of the type now in use at a number of secondary schools and colleges, such as Oak Park High School, Oral Roberts University, or Oklahoma Christian College. The reasons are straightforward and fall into several categories. First, such systems are many times more expensive than the one we envision. The costs of a unique cable to each student room are very high indeed. We propose a common coaxial cable to all sites. The costs of an automatic telephone type switching system to link a given location (say a student's room) with a given source of information (say a videotape playback unit) are also very high. We propose to use a manual switchboard operated by students.

Second, dial-access equipment is manufactured for the educational market. The components for the system we propose are manufactured principally for two markets—the home television receiver market and a professional market consisting of operators of community antenna television systems. The receiver market is highly competitive, resulting in lower prices and good reliability of equipment. There are also enough different suppliers of equivalent equipment to enable significant cost savings through competitive bidding.

There are definite differences between the system we propose and the more conventional multichannel distribution system found in increasing numbers on school campuses. For example, our system is designed eventually to reach student rooms, faculty tutorial offices, *and* classrooms and lecture halls. Most systems are designed to serve only classrooms and lecture halls, thus failing to serve the individual study needs of students and the many educationally valid programs which are broadcast on open-circuit television. The Hampshire curriculum is designed to include large amounts of independent study, even at the level of the entering student.

Thus media support for independent study is as crucially important to the Hampshire program as media support for large group instruction is at other institutions with different curricular patterns. In addition, we propose to permit users of the system to control remotely the device which originates the signal they are using. The inability to stop, start, and reuse portions of, say, a videotape, is one of the principal reasons that teachers and students have not found these devices more useful in classroom and independent study up to now. We seek in our system what the Carnegie Commission on Educational Television observed as the promise of low-cost storage devices, for example, EVR.

> [The user] can select the program, play it at the moment of his own choosing, replay it at will in whole or in part, interrupt it for his own comments—in sum, fit the program to [his own needs].[19]

Pilot System Design

The total network is designed to link the Library Center with the Academic Building, residence houses, Dining Halls, and the Masters' Houses for television, audio and data communication. Figures 6–1 and 6–2 illustrate the general systems layout. The pilot system will make the same linkages, but will have fewer receiving locations, about 30 as a start, and less terminal equipment at the head end in the Library Center. The system is two-way in character, conveying signals from appropriate locations to the Library Center, through a switching matrix into which additional signals are inserted, and out again to various reception locations, the number of which may be expanded to connect additional spaces.

The television reception portion will contain broadcast channels from the three major networks, one educational channel, and the FM radio band, as well as four on-campus closed-circuit television channels and one audio-only channel for reception through ordinary television sets. One channel will be a "bulletin board" for daily announcements, classified ads, local news, and so on. The bulletin board is a device which televises printed messages in sequence. It consists of a large wheel—a sort of a Ferris Wheel—into which 3 x 5 cards are inserted, rotating around a center-mounted television camera. Cards may be shown in sequence for a predetermined period of time, the machine may be operated manually, or an audiotape recorder can be utilized to automatically synchronize the printed messages with audio on a single closed-circuit channel.

On another channel we will have a continuous presentation of a national newswire service. At present this is a straight Teletype news service with television camera to convert the Teletype image into video signal for transmission through the system. It is possible—at added ex-

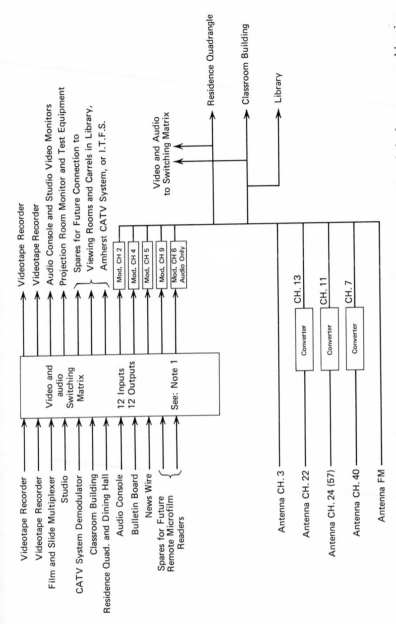

Figure 6–1. Cable network functional diagram (Note 1. Any input may be switched to any combination of outputs.)

167

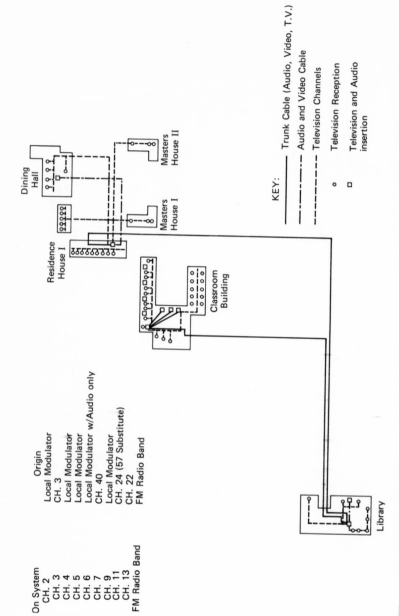

Figure 6–2. Cable plan. Key: —— Trunk cable (Audio, Video, T.V.); — · — Audio and Video Cable; — — — Television Channels; ○ Television Reception; □ Television and audio Insertion.

pense—to utilize the community antennae television services of the national newswire service which convert the digital wire information directly into video signals, providing better resolution and convenience. Our principal concern here is to see if such a news service has usefulness in our context.

By routing all signals, through the video and audio switching matrix, Hampshire's existing equipment (two videotape recorders, film and slide television projectors, the studio, and possibly channels from the Amherst CATV system) may be seen at any of the receiving locations. In addition portable television camera equipment may be utilized in the Dining Commons, in any of the lecture halls, or in classrooms to transmit "live" presentations to all viewing locations or to record events on either of the video-tape recorders in the Library Center.

Spare capacity is built into the system to accept images from Touch Tone telephone-operated microfilm readers, and to feed any of the input signals directly to viewing rooms in carrels in the Library Center, into the Amherst CATV system, and possibly to an Instructional Television Fixed Service transmitter for transmission to the other four colleges.

By adding terminal equipment such as film chains and VTR's the capacity of the trunk cable network may be expanded in the future to accommodate 20 or more conventional television channels outbound from the Library Center and additional channels inbound from the classroom building and residence quadrangle. Spectrum within the cable may also be utilized for nontelevised services in either direction such as data transmission, multiple audio channels for individual use, remote control of apparatus, or the monitoring of building service equipment. The addition of Touch Tone telephone pads to instruments in the existing telephone system with suitable interface equipment at the receiving end appears to be the most economical remote machine control method for purposes such as the control of microform readers. At minimum the Touch Tone system, based on a filter at the head end to detect tones, can be used to stop, start, and reverse a program. This, of course, is operable only if control has been turned over to the user. Eventual development of this attribute can be used, for example, to zoom cameras, or, with special logic circuits, to provide a memory for queries in information retrieval using microforms as the basic storage unit. The combination of tones would provide the specific search requirements.

Programs of Experimentation

There are many uses for the system described here. Some of these are straightforward, and have a high probability of utility given present information. Others are less well-defined; and it is with these that experimentation will produce the most valuable information, not only for our own future development but for other institutions which may wish to make use of our experience.

1. *How can users of communication media best be given means to control transmission of information?* We envision a system which operates in this fashion. A user at his desk decides (for the purposes of example) to watch a videotape of a lecture given a week ago at one of the other colleges in this area. Using his telephone he calls the Library Center and requests this tape. The attendant gets the reel of videotape, places it on a playback device, switches the output of that device to a vacant channel of the distribution system, and notifies the user over the telephone which channel to select on his television receiver. The attendant then transfers control of the playback device to the user, who can start, stop, and rewind the device using the touch-tone buttons on his telephone. This "demand" mode of operation may pose a useful and economic alternative to dial-access and possibly even to the individual storage and viewing concept of EVR, Selecta-Vision, and similar packages.

2. *Can a relatively small number of channels serve the needs of a population the size of Hampshire's?* The usual dial-access model assumes that each user needs a "free line" at all times to the library. The EVR model assumes a playback device at each location, thus assuring the equivalent of a free line. Our design does not provide such a guaranteed access, but requires all users to share a common set of lines. We believe we can develop procedures for the allocation of channels between "demand" mode and the more usual "scheduled" mode, to minimize the problems of queuing. If this is possible and valid, then the cost savings are appreciable.

3. *Is the concept of "each student's room a learning center" valid?* Some 80 percent of Hampshire's students live in single study-bedrooms. But the issues of availability of information and environmental "set" for study are vexing ones, and the data we collect on the use of the system will help determine whether students can indeed use the rooms for some of the purposes formerly requiring them to go to the library.

4. *What formats of information presentation are both effective and economical?* Television commercials use extremely effective information (cognitive) and attitude (affective) transmission techniques. But the cost of a one-minute commercial may be several hundreds of thousands of dollars. Even present "conventional" educational television may cost $20,000 per hour.[20] These rates are far too high for an institution such as Hampshire College. One possible answer to this question may lie in

"static" television—transmission of still images with an accompanying sound track. This idea, and several extrapolations on the future of television as a transmission system, are described in the article "Televistas" by J. C. R. Licklider, included as an appendix to the Carnegie Commission Report.[21] It is encouraging to note that the basic system outlined here could be modified to permit experimentation even with some of Licklider's more advanced ideas, especially those dealing with interactive and selective television.

5. *How can we provide for user responses during the course of a presentation?* The use of touch-tone buttons to make responses (in a mode approaching programmed instruction) and the use of voice feedback (similar to the format of a radio "talk show") are two models for user interaction with information while it is being presented. We hope to be able to experiment with these and other means for insuring active participation by users within the total system.

6. *Can we provide access through such a system to material not usually associated with television?* One project under consideration involves remote scanning of microfilmed materials by a television camera with control of the scanning camera and movement of the microfilm left to the user through his touch-tone buttons. If this proves to be a viable way for users to gain access to microform materials, then we are well on the way to making the Library a process as well as a building, and a switching center of the highest importance to the intellectual life of the College.

Educational Technology and the Academic Program

The availability of such techniques for teaching and learning will have effects—possibly profound effects—on the patterns of learning and teaching at Hampshire College. Examples of some of the possible new uses of these techniques will illustrate, we believe, the changes that could take place in the teaching process. It is worth noting that these place greater responsibility on the student for maintaining currency in a course than is usually the case with traditional formats. Note also, however, that the mix of communications system and over-the-counter distribution offers more options to both student and teacher to view, to listen, or to read. It says, of course, nothing about motivation. However, our assumption— and a reasonably valid one at the moment—is that good teaching, combined with the options discussed here, provides the context for making a subject three-dimensional, susceptible to a variety of approaches, and hence more interesting. No one will deny that success depends on imaginative and creative use of any medium. A poorly written book, a boring lecture, a hack video production, a sloppily produced film: all have a deleterious effect on learning and motivation. We must assume that the experimenting and creative environment of Hampshire College will maintain a critical awareness of excellence and will demand that excellence. Any other assumption is self-defeating. Some of the possible uses of this mix of systems are outlined here.

Students in a Human Ecology course watch a news special on pollution, broadcast on Monday evening. During a seminar discussion on Wednesday, the instructor uses portions of the program—which was recorded off the air—to spur discussion of important issues.

A visiting speaker at Smith College in Northampton is videotaped. The tape of his presentation is watched at various times during the following week by interested students and faculty in their offices and rooms. The tape is erased after one week.

The Amherst Town Meeting is broadcast over the town community antenna television system. Political Science students at Hampshire watch, and after the meeting ask questions of town officials in a telephone conference call. The session is also recorded off the air and replayed for individual viewing and class discussion.

A series of basic demonstrations of field specimen gathering techniques is filmed by a Hampshire faculty member in the Lawrence Swamp Conservation Area of Amherst. The films—10 minutes in length—are put in the Library for students to view at their convenience before performing these activities themselves.

One channel of the television system shows a continuously changing college bulletin board, described above, with academic, social, and classified ad type notices. The audio on this channel would carry WFCR, the existing Five-College radio station.

During course registration students watch a continuous showing of instructors describing their courses in short three-to-five minute video format. This was done, in September 1970 when the College opened, on a single VTR in the Library Center with tremendous success. It offers great potential for putting flesh and life on the bare dry bones of usual course descriptions.

Language students check out cassette tape recordings of teaching materials in a foreign language. They use these cassettes in their rooms, with their portable playback units attached to the high-quality sound systems of their television sets.

Students check out portable teletype terminals and use them in their rooms, connected to the computer at the University of Massachusetts through an acoustic coupler to the telephone instrument in their rooms.

Art students view slides with accompanying recorded commentary in Library carrels; these presentations completely take the place of lectures in art history. Class time is spent in discussion.

COMPUTERS AND COMPUTER USE[22]

In developing a computer policy relating to education and research at Hampshire College, we realized early in our planning that there were four intertwining factors: the time-sharing system at the University of Massachusetts; the potential development of a four-college administrative computing center; the Program in Language and Communication at Hampshire; and the need to develop a humanistic approach to the computer.

1. The time-sharing system at the University of Massachusetts is available to Hampshire College, as it is to the other colleges, by on-line terminals. The UMASS (Unlimited Machine Access from Scattered Sites) system provides remote access to the Control Data Corporation 3600 computer. At the present time (Fall 1970) the computer facility has 64 ports; that is, it can be simultaneously shared by up to 64 users, operating under the UMASS control system.[23] The system has regular users not only in the Amherst area, but also on the Boston campus of the University. The UMASS system will continue to expand. We can expect, however, that computer use will grow even more rapidly. This may in time present some dislocations in servicing extensive requests for time, especially at peak use periods.

2. There was no single administrative computing center in 1968 with the power and capacity to take care of the larger requirements of the five colleges. The University, with an IBM 360/40 for its administrative data processing, could do little more than keep up with its own needs. It is worth noting that the Library at the University has developed and is using the 360/40 for an on-line acquisition system.[24] Amherst College uses an IBM 1401 for its administrative computing. Although open to the other colleges for batch processing, its capacity and usefulness are limited. By mid-1970 there were definite and solid plans for a four-college administrative computing center, with time-sharing capabilities, to be located at Amherst College. Although not primarily of concern to the intent of this chapter on educational technology, administrative data processing has several implications. First, such a center will provide better servicing of standard library system needs discussed in the preceding chapter, and hence will allow us to move more rapidly into the exploration of retrieval and dissemination potentials for the Library. Second, as a self-critical and self-conscious institution, Hampshire College desires to develop a continuing program in institutional research, both alone and in cooperation with the four other institutions. This will

require extensive data storage, manipulation, and analysis of student, faculty, and financial data in cooperation with those responsible for administrative data processing.

3.   Our third point is that we view the computer not only as a tool for the solution of primarily quantitative—or quantifiable—problems, but as an important and influential artifact of late twentieth century culture. This fact has been missed by most observers. For example, in the report of the President's Science Advisory Board on *Computers in Higher Education* in 1967 the major thrust was the computer as a tool for solving problems. Tucked away in Appendix K is a statement by H. W. Johnson, Jr., which is worth excerpting here, for it addresses some of the problems of the computer in and of our culture.

> A person for whom the computer is merely something to be used gains from his contact with it no appreciation of the nature of the contemporary world. . . . At your symposium (the computer symposium presented at Bell Laboratories in June 1966), I was fascinated by the particular applications that we are making of computers. What impressed me most deeply was that in the number of these applications we have reached a turning point. The use of the computer has all at once spread to all aspects of our culture. It is this that struck me as being of primary philosophical relevance. What is relevant is the way the computer has changed the quality of contemporary life—not so much in satisfying our material needs as in causing us to think about ourselves in a new way.[25]

It is important to see the computer not only as an instrument which solves problems but also as a cultural and social artifact. It is in this context that a liberal arts college such as Hampshire must use and view the computer. The computer and related information technology, we believe, will be a pervasive influence in the culture of the latter part of this century. All students and faculty at Hampshire should be exposed to it. Some will use it as a tool in problem solving. Some will study its architecture and its languages. Some will use it as a teaching device. Others will study it historically, or culturally. But all should have exposure, seeing it not only as a useful tool but as a trigger for change: its effect on social, political, and economic organization; its implications for our concepts of mind and intelligence.

Consequently in the first year of the Program in Language and Communication all students in the College will be expected to become acquainted with simple programming, probably in BASIC. We find that a not inconsiderable portion of the students coming to Hampshire have had some exposure to computers and to elementary programming. This portion, we are sure, will grow and will not be limited only to those interested in natural sciences and mathematics. Students and faculty in

Language and Communication will use the computer in different ways from those in the sciences. They will tend to require different types of compilers and larger memories (both core and storage) than those working in conventional numeric processing.

There is no doubt that the College will wish to maintain close knowledge of and, where feasible, to exploit programs in computer assisted instruction (CAI). The basic concept of CAI is that the computer aids the instructional process and adjusts its response to the progress shown by the student at the terminal.[26] In this process the computer presents information to the student, asks questions, evaluates answers, and, most importantly, adapts the instructional process to the student's individual needs "in a manner that rivals and promises to surpass the best efforts of a gifted teacher."[27] The long-range importance of the CAI concept should not be overestimated; but like all technological promise we tend to confuse long-range potential with short-term usefulness. Extensive use of CAI in undergraduate liberal arts education is a long way off. The current state of CAI for use in higher education probably precludes any significant use of such systems in the early years of Hampshire College. We can foresee, however, several eventualities for CAI-type systems.

In this context CAI should be viewed as a series of modules, ranging from the explication of a single problem to, much less frequently, whole units or even courses. First, it can be used for review of already learned material, especially in mathematical formulations. This has immediate potential if the design is conceived in small well-defined modules. Second, it can be used for learning certain types of material in courses that are primarily progressive; that is, built on previous axioms and statements, such as logic. In this context it can also be used for teaching certain skills such as programming. Third, there is a potential in the branching structure of CAI-type programs that we suspect may be useful as a basis for information-seeking in libraries. The ELIZA program and its refinements developed by Joseph Weizenbann[28] and the GRINS program by James Green[29] are examples of the potential. True, public usage of these programs is some distance down the road, but their development may prove to be a significant pedagogical event in the life of a student. This, in a sense, is the fourth possible use of CAI. As a form of experimentation the translation through programming of a limited, specific, and well-defined concept into a useful tool for others, may be an extraordinarily rich learning experience for a student. Here he must think deeply and analytically about a specific problem, arrange it logically so that other students can learn from it, program it on the computer, and finally evaluate its usefulness as a pedagogical tool.

Now, how do we translate these needs into systems? The Hampshire interest in Language and Communication will place some emphasis on computer usage and computer appreciation. The Natural Sciences and Mathematics and the Social Sciences will undoubtedly use the power of the computer extensively to analyze data and to solve specific problems. Thus, within the constraints of economic and physical feasibility, the student should have easy access to a computer when he needs it. Access does not necessarily mean the physical presence of a central processing unit, but rather remote on-line access to a time-sharing system. Hampshire College will probably not require an independent computer center under these circumstances, certainly not in the beginning years of the College. This does not preclude the possibility of small free-standing computers which can also be used as input/output terminals to a larger system.

Within this environment and with these constraints, it appears that the College's requirements can best be served by a mix of systems. Major emphasis should be placed on the use of consoles, teletype at first and CRT devices when feasible, which will allow access to memories and software in other locations. At present the Research Computing Center at the University of Massachusetts offers the best opportunity. Other locations, such as the Computing Center at Dartmouth College, or commercial time-sharing systems, can be used, utilizing regular or leased phone lines and multiplexor as necessary. Most consoles, especially of the Teletype variety, should be portable. Such portability, based on available telephone outlets and acoustic couplers, will allow units to be moved around campus so they can be concentrated or dispersed as the need arises.

REFERENCES

1. As quoted in *The New York Times*, October 15, 1970, 10.
2. Anthony Oettinger, *Run, Computer, Run, The Mythology of Educational Technology*. Cambridge, Harvard University Press, 1969, 39.
3. Fred W. Friendly, Asleep at the Switch of the Wired City, *Saturday Review*, **53** (41):58–60 (October 10, 1970).
4. *Ibid.*, 58.
5. Oettinger, *op. cit.*, 171–173.
6. Gabriel D. Ofiesh and Everett C. Rompf, *Dial Access Information Retrieval Systems: Guidelines Handbook for Educators*. Washington, D.C., Center for Educational Technology, Catholic University, July 1968, 26.
7. See *Ampex Readout*, **9** (2):5; and Ampex Corporation literature on random access systems, Pyramid preliminary information sheets; also M. J. Kuljian, A True Random Access Audio Video Retrieval System. A paper presented to the Society of Motion Picture and Television Engineers, April 24, 1969.

8. Robert R. Stevens, The Vincennes Project: A Study in ETV-CATV Relationships, *Educational Television*, **3** (7):12–14 (July 1971).

9. Anthony W. Oettinger, on the dust jacket of his book *Run, Computer, Run, op. cit.*

10. As quoted in W. J. Parente, Videotape and the Academicians. *Antioch College Reports*, February 1969.

11. S. N. Postlethwait *et al, The Audio-Tutorial Approach to Learning*, 2nd ed., Minneapolis, Burgess, 1969.

12. Oettinger, *op. cit.*, 155.

13. As quoted in *To Improve Learning, A Report to the President and the Congress of the United States by the Commission on Instructional Technology*. Washington, March 1970, 91.

14. See especially pages 205–208 in F. Patterson and C. R. Longsworth, *The Making of a College: Plans for a New Departure in Higher Education*, Cambridge, M. I. T. Press, 1966.

15. *Ibid,* 166.

16. This section is derived in large part from the Hampshire College Planning Bulletin *Educational Technology and Information Transfer* by Richard L. Muller, Amherst, Mass., Hampshire College, May 1970.

17. Wilbert J. McKeachie, Higher Education in P. H. Rossi and B. J. Biddle (Ed.), *The New Media and Education*. Garden City, N.Y., Doubleday, 1966, 285–328; see especially 310–311.

18. W. P. Davenport, Touch Tone, *Data Processing Magazine*, 7:36–38 (October 1965).

19. Carnegie Commission on Educational Television, *Public Television, A Program for Action*. New York, Bantam Books, 1967, 82.

20. *Ibid.,* 188.

21. *Ibid.,* 201–255.

22. This section is based on the Hampshire College Planning Bulletin, *Computers and Computer Use,* by Robert S. Taylor, Amherst, Mass., Hampshire College, January 1969.

23. *UMASS User's Manual,* Amherst, Mass., Research Computing Center, University of Massachusetts, Revised January 1970.

24. James H. Kennedy and James S. Sokolski, Man-Machine Considerations of an Operational On-line University Library Acquisition System, in American Society for Information Science, *Proceedings,* 7, 1970, 65–67.

25. *Computers in Higher Education, Report of the President's Science Advisory Committee,* Washington, D.C., February 1967, 77–78.

26. Patrick Suppes, The Uses of Computers in Education, *Scientific American,* **215** (3):206–220 (September 1966).

27. Entelek Inc., *Computer-Assisted Instruction Guide.* Newburyport, Mass., Entelek, Inc., 1968, Preface.

28. Joseph Weizenbaum, ELIZA, A Computer Program for the Study of Natural Language Communication, *ACM Communications,* **IX**:36–45 (January 1966).

29. J. S. Green, *GRINS, an On-line Structure for the Negotiation of Inquiries.* (Report No. 4, Studies in the Man-System Interface in Libraries). Bethlehem, Pa., Center for the Information Sciences, Lehigh University, September 1967.

Chapter Seven

Library Networks
and Cooperation

Cooperation and networks have many faces. Networks basically are concerned with the physical arrangements necessary for the movement of messages among a group of institutions. These arrangements may be barefooted boys racing down cobbled streets or telephone cables stretched underground; red, white, and blue panel trucks with "U. S. Mail" lettered on the side or a series of microwave towers across the hills. They connect a set of institutions for the purpose of moving messages. The messages may vary from clay tablets to bibliographic data in digital form, from physical books to television images. Institutions, in our context, may vary from the small college library to a poison control center in Chicago, from a bank of MARC tapes in Boston to a television studio in Atlanta, from a museum in New York to a computing center in Berkeley. It is necessary to understand that though we speak in terms of bibliographic networks, it is the larger information and media net which is the eventual goal.

The significant and interesting thing about the concept of networks is that, if data exist, we can begin to understand networks in scientific fashion as switching configurations. Such an approach provides the framework and criteria to ascertain the most efficient manner of transmitting a message. We need first to develop models of library networks: configurations, that is, nondirected or directed; types of transactions; message formats; types of nodes; traffic requirements. A good beginning in this model-building has been made by Maryann Duggan of Southern Methodist University in her work on library network analysis and planning.[1] A measure of network effectiveness—at least a range of effectiveness criteria in varying conditions—should be derivable from these models. To make such models useful it is necessary to be able to isolate and define all the elements of the system. This is a difficult, but not impossible, task. We need to have data on the number of messages, their types and qualities, the speed required, the sociological nature of the institutional nodes, and the relative costs of these different requirements and channels. We do not have these data now in any significant form.[2] When we begin to understand a little better the models, or their derivatives, which Miss Duggan explicates, and to know the valid range and kinds of data, then we can simulate networks, not just to play games but to derive useful bases for the analysis, projection, and perturbation of networks.

It is quite obvious that the total electronic network is not possible *at this time,* especially one geared to a variety of media, both print and nonprint, ranging from rare manuscripts to CAI programs. We must therefore think in terms of hybrid networks, utilizing all modes of transmission and transport, including those for physical objects, choosing those that best match the message format, the use requirements, and the situation economics for that item at a particular time. This leads us to the problems of cooperation.

Cooperation then is the package of agreements, standards, regulations, and both overt and covert political agreements among groups of institutions necessary to allow a network to operate and messages to move. It must do this without appearing to destroy the image of local autonomy and local choice. We tend, mistakenly, to think of cooperation in this context only as a way of speeding interlibrary loans, facsimile transmission, or referring inquiries to other centers. There are many other forms of potential cooperation which, though related to the technology of networks, solve other problems and require other approaches. Agreements for cooperative processing, discussed briefly in Chapter 5, and formal acquisition agreements in a variety of media are certainly two of these. Both of these kinds of mutuality also imply a loss of local autonomy and choice. And one may legitimately ask if we can any longer afford the expense of local autonomy when it adversely affects the finances of the local institution and eventually the capability to serve the user. This is of course a problem of priorities; but we can expect that, as the economics of colleges become tighter, libraries and similar agencies will be asked to justify themselves in what may well be unpleasant ways. Cooperation, however difficult and traumatic for the institution, is one of the major roads at this juncture unless the whole frame of reference of higher education undergoes radical and revolutionary change, a result we cannot truly anticipate and one we cannot plan for anyway. Cooperation means standardization of processes and formats, as well as a loss of local autonomy. In speaking of the five-college community Carl Overhage, Director of Project INTREX, stated the point well at a 1968 meeting at Hampshire.

> As long as you can continue the present autonomous, comprehensive and cumulative procedures, you will of course continue because the faculty will not allow you to stop. But the day will surely come and it is coming to Harvard, as it has come to MIT, where you cannot continue. Here you are in the unique position of creating the awareness at the start, you see, and not waiting until you are pushed into it, but designing from the beginning for something that will ultimately be more stable and more satisfactory. You really have to create the climate for this kind of change and the institutions here have the opportunity now, particularly with the emergence of Hampshire.[3]

MIXED MEDIA NETWORKS

For libraries, cooperation and successful (however defined) networks require data standardization in a format that can lend itself to the efficient performance of as many necessary functions of the network as possible. These data, among other purposes, serve to inform an inquirer (library, information center, etc.) about the status (location, ease of access, etc.) of a specific package in which desired information is presumed to exist. They should also furnish continuing clues as to the performance of the system. The data, by its storage format and systems linkages, may also provide exact duplication of itself at a remote location, both automatically and on demand. The Card Division of the Library of Congress is an early example of this kind of service. Bibliographic data in MARC format will do the same thing, but it has the potential to do many other things: provide location information, generate products such as specialized lists, customized notices to individuals according to their interests, and so forth. It will take the MARC concept a number of years before it touches the broad spectrum of libraries, media centers, and information centers in significant areas of their interests. Pre-1968 bibliographic records, nonprint formats, gallery and museum needs, and other related activities all require large extensions in, or even alterations of—the present concept of the MARC system. This is, of course, an unfair criticism. It is made principally to indicate that there are a great many needs of libraries necessary for change and growth which may not be met by MARC in the foreseeable future. For a library such as Hampshire's it means that a few areas of cooperative effort, for example, the book-based operation will become highly efficient while the other areas will undergo ad hoc solutions, with a tendency to develop their own separate systems, adversely affecting the integration sought. Its internal effect for the Hampshire Library Center has been discussed in Chapter 5. Such an argument can of course easily lead to inaction. Not wishing to be classified as alienated and despairing, we merely point to these needs in order that they may become inputs to network decision-making in the future.

John W. Meany of the University of Notre Dame discussed this at length in his paper presented at the Interlibrary Communications and Networks Conference in September 1970.

> In view of our past history . . . we may suspect that our choice is not between a mixed media network and an unmixed one. We may safely assume that we will always have a somewhat mixed system, try as we will to unmix it and to come to some common denominator. Our choice seems to relate more to the question of how gracefully or efficiently we are prepared to live within the mixed media system. There are things that we can do—standardization, for instance—that will considerably relieve the difficulties of mixed media operation. There may also be steps that we must take to reduce the confusion in such a system and to keep the mix within manageable bounds . . .
>
> A mixed media situation offers its administrators a relatively complicated bibliographical indexing and control process. They will have to know where the pictures, films, tapes are, how to get at them, what is in them, how to index them. Something very radical is implied in all this. We know how to index a book, but how do you index pictures? By a verbal description of what they contain, or by a truly pictorial representation—or by some combination of the two? Along with the technological interface between media we need to develop what we might call transmedia analogs. And here we are up against the ancient problems of synaesthesia. The ears and eyes of men represent two senses with certain areas of radical and perhaps irreducible difference, even though we reduce them physiologically to similarly transmitted impulses in our nerves . . . the sound and picture fringes of our libraries continue to present us with enormous problems of day-to-day bibliographic integration . . .
>
> The prospect of living indefinitely with a mixed media system should bring us to face certain needs which are inherent in such a situation, needs which induce standards, new research, depositories, and demonstrations . . . .[4]

There is no doubt that nonprint packages, media storage and transmission, and media description need standardization. To be left at the mercy of commercial competition for markets, with resultant incompatibility among systems and formats, is the result not only of indecision on the part of librarians and media specialists, but also of the failure to understand the communications revolution surrounding us and to which essentially this book is one response. Until we recognize the unity of these processes and of those professions which work within these contexts we will be dealing with ad hoc and very expensive solutions. These are immense and very intricate problems, a fact which merely underlines the necessity that we emerge from our insulated boxes in order to give substance to the concept of cooperative networks—locally, regionally, and nationally. Merely to state its complexities, however, is not to solve its problems, or even begin to work toward solutions. There are, then, several areas toward which it is necessary to project work and efforts.

1. We need standardization of the elements of description for items other than print which will be handled in a network. It may be a practical solution at this time to extend MARC formats to include media other than print, but we should be aware that this format may not meet actual requirements for nonprint media, for galleries, or for computer programs, certainly necessities in any information system.

2. We need standardization of equipment and systems, and compatibility, both in the computing field and in the spectrum of nonprint media formats, especially video.

3. We need a better understanding of the role—or, more importantly, potential roles—of various media formats in education, decision-making, everyday living, and research and scholarship so that the planning and operation of networks can be better directed.

4. We need hard data on the relative costs and relative advantages or disadvantages of different formats, of different transmission channels, and of varying modes of interfacing with the users.

The development of networks among information and media centers, including libraries, will be a terribly expensive process. To add to these expenses by imposing a lack of standards and an artificial divergence of professional viewpoints seems absurd. It will be necessary, however, to proceed without anywhere near a full understanding of the processes we are dealing with for these are basically empirical systems. If anything this is a plea for parallel large-scale studies to accompany the development process, so that we will have constant feedback to provide benchmarks. It is also necessary to pursue analysis from both ends of any network, for example, at the national level as well as at the regional or local level. To neglect the local level, the node, is to cancel out the true objective of the system—the individual user.

Eventually we are concerned with very large, very complex mixed data systems. But our real concern right now is how to get from "here" to "there." At this point it is worth reminding the reader again that we are talking about the "extended library"—total media library, bookstore, gallery, computing facilities, television systems. It is obvious that, within the network context, these functions will have different rates of development because of their needs, their formats, and their present state of activity. Remotely accessed computing and television systems, for example, obviously are networks already. The media library itself, as we have already pointed out, is at different stages of development in anticipation of networks, with printed materials gradually building up a solid data base for networking and other formats in various stages of limbo. Despite the variety of uses and formats we are really concerned at this time with the ways we describe items physically and the way we name or label them for retrieval. This is true whether we include only books or also video tapes, films, audio tapes, slides, paintings, archeological artifacts, realia, and computer programs. These are all items about which information is required and *they* must be in our networks, too. To match our requirements for across-the-board integraton, this means that there must be compatibility among the machine formats for all of these forms. Equally important is the need to have an easy and acceptable interface between man and the system. This interface must not only use natural language, but be as close to standard English (in our case) as possible.[5] With these cautions, extensions, and limitations in mind we can begin to sketch the variety of major uses to which a network will be put.

    1.   The institution (library, etc.) needs to have access to a data base which will supply processing information on newly added items in its collection. This is necessary so that some form of condensed representation of any format can become part of the institution's files, be they manual and visually scanned as in a card catalog, or in machine form for later manipulation.

    We are beginning, of course, to have this data base for current printed materials through the MARC system, commented on in Chapter 5. The MARC format is also hospitable to other media forms, if we use a basically book-oriented description for those media. Inevitable in the start of any system of this sort is the amount of work, with its incompatibility, that was accomplished before and while the MARC system was getting established. It is interesting—if disheartening—to note, as Henriette Avram and Josephine Pulsifer have pointed out, that

> . . . approximately 3 million records are already in machine-readable form in 33 libraries in this country alone. Of this total, 2.5 million are monograph records. The preliminary analysis performed up to this

time indicates that the *bibliographic conformity across data bases is virtually non-existent.* Considering the resources expended to create the existing data bases, the resultant duplication of titles and the non-uniformity of the machine-readable records, it is urgent to take action.[6] [Italics added]

One can say that this is the result of unsystematic planning, or planning and action happening too late with too little support, and a failure of the library profession to back a national commitment. More than likely it is the way such systems must start, with a good deal of energy and money expended in probing, exploring, and testing because the resultant system must rest on an educated profession and a widely acceptable standard.

2. The user (possibly through the institution) must have access to data which tells him where a specific package is located, what its cost or conditions of use are, and how soon it can be made available to him. By "package" we mean the range of information package from the CAI programs to 13th-century manuscripts. This also includes bookstores, to add to their stocks, and galleries, to add to their display capabilities.

This MARC base of course provides a beginning, if limited, answer to this type of need, the union catalog for printed materials. It may, by use of the Standard Book Number, also provide the basis for faster service between bookstore, jobber, and publisher. This will depend in considerable part on the economics of publishing and on the cooperative bases that can be developed. Again this does not begin to solve, at this time, the problems of nonprint media formats.

3. The individual user needs access to computer systems (a) which will help him solve complex quantitative problems, (b) which will aid him in finding specific items of information, for example, factual data, possibly from on-line highly dynamic encyclopedias, and (c) which will aid him in specifying his information needs, basically highly interactive question-answering systems.[7]

The beginnings of a possible answer to this need for highly interactive networks can be seen in the multicomputer network now an object of research and development by the Advanced Research Projects Agency of the Department of Defense.[8] The network, according to J. C. R. Licklider, will be used mainly to give research workers access to (a) remote complex computer programs, (b) specialized hardware at a distance, (c) remote dynamic files of data, and (d) colleagues scattered across the country, with programs and data necessary for a computer-supported "teleconference."[9] When fully developed in the next 10 to 15 years such a network may well change the style of research and development in this country, and also the formats of conferences, symposia, and meetings. It will eventually alter the scientific and scholarly paper as we know it, from its published state, as it is today, to a formal addition (as data, comment, analysis) into a computer-stored highly specific and highly dynamic set of statements concerning a precisely defined problem.[10] This will make a problem highly fluid, as new data are added or changed. It will not, however, solve the question of possible cross-disciplinary benefits from problems in one field to those of another.

Though not specifically oriented toward the solution of library-media-information problems, such a network, when developed, will be a paradigm for the kinds of nets we are describing. The development also emphasizes the need—the urgent need—for modeling and simulation of interlibrary switching and communications systems.

4.   The user and the institution both need access to telecommunication systems which will allow them to call up visual and audio programs at will for educational, managerial, research, informational, and entertainment purposes. This fourth need may have a whole range of possible —and partial—solutions. The best answer, or at least the most apparent, may be a hybrid system, such as the library projected in these chapters. At this point, however, we are principally concerned with the extension of the lending/selling functions of the library to a new form of dissemination—new at least for the traditional library. The "wired city" concept discussed in Chapter 6 is one possibility, although limited by the number of usable channels in a physically feasible cable system.

5.   The user especially needs access to telecommunication systems which will allow him to interact fruitfully with colleagues in other locations. The concept of an "electronic highway" connecting a number of physically dispersed institutions was explored recently by the WGBH Educational Foundation with support from the Ford Foundation.[11] The purpose was to examine the feasibility of interconnecting via microwave a group of academic and commercial groups in the Boston-Cambridge area with a similar set of groups in the Montreal-Ottawa area, with links to Yale University in New Haven and to Hampshire College in Amherst. As usual, it was found that the technology generally exists for such a system, with two caveats. First, the special requirements of personal interaction (watching another person's eyes and gestures, *and* having him be aware of that) poses some real technical problems at this time. Second, although there were many suggestions as to how the system might be used, one has the uncomfortable feeling that the system would be strange enough and perhaps uncomfortable enough to inhibit the kind of interaction it was supposed to encourage. It may be that, on a smaller

scale, we first need experience with something like the Picturephone, and conferences with participants scattered across a single large campus or group of geographically proximate campuses.

In all these schemes, projects, and potentials one cannot help but ask —and we must ask—what the role of the small academic library can be. Can we do anything more than sit and wait? It is obvious that we lack the talents available, say, to a Project Intrex, nor have we the internal capabilities for participating in an ARPA Computer Network. We have the advantage of starting *de novo,* with all its attendant risks. In the case of Hampshire, we can and are redefining the library within the College. But participation, or better said preparation for participation, in larger networks is another matter. If we push too far and too fast in assuming a role in the larger context will we find ourselves not only isolated but possibly marching to a different drummer, in a direction not taken by other libraries? Will we find ourselves assuming a financial commitment we are unable to carry? These are critical questions when we speak of networks and cooperation from the standpoint of a very small but dynamic library. It is one we have not yet solved to our satisfaction.

COOPERATION AMONG THE FIVE COLLEGES

> Hampshire is the result of an act of cooperation; it represents and will seek actively to express a view of cooperation as creative collaboration, in which all concerned can find advantage.
>
> *The Making of a College*[12]

It is a bit difficult—and even uncomfortable—to climb down from the heights of "finger-lickin" anticipation of the last section to the realities of everyday operations where people are naturally recalcitrant, money is in low supply, and the technology is frequently out of order. But this we must do, for this is the world in which we hope these systems or reasonable facsimiles of them will work. This section attempts to translate some of the ideas expressed in the preceding section to the local and regional level.

The idea and actuality of cooperation among the five institutions began early, with the founding of the colleges. Mount Holyoke and Smith Colleges, and the original Massachusetts Agricultural College (now the University of Massachusetts) were all assisted in their early days in the nineteenth century by faculty members and administrators from Amherst College. Hampshire College itself is the fruit of cooperation; and again Amherst College provided much of the original impetus, and some of the initial administrators.

In 1914 a Committee on University Extension of the Connecticut Valley Colleges was established, composed of representatives from the four institutions plus the International Y. M. C. A. College (now Springfield College). Among other activities this Committee in 1922–1923 sponsored the first courses of instruction given by radio in this country and later took an active part in the organization and incorporation of the Western Massachusetts Educational Television Council.

The three colleges and the University also had informal programs of faculty and student exchange from at least the 1930's. Student course exchange among the four institutions was over 1,000 in 1969–1970. The field of astronomy was developed as a five-college department. Several joint appointments have been made in other fields.

An educational FM radio station (WCFR) was founded in 1962 and receives support from all of the institutions. The *Massachusetts Review,* its first issue in 1960, is also a cooperative venture. The first coordinator for four-college cooperation was appointed in 1957. The present coordinator, the first full-time coordinator, was appointed in the fall of 1967 and has office space for himself and staff at Hampshire College.

In 1968 the five Presidents established the Five-College Long Range Planning Committee which included representatives of the faculties and administrations of all five institutions. Its purpose was to review the strengths and weaknesses of present cooperative programs, and to make recommendations for the future of cooperation among the five institutions. Its *Report* was published in 1969.[13]

HAMPSHIRE INTER-LIBRARY CENTER

Cooperation also is not new to the libraries of the region. The Hampshire Inter-Library Center (HILC), incorporated in 1951, was established to provide a jointly owned research collection to supplement the holdings of the libraries of the participating institutions.[14] Its original members were Amherst, Mount Holyoke, and Smith Colleges. The University of Massachusetts was admitted to membership in 1954. The Forbes Library, the public library of Northampton and one which Charles Cutter directed for many years, became a member in 1962. As the local regional library of the Massachusetts Western Regional Public Library System it links HILC and its members with 110 public libraries in the four western counties of the state. Hampshire College was admitted to membership in 1970. The members share in providing financial support. The collection exceeds 50,000 volumes, and is growing at a rate of about 2500 volumes a year. It is housed, together with director and staff, in the Goodell Library at the University of Massachusetts. It operates a daily messenger service among the seven cooperating libraries. This service, under optimum circumstances, can provide interlibrary loans on a half-day basis. The usual turnaround time, however, is 24 to 72 hours. There is no union catalog, and Keyes Metcalf, in his 1957 *Survey*, argued against it.

> Such a catalogue would undoubtedly save time for users and encourage the interlibrary lending of publications. But, even if only one copy of such a catalogue were made (instead of one for each of the member libraries), its cost would threaten to bankrupt the organization . . . .
> It is recommended, instead, that a partial union catalogue be created.[15]

It is interesting to note that Metcalf recognized that the user's time would be saved. This again raises a point made previously. Our present systems, and the assumptions supporting them, place the costs on the user. Little wonder that users, for a small fee, are turning to specialized information agencies. Until users are considered an integral part of systems we will have this dichotomy between the organization of the library and the naturally antagonistic users storming the gates.

Metcalf went on to recommend[16] that the following types of materials be included in the partial union catalog: HILC holdings; serial holdings of all members; large or expensive sets; rarities; and descriptions of special collections. The first is available. A computer based union list of serials, based on the University's *Catalog of Journal and Serial Holdings,* was started in 1969, and a second more inclusive edition was issued in 1971. The others have not been accomplished. Hence the target by an individual library for a specific item rests largely on the personal knowledge and acumen of the interlibrary loan personnel. The *Report* of the Long Range Planning Committee had the following to say about HILC:

> Although HILC has been remarkably successful in achieving its goals, some critics claim that it no longer meets the needs of the institutions as their own collections expand. The University alone is projecting a collection of two and a half million volumes by 1980, for instance, whereas the HILC collection is only fifty thousand volumes. It has been suggested that the purposes served by the Center should be assumed by the University in the future, especially since the University collection already duplicates a number of the titles in HILC and purchases many titles which might otherwise have been considered appropriate for HILC.
> This line of argument, by concentrating upon specific titles which are

bought or not bought, fails to take into account the buying policy of HILC which serves as the justification for the cooperative venture and as a guide for its operations. The policy is designed to be flexible enough to accommodate to changing circumstances. Titles are dropped or added to the college and the HILC collections depending upon judgments concerning the type, location, and extent of use they are likely to have.

The LRPC believes that HILC will continue to be useful even with the changing nature of the five-college community and that it should be continued as an independent library with the University retaining its full membership. Its functions might be expanded . . . . Its limited budget may, in fact, have kept it from fully discharging its primary responsibility.[17]

There appears to be little doubt that HILC has reached a point where major decisions must be made concerning its direction, responsibilities, management, and cooperative functions for the next decade. This is not a unique situation, for it is true of all cooperative library ventures today as they face the problems of automation, communications, and their attendant costs.

There is, as implied in the quotation above from the Five-College Long Range Planning Committee *Report,* a question about the very existence of HILC. This is a legitimate question, but only when the Center is conceived in the restricted sense of past operations and policies. That is to say, when viewed *only* as a collections point, as a center for research materials, one may well question its continued existence. The full potential of even the limited scope of the HILC concept has not really been approached—"to provide a jointly owned research collection to supplement the holdings of the libraries of the participating institutions."[18] The key words here are "provide," "research," "supplement," and "holdings." And it may be the phrase "holdings of the libraries of the participating institutions" that needs redefinition. In the 1950's and early 1960's there was evidently a fairly strong, if limited, program of shifting journal runs from the individual libraries to HILC. This policy should be reinstated and reenforced, with the eventual intent of making the individual libraries' collections only high use materials, supplemented by local responsibility for special subject development.

Admittedly such a change will require reassessment by the institutions themselves and by the various faculties of their instructional and research goals. Politically libraries are not in a position to do this and hence, in the past, have been at the mercy of frequently impossible demands. More than most elements in academe, the library has the best knowledge of the costs in labor, space, and acquisitions of the faculty demand that everything be at one's fingertips. Yet they are seldom asked.

We won't discuss here the reasons for this state of affairs. Suffice it to say that, as financial support becomes tighter, it will be necessary for librarians to be in a position to ask embarrassing questions, to state viable options, and to expect real if not solid answers.

Such a process during the next 10 years is one of the elements for a rejuvenated Hampshire Inter-Library Center. However, this is only one side of the coin. The other side requires that HILC be able to respond to demands quickly and efficiently. HILC must be able to provide as good a service as the individual faculty member or student thought he had when the material was in the library of his own institution. Such service in whatever forms it may take—easy access to surrogate information and quick delivery—is a requirement for such a change.

Within the cooperative framework of the present five institutions, there are a number of possible areas by which present interlibrary cooperation can be extended and possible new areas of cooperation just beginning to surface can be encouraged. We have already mentioned in Chapter 6 the time-sharing computer system at the University of Massachusetts and the possibility of a four-college administrative computing center. In addition the development of a pilot telecommunications system within Hampshire College, also described in Chapter 6, can be viewed as an incipient network model and as a potential node for a CATV system with links outside the College. Within the context of the Hampshire Inter-Library Center, including possible cooperative accretions around it, there are several potentials.

There is no central source for statistics and data, especially those pertinent to the interlibrary loan process. HILC has not done this, principally because it has not been looked on as anything more than a "jointly owned research collection." No attention has been paid to the interlibrary process. It would be highly desirable to have not only a central source for statistics relevant to these processes, but also a mechanism for producing analyses of these data on a regular basis. These analyses are absolutely necessary as we begin to plan the future of HLIC.

We need to know, for example, the relative rates of borrowing and lending among the institutions. We need to know the speed of the process and the mechanics. We need to know what the role and costs of teletype are within the HILC context. We need to know something of the mobility of students among the five campuses and their use of libraries. The HILC libraries are in the position of serving, through the Forbes Library of Northampton, more than 100 small public libraries in Western Massachusetts. We know very little about this interesting mix of public and private, collegiate and noncollegiate institutions, a unique model for other regional networks. John Humphrey's report[19] on cooperation among private and public libraries in Rhode Island might have relevance here. It appears, however, to be more a survey and a series of recommendations than the study of an ongoing mixed system.

The Massachusetts Library Planning study made by Arthur D. Little, Inc. in 1967[20] had really very little to say about HILC, about the interchange that does take place among its cooperating libraries, about the public-private mix of libraries, or indeed about the dynamics of the interlibrary process anywhere in the state. It was an organizational study, one based on the regulations of the libraries studied, rather than on the sociological realities of the situation.

In 1957 Metcalf recommended that "Detailed descriptions . . . should be provided for special collections of research interest that are owned by member libraries."[21] This very necessary survey and description of the collections in the seven libraries (including HILC and Forbes) has not been done. The information derived from all of these studies is a necessary base not only for any future planning, but for current operations and daily decision. The Hampshire Inter-Library Center is the obvious place for the development (and analysis) of these data especially if it moves from being a warehouse only to being consciously an active participant (which it already is but in an unrecognized fashion) in the cooperative net among the libraries.

Another area of possible concern within the HILC context is the growing pattern of overlapping cooperative agreements and networks. There are at least three incipient library networks which overlap in some degree the HILC circle. The first is the NELINET (New England Library Information Network) concept which, at least in its beginnings in 1966–1967, included the University of Massachusetts. Its potential is largely unrealized as yet, although a recent report[22] explores the positive potential of a New England union catalog using previous experience in developing and experimenting with MARC.

A second cooperative circle stems from the interests and activities of the University of Massachusetts, in this instance on the processing side with some 28 state college libraries. This is discussed at more length below. A third overlapping cooperative activity may touch HILC more specifically and, at least in part, formed one of the recommendations in the Metcalf report, in which he wrote

> . . . It is recommended that invitations to join [HILC] as associate members be extended to Dartmouth, Trinity College of Hartford, Wesleyan, Williams, and the Forbes Library of Northampton.[23]

The Forbes Library has already been admitted. In the past several years a new group, the Connecticut Valley Libraries (CONVAL) has gradually become a factor.[24] Its overlap with HILC can be seen in its membership: Amherst, Smith, Williams, Bowdoin, Dartmouth, Wesleyan, and Trinity; Mount Holyoke College is also associated with CONVAL.[25] At the time of writing, CONVAL is a paper organization. The Balliot report, finished in June 1970, describes a program for cooperative acquisition and use among the CONVAL libraries. It makes extensive recommendations, curiously with very little attention paid to HILC, the only true operating cooperative arrangement among any of the institutions.

Among the Balliot recommendations are incorporation of CONVAL, a director and office staff to be located in the Amherst-Northampton area, assignment of collecting responsibilities, installation of Teletype, relocation of collections, development of compacts with HILC and the New England Depository, reclassification of several libraries not on the L. C. system, and automation research to be centered at Dartmouth.[26] This is, to coin a phrase, quite a mouthful. There is little doubt but that the pressure for cooperation is growing; and that the libraries are generally in front of their parent institutions because networking (under a variety of nonstatus names) has been a way of life for libraries over the past half-century.

There is, however, an implicit danger in this tradition of interlibrary cooperation. The commitment to cooperative agreements in the past now has a tendency to bind institutions to patterns which attempt to solve past rather than future problems. In other words, libraries react in rather fixed ways, partially because of their own traditions and partially because of institutional inertia. The CONVAL report and the HILC organization are cases in point. It is for these reasons that the scientists and technologists have had to establish their own information networks outside the confines of the conventional library, that media networks have had a separate development, and that most advances in interlibrary networking will probably come from outside the profession. The HILC organization provides, however, a basis for increased cooperation, albeit of a traditional type. Some sort of collaboration with the CONVAL Libraries would seem to offer the best base for a wider type of bibliographic net with direct connections into other networks: through the University of Massachusetts to the state colleges of Massachusetts, through the colleges in Connecticut to the network of that state, through the Forbes Library to the public library network, and through Dartmouth College to the medical information net. In addition, as NELINET is resuscitated then there is real potential for relationship to the state university network throughout New England with parallel contact within each state. Needless to say such a broad effort is not one to be taken lightly for it has the potential, over the next decade, of truly developing a regional base for cooperation. The variety of efforts will tend to dissipate the energies, however, and, unless a clear pattern emerges soon, the chance for a six-state network, including processing, may disappear.

The Hampshire Inter-Library Center should probably be limited, even in a wider regional context, to the acquisition of research materials, to the encouragement of cooperative agreements on subject coverage, to the organization of better means of communication and transport, and to the development of quicker means for locating specific materials. There are several other avenues of cooperation and networking.

STUDENTS, SYSTEMS AND MEDIA

Increasing mobility of students, coupled with recent demands for open access to all five libraries, poses a very real need to develop means through which the undergraduate student in particular can benefit from library cooperation. A freeing of interlibrary loan restrictions, a limited undergraduate pass system from one library to another, and a liberalization of use controls for Hampshire students—all recent developments—have begun a process which will be impossible to reverse. However, it may end in a chaos of time-consuming paperwork and petty bureaucracy. This is complicated by the fact that about 73 percent of the students in the area are from the University of Massachusetts, and 27 percent from the four private institutions. This ratio will gradually change with the University growing to about 80 percent of the total population by 1975. This ratio is reversed, however, in size of collections, with about 35 percent located at the University and 65 percent in the four colleges. This ratio will probably change with the University portion gradually increasing to possibly 50 percent by 1980. Approximately 30 percent of the total library seating is at present in the University Library and 70 percent in the colleges. This ratio will alter radically when the University's new library is finished in 1972–1973 and will give the University about 57 percent of the total library seats.

This question of easy access to materials *and space* will probably become the major problem facing libraries in the next decade, not only in five-college surroundings, but in the context of student mobility everywhere. The present library is ill equipped to solve these kinds of problems. Larger collections with high duplication and bigger buildings have been the usual response. Until the truly on-line library has been developed, several decades hence, it may well be cheaper and far more efficient to distribute high-use material in paperback or copied form freely or at token cost to the student.

A second area of necessary cooperative effort outside the HILC context exists in systems and automation efforts. A systems staff is already in existence in the University of Massachusetts Library. It will be necessary to build a parallel staff for the four college libraries because no single one can afford the necessary personnel. The function of such a staff would be to develop, in collaboration with the individual libraries, systems in support of local operations, with the assurance that such systems will have some degree of internal compatibility among themselves, and that they would also interface comfortably with systems developed at the University. Such a development will allow a more rational and parallel systems growth to take place, with a high degree of compatibility and interchangeable information. With the development of a four-college administrative computing center, discussed briefly in the preceding chapter, the potential for such cooperation is high. The time may come, however, when a cooperative library computing center may be necessary. By the latter part of this decade the load of five libraries in ordering, processing, locating, listing, controlling, and retrieving bibliographic material and printed information will easily be large enough to justify serious consideration for a separate computing center devoted primarily to alphabetic, rather than numeric, information. This does not include the other formats; that is, nonprint, which will become part of the total information network. In addition such a center will provide a base for larger cooperative nets such as CONVAL, and as a major node in the larger national library nets and in such incipient developments as the Museum Computer Network.[27] It is not too early to sketch the elements and requirements of such a center now.

The Library of the University of Massachusetts has recently begun a project to acquire and process books to improve the collections of the libraries of the 28 state-supported institutions of higher education.[28] Using several data bases selection lists are prepared for each library, orders placed, and computer-generated catalog cards and spine labels are produced. The project, currently under way, is expected to handle some 600,000 volumes during the year. Tapes from Richard Abel & Company, internally generated records, and MARC tapes are all used as the data base. This, together with the automated Book Order System,[29] will provide an extraordinarily experienced and useful base for any attempts at cooperative processing among the five libraries.

It is noteworthy, and a theme we have mentioned several times before, that what has been discussed so far within the five-college context is limited to printed materials. Yet there are within the five-college complex literally tens of thousands of discs and audio tapes, hundreds of thousands of art and related slides, hundreds of films, and untold numbers of paintings, artifacts, pieces of sculpture, and museum realia about which, as a group, we know very little. These, too, are information-potential media as is the book. Their dispersion and chaos not only represents something intrinsic in the nature of the medium but also says something about the acquisitive society that hoards without knowing what it hoards.

Film networks are already aborning. The work by the Center for Instructional Communications at Syracuse University[30] on a computer-based statewide film library network is a first step toward serious development in this area. It is, however, typical and disheartening, but instructive to note that, as the report states, "target dates for real-time systems are usually off by one-hundred percent or more."[31] The familiar sounds—change in computer, delays in deliveries, rewriting of programs, retraining of staff, lack of continuing funding—pose the real problems for imaginative and well-meant projects. These problems must be recognized, and at least funding problems solved before true networks at any level of automation are operable.

Museums, with very little exception, have not thought of themselves as lending, and therefore educationally oriented, institutions, but rather as collecting and displaying institutions. In this sense they differ markedly from the library which, especially since the mid-nineteenth century, has been education oriented. The conference held by the Smithsonian Institution in 1966 on museums and education represented a real break with tradition.[32] It is interesting to note, however, that almost no mention was made in the papers presented at that conference of cooperation among institutions as a means of supporting the educational objectives. At about the same time, in early 1967, a group of 15 museums in the Eastern United States conducted a series of discussions at the Whitney Museum of American Art in New York which culminated in the formation of a consortium known as the Museum Computer Network to investigate the adaptation of computer techniques in the development of "a comprehensive communication system for the fine arts."[33] Such an effort can be seen as a very early attempt to begin cooperation as a computer-based operation. It will be necessary first to be able to establish acceptable standards for description of a wide variety of objects which can also be translated into digital form for computer storage.[34]

However, there may be other ways of attacking this problem, viz., the use of images in microfiche which are computer manipulated.[35] There are also aperture cards (punched cards with inserted negative photograph) but they would be too bulky a file for easy scanning. Recent efforts among the college art museums of New England appear to point toward the possibility of a centralized holdings file, built from a gross rather than a precisely defined and itemized base.[36] Such a project, if carefully defined and maintained currently, could provide a beginning base for larger networks. Like libraries museums and galleries will have to break the acquisitive and hoarding syndrome that presently inhibits the development of standards necessary for cooperation. This does not mean that the responsibility for conservation is abandoned; rather, as we realize that education is the basis for our knowledge-producing and -distributing society, conservation takes on another aspect—that of sharing, if not the physical item at least the knowledge of its existence, location, and conditions of use.

REFERENCES

1. Maryann Duggan, Library Network Analysis and Planning (Lib-Nat), *Journal of Library Automation,* 2 (3): 157–75 (September 1969).

2. See, for example, Norman Meise, *Conceptual Design of an Automated National Library System.* Hamden, Conn., Scarecrow Press, 1969.

3. Robert S. Taylor, Ed., *Relationship of Information Transfer Systems and Experimentation to the Design and Function of the Library,* Amherst, Mass., Hampshire College, April 1969, 45.

4. John W. Meaney, "The Implications of a Mixed Media Network for Information Interchange," in the unpublished papers of the *Interlibrary Communications and Information Networks Conference,* Airlie House, September 1970, Paper C-5, 3–4, 17–18.

5. See W. C. Watt, Habitability. *American Documentation,* 19 (3):338–351 (July 1968); and Michael P. Barnett, *Computer Programming in English.* New York, Harcourt, Brace & World, 1969.

6. Henriette Avram and Josephine Pulsifier, "Bibliographic Services for a National Network", in the unpublished papers of the *Inter-Library Communications and Information Networks Conference, op. cit.,* Paper B–1, 17.

7. See discussion of question-answering systems in Carlos Cuadra (Ed.), *Annual Review of Information Science and Technology,* 3 (1968); G. Salton, "Automated Language Processing," 169–199, especially 177–181; and *ibid.,* 4 (1969); C. A. Montgomery, Automated Language Processing, 145–174, especially 161–164.

8. J. C. R. Licklider, "A Hypothetical Plan for a Library-Information Network," in the unpublished papers of the *Interlibrary Communications and Information Networks Conference, op. cit.,* Paper E-3.

9. *Ibid.,* 12.

10. Carl F. J. Overhage and R. J. Harmon, *INTREX: The Report of a Planning Conference on Information Transfer Experiments.* Cambridge, M. I. T. Press, 1965. See especially "The On-Line Intellectual Community," 25–41.

11. *International Electronic Highway,* Report of a feasibility study for an experi-

ment in international communications for education involving Boston and Montreal. Boston, April 6, 1970.

12. F. Patterson and C. R. Longsworth, *The Making of a College*. Cambridge, M. I. T. Press, 1966, 220.

13. *Five-College Cooperation, Directions for the Future,* Report of the Five-College Long Range Planning Committee 1969. Amherst, Five Colleges, Inc., 1969.

14. *A Guide to the Hampshire Inter-Library Center,* Amherst, Mass., HILC, 1968.

15. Keyes D. Metcalf, *The Hampshire Inter-Library Center, A Survey of its Background and its Problems with Recommendations for the Future.* South Hadley, Mass., HILC, 1957, 23.

16. *Ibid.,* 23–24.

17. *Five-College Cooperation, op. cit.,* 143–144.

18. *A Guide to the Hampshire Inter-Library Center, op. cit.*

19. John A. Humphrey, *Library Cooperation: The Brown University Study of University-School-Community Library Coordination in the State of Rhode Island.* Providence, Brown University Press, 1963.

20. Arthur D. Little, Inc., *Library Planning Study: Massachusetts.* Cambridge, Arthur D. Little Inc., August 1967.

21. Metcalf, *op. cit.,* 24.

22. Goldstein et al., *Development of a Machine Form Union Catalog for the New England Library Network,* Wellesley, Mass., New England Board of Higher Education, September 1970.

23. Metcalf, *op. cit.,* 9.

24. Robert L. Balliot, A Program for the Cooperative Acquisition and Use of Library Materials of Seven New England Liberal Arts Colleges (CONVAL) Based on an Analysis of their Collections, *Final Report.* USOE Grant, 9-A-046, June 1970.

25. Communication from Anne C. Edmonds, November 1970.

26. Balliot, *op. cit.,* 60–67.

27. Museum Computer Network, Interim Progress Report, April 1, 1968.

28. *Library Newsletter,* University of Massachusetts at Amherst, October 1970, 6.

29. James H. Kennedy and James S. Sokolski, Man-Machine Considerations of an Operational On-Line University Library Acquisitions System, in American Society for Information Science, *Proceedings,* 7, 1970.

30. C. M. Bidwell and D. Auricchio, *A Prototype System for a Computer-Based Statewide Film Network: A Model for Operation,* Syracuse University, September 1968. And C. M. Bidwell and M. L. Day, *Statewide Film Library Network: User's Manual,* Syracuse University, September 1968.

31. *Ibid.* 25.

32. Eric Larrabee, Ed., *Museums and Education,* Washington, Smithsonian Institution Press, 1968.

33. Correspondence, Everett Ellin, January 12, 1970.

34. See Everett Ellin, "An International Survey of Museum Computer Activity," *Computers and the Humanities,* 3 (2):65–86. Also for a single system description, see *Systematics for the Swedish Documentation Centre of Modern Art.* Lund, November 1969.

35. See material on SRD/COMPCARD, Image Systems, Culver City, Cal. A microfiche storage and retrieval system, combined with a mini-computer with 8K bytes of memory and an instruction repertoire.

36. Report, Twelve-College Art Conference, Estelle Jussim, November 1, 1970 (typescript).

Chapter Eight

Innovation: Implications and Alternatives

We, in the Twentieth Century, are concluding an era of mankind five thousand years in length . . . . We are not, as Spengler supposed, in the situation of Rome at the beginning of the Christian West, but in that of the year 3000 B. C. We open our eyes like prehistoric man, we see a world totally new.

Kurt W. Marek[1]

On reading a quotation such as Marek's cited above one nods his head in agreement, and then, if he has time, wonders what he has agreed to. Modern man has never really adjusted to historical time, a sense lack strengthened by our technological bias for instant progress, which, being ephemeral, gives the illusion of change. When Marek speaks of "concluding an era" 5000 years in length, it does not mean that, with a crash of cymbals, this happens next Tuesday, or at the toll of a midnight bell (electronic) ushering in the year 2001, or at any specific time. The point is that it is a process and we are going through it. "I seem to be a verb," says Buckminster Fuller. Our vocabularies are not suited to talk about change. Our grammars allow only pasts, presents, and futures, not process, not movement in time. We can speak of "here" and "there," but very little of the road between. We do not quite know where "there" is, nor when we might arrive. In fact we may never arrive—or rather, if we do arrive, we will not know it, for we will be on the road to another "there."

This, in metaphor, is the process of transition. It is a principal theme throughout this book, though sometimes hidden in the thickets of pro-

199

fessional verbiage. It is the process of planning and designing in a period of change and of being able to adapt to demands and opportunities as they are sensed and isolated. Though we may not quite know where "there" is, we have some conception of what this way-station might look like: *a social institution, or combination of institutions, which will raise the probability of effective use of data, information, knowledge, and artistic form in all media in support of education (both formal and serendipitous), leisure enjoyment, research, and decision-making.*

It is worth noting that so far in this chapter the word "library" has not been used. There are moments, and this is one of them, when we wish we did not have to use the word "library." The word carries too many connotations which, partially truth and partially myth, may not let the library get to tomorrow, may inhibit its adaptability. The term exaggerates the difference between print and other media. It emphasizes the static warehouse rather than the dynamic process. It focuses on physical objects rather than on people. It impedes communication. It provokes a dichotomy between people who should be working together. All of these disadvantages have implications for operations and effectiveness, both now and in the future. We will, however, continue to use the word, but the reader should flag it in some way—perhaps quotation marks—so that he will stumble over it and begin to encase it in other contexts.

There are many dimensions in our exploration of the road from "here" to "there." These dimensions cannot be well and precisely defined. Frequently, like the word "library," they carry a great deal of excess baggage. They have rather less to do with direction than with the style and nature of the process. These dimensions are explored in this chapter and should be understood in the spirit of the remarks of Professor John Tukey of Princeton at the 1966 International Symposium on Information Theory.

> I will have done my part well if the message I bring you is *not* any of the messages you expect . . . . The messages that I try to bring you tonight are *vague* messages, not precise ones. They are vague, not because I could not try to substitute precise ones for them, but because *important messages are likely to be vague,* are likely, indeed, to lose their value when replaced by precise, inadequate substitutes.[2]

This is not to say that all vague messages are important. We have the temerity to believe that the messages of this chapter, indeed of this book, have importance. It is within this context that these explorations should be understood.

PREDICTING AND FORECASTING

> It's poor sort of memory that only works backwards.
>> The White Queen in
>> *Through the Looking Glass*

Memory of the future, some may say, is a contradiction in terms. And Alice found it as difficult to understand as we do, as she watched the White Queen put a bandage on her finger for a pinprick that was going to happen in a few moments. But this is not just juvenile silliness or make-believe. In our culture we are forever living in anticipation of future events, whether it be good deeds to assure entrance into heaven, societal planning based on technological progress, or the design of communication networks to carry future messages. As Bertrand de Jouvenal has pointed out in his book, *The Art of Conjecture,*

> . . . The reason why we give forecasts is not that we know how to predict: decision makers mislead the public if they suggest to it, or even allow it to think, that this is so. We do not make forecasts out of presumption, but because we recognize that they are a necessity of modern society. And for my part, I would be willing to say that forecasting would be an absurd enterprise were it not inevitable. We have to make wagers about the future; we have no choice in the matter. We are forever making forecasts—with scanty data, no awareness of method, no criticism, and no cooperation. It is urgent that we make this natural and individual activity into a cooperative and organic endeavor, subject to greater exigencies of intellectual rigor.[3]

Society is beginning to ask, indeed demand, that consideration be given to the impact of new industry and of application of technology. This is a relatively new idea, especially as it becomes a significant form of societal pressure. It will require that we "know" the future in ways possibly analogous to the ways we "know" the past. It is not our intent here to examine this question; besides it is beyond our competence. We do wish, however, to explore the methods used for reasonable prediction in technology. The imposition of technological innovation on various systems in society, such as information institutions like the library, will cause changes in the institution itself. This ordering of change—technological first, then institutional—poses some critical concerns, for, as society thinks about the quality of life, it must also determine gross priorities in technological application. This is a period in which the norms are no longer normal, in which we cannot rely wholly on past experience, on precedent, a time in which we must think "as though we were the first persons ever to think." This exaggerates of course, but with a purpose. The point is principally that we are entering a new arena, where cultural, and institutional assumptions are totally different from the ones we have known and operated from. The social landscape is different, and yet we act and make decisions as though these were familiar streets and hills. This is, in economist Peter Drucker's words, an Age of Discontinuity, where

> . . . discontinuities which, while still below the visible horizon, are already changing structure and meaning of economy, polity, and society. These discontinuities, rather than the massive momentum of the apparent trends, are likely to mold and shape our tomorrow, the closing decades of the twentieth century. These discontinuities are, so to speak, our "recent future"—both already accomplished fact and challenges to come.[4]

Drucker points out that major discontinuities exist in four areas.[5] Although these are stated in basically economic terms, they have relevance to our argument.

1.   Genuinely new technologies are upon us. The growth industries of the last decades of the twentieth century are likely to emerge from the knowledge discoveries of the first 50 and 60 years of this century: quantum physics, the understanding of atomic and molecular structure, biochemistry, psychology, symbolic logic.

2.   There are major changes taking place in the world's economy. Imperceptibly there has emerged a world economy in which common information generates the same economic appetites, aspirations, and demands—cutting across national boundaries and languages and largely disregarding political ideologies as well. The world has become one market, one global shopping center. This world economy almost entirely lacks economic institutions, with the important exception of the multinational corporation. It is not yet a viable economy, with the dangerous dichotomy growing between rich and poor nations, and between the rich and poor in a single country.

3.   The political matrix of social and economic life is changing fast. Today society and polity are pluralistic. Every single social task of importance today is entrusted to a large institution organized for perpetuity and run by managers. Our assumptions are based on 18th century liberal theories, but the reality governing our behavior is that of organized, indeed over-organized, power concentrations. There is disenchantment with these institutions and cynicism regarding their ability to perform.

We have created a new sociopolitical reality without so far understanding it. This new pluralist society of institutions poses political, philosophical, and spiritual changes of profound consequence.

4.   The most important of these changes or discontinuities concerns knowledge, which, during the last few decades, has become the central capital, the cost center, and the crucial resource of the economy. This changes labor forces and work, teaching and learning, and the meaning of knowledge and its politics. It also raises the problem of the responsibilities of the new men of power, the men of knowledge.

It is principally the last two discontinuities which concern us, for libraries (a) are part of the institution (establishment?) of education, one of the major power concentrations in our society, and (b) have a role, as yet undefined, to play in the knowledge economy. Although Drucker does not mention them specifically, there are at least two more discontinuities which pervasively underlie the preceding four points he has mentioned.

5.   The change in media and communications technology, as has been abundantly pointed out by Marshall McLuhan and others, has and will continue to change our perceptions of the world around us. A major event anywhere in the world can be known to a multinational audience in a matter of hours if not seconds, and not only known but frequently watched directly. This has created a sense of immediacy never known before. It tends to erase history, replacing it with something we are far less sure about—contemporaneity, future anticipation, and a visiual rather than a linguistic sense of events.

6.   The reaction to scientism and technology that takes its present form in such ideas as "alternate culture" and "Consciousness III"[6] may not have immediate impact. It will, however, affect the way we look at application. These cultures will become our conscience, a function that traditional religion has largely abandoned. The media culture will increasingly reinforce these new religions and, by so doing, alter them. It is doubtful, however, that, without major human catastrophe, these alternate cultures will play much of a role. But then in such a case all bets are off.

The question then is are there methodologies suitable for predicting technological change in libraries? What kinds of changes can we anticipate? Can we reliably predict a rate of change? Can the library adapt meaningfully to those changes? In predicting change in libraries, are we dealing with too small a unit and too short a time span? It may really be too small a unit, unless, if we dare, the library becomes a change agent, as we will suggest. But our concern here is, for the moment, more passive—to examine ways of forecasting the technological future. The Delphi method developed at the RAND Corporation[7] is one such predictive approach.

> It derives its importance from the realization that projections into the future, on which public policy decisions must rely, are largely based on the personal expectations of individuals rather than on predictions derived from a well-established theory . . . . In view of the absence of a proper theoretical foundation and the consequent inevitability of having, to some extent, to rely on intuitive expertise—a situation which is still further compounded by its multidisciplinary characteristics—we are faced with two options: we can either throw up our hands in despair and wait until we have an adequate theory . . . or we can make the most of an admittedly unsatisfactory situation and try to obtain the relevant intuitive insights of experts and then use their judgments as systematically as possible.[8]

In a typical Delphi investigation, the expert participants are sent a series of questionnaires. They might be asked when, in their best judgment, a group of events or developments might take place. For example, the participants might be asked when the following potential development might take place: establishment of a central data storage (or several regional facilities) with wide public access (perhaps in the home) for general or specialized information retrieval, primarily in the area of library, medical, and legal data.[9] They might also be asked to estimate the consequences, both good and bad, of such a development. Response to such questions normally shows a range of opinions. A second questionnaire, showing the data derived from the first, is then sent out. In it, the participants are asked to revise their estimates in view of the group response. If this second response falls outside the range of the majority, they are then asked to provide reasons for their position. The results are again collated and a third questionnaire, in the same pattern, is sent out.

> A convergence of opinions has been observed in a majority of cases where the Delphi approach has been used. In the few instances in which no convergence toward a relatively narrow interval could be obtained, opinions generally polarized, so that independent schools of thought regarding a particular issue could be discerned. This may have been an indication that the opinions were derived from different sets of data, different interpretations of the same data, or different understanding of the question . . . .

> Even though this technique has been used with some success . . . it should not be interpreted as a device that produces "truth about the future." The Delphi method is designed to produce consensus judgments in inexact fields; it would be a mistake to consider such judgments as complete or precise descriptions about the future.[10]

There are, of course, several difficulties with the method and its interpretation. Certainly one is the lack of precision in the wording of questions, with the result that participants may respond on different levels and, consequently, to essentially different questions. A second difficulty concerns the limited definition of experts who participate in the forecasting process. For the most part they are scientists, essentially isolated from the decision-making patterns, from marketing contexts and the social demands which will actually determine acceptance and timing of real social application of a specific technology. And this is a much more difficult question, but it is really the one which those at the operating level must consider. It would be worthwhile to follow up the original Delphi probe, with a second one utilizing those in decision-making positions, asking not only when, but under what conditions or within what constraints, a given technology will be accepted *and* used.

The study by Theodore J. Gordon and Robert H. Ament of the Institute for the Future from which the preceding quotations were taken was directed toward the forecasting of certain technological and scientific developments and their social consequences. Figure 8–1 is an excerpt from that study showing their results in predicting the probable occurrence in the future of certain physical developments relevant to libraries and information systems.[11] Figure 8–2, likewise excerpted from that study, considers the possibility of intervening in the processes where certain consequences were thought to follow a given event.[12] The authors' comment on this portion of the study is pertinent.

> There was agreement among the panelists that some of the likely results of scientific and technological progress will be desirable. Society as a whole would probably agree on that point. A great deal more thought is required, however, on how to distinguish the desirable from the undesirable on a democratic basis and, having determined this, to design programs which promise to accomplish the intended ends. The programs . . . undoubtedly include some which are impractical, which are pointed to ends not acceptable to society, and, finally, which are unlikely to produce the desired result. Nevertheless, the need for thinking about such actions is clear, and the time available for their consideration is very short.[13]

Figure 8–3, also from the Gordon-Ament study[14] shows the respondents' list of prospective consequences, with likelihood and effect, which they felt might be expected as a result of forecasted developments in automation and communication techniques.

From these forecasts and their consequences the authors develop "scenarios" for the years 1985, 2000, and 2025.[15] Relevant portions of these forecasts are included here.

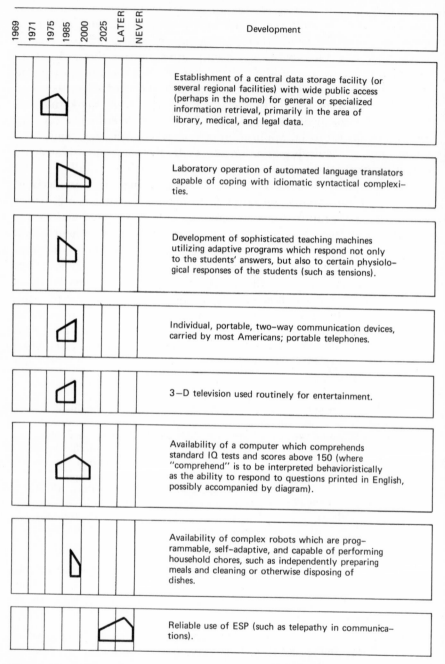

1969	1971	1975	1985	2000	2025	LATER	NEVER	Development
								Establishment of a central data storage facility (or several regional facilities) with wide public access (perhaps in the home) for general or specialized information retrieval, primarily in the area of library, medical, and legal data.
								Laboratory operation of automated language translators capable of coping with idiomatic syntactical complexities.
								Development of sophisticated teaching machines utilizing adaptive programs which respond not only to the students' answers, but also to certain physiological responses of the students (such as tensions).
								Individual, portable, two-way communication devices, carried by most Americans; portable telephones.
								3–D television used routinely for entertainment.
								Availability of a computer which comprehends standard IQ tests and scores above 150 (where "comprehend" is to be interpreted behavioristically as the ability to respond to questions printed in English, possibly accompanied by diagram).
								Availability of complex robots which are programmable, self–adaptive, and capable of performing household chores, such as independently preparing meals and cleaning or otherwise disposing of dishes.
								Reliable use of ESP (such as telepathy in communications).

Figure 8-1. Approximate times of future physical developments

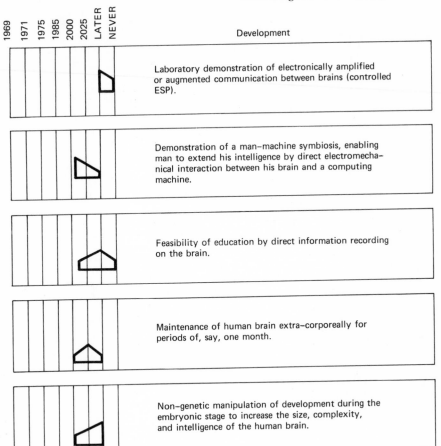

Figure 8-1. (Continued)

The Technological World of 1985

There will have been an enormous increase in information-handling machines and in the complexities and pervasiveness of their operations. The importance of skilled programmers will have been enhanced. Central data storage facilities with wide public access will have been established and will provide library, medical, and legal data. Privacy will have been challenged by the large data banks, and new methods of computer-aided crime will have come on the scene. New computer and automation uses will include automated language translation capable of coping with idiomatic syntactical complexities and sophisticated teaching machines which utilize adaptive programs responding not only to the students' answers but also to certain physiological responses, such as extreme tensions.

Potential Development	Potential Consequence	Panel Value Judgment					Chance of Intervention			Suggested Means of Intervention
		1	2	3	4	5	A	B	C	
Development of sophisticated teaching machines utilizing adaptive programs which respond not only to the students' answers but also to certain physiological responses (such as extreme tensions).	Significant decrease in those aspects of education transmitted uniquely by a human teacher (including humanistic values and the stimulation and excitement possible in intellectual pursuits).									1. Use of human teachers to teach humanistic aspects of education; teaching machines reserved for information transfer.
										2. Establishment of better techniques for measuring educational attainment, beyond simple monitoring and the transmittal of information to the student.
										3. Establishment of programs which permit political leaders, industrialists, intellectuals, and others to record their thoughts for inclusion in later computer–controlled teaching machine programs.
										4. Establishment of private or public "learning centers" using teaching machines and offering personal tutoring to preserve humanistic aspects of education.
										5. Beginning of a dialogue between groups representing teachers and those representing teacher–machine interests, to establish desirable roles and missions of each.

Figure 8-2. Selected intervention techniques

Potential Development	Potential Consequence	Panel Value Judgment						Chance of Intervention			Suggested Means of Intervention
		1	2	3	4	5		A	B	C	
Establishment of a central data storage facility (or several regional or disciplinary facilities) with wide public access (perhaps in the home) for general or specialized information retrieval, primarily in the areas of library, medical, and legal data.	The rise of new methods of computer-aided crime.										1. Antitrust laws to limit corporate power derived from control of computers and data banks. 2. Computer design which guarantees against criminal tampering.
	Invasion of privacy (assuming data associated with individual people can be retrieved).										1. A computer-oriented definition of privacy. 2. Computer-oriented legislation to guarantee the right to privacy. 3. Individuals assuming independent identities for different spheres of activity.

Key: 1 = Very Favorable; 2 = Favorable; 3 = Little/No Importance; 4 = Detrimental; 5 = Very Detrimental
A = Significant; B = Slight; C = No Chance.

Figure 8-2. (Continued)

NEW AUTOMATION AND COMMUNICATION TECHNIQUES

IF THESE DEVE-LOPMENTS WERE TO OCCUR,	THEY MIGHT RESULT IN:	VIRTUALLY CERTAIN	PROBABLE	POSSIBLE	ALMOST IMPOSSIBLE	VERY FAVORABLE	FAVORABLE	LITTLE OR NO IMPORTANCE	DETRIMENTAL	VERY DETRIMENTAL
New automation and communciation techniques, in general.	A. Increased standard of living for most people in affluent societies.									
	B. Increased unemployment of certain types of employees, necessitating wide-spread retraining programs.									
	C. Great increase in economic productivity.									
	D. Belief that we are being increasingly "programmed" and dehumanized.									
Laboratory operation of automated language translators capable of coping with idiomatic syntactical complexities.	E. Increased technical and scientific communications, e.g. reorientation of scientific journals.									
	F. Changes in language teaching at all education levels.									
	G. Real time television translation service.									
	H. Further ethnic separation between countries speaking different languages: fewer linguists and less intimate understanding of vocabulary nuances.									
	I. Decrease in the number of extant languages.									

Figure 8-3. Prospective consequences—automation and communication techniques

NEW AUTOMATION AND COMMUNICATION TECHNIQUES

IF THESE DEVELOPMENTS WERE TO OCCUR,	THEY MIGHT RESULT IN:	VIRTUALLY CERTAIN	PROBABLE	POSSIBLE	ALMOST IMPOSSIBLE	VERY FAVORABLE	FAVORABLE	LITTLE OR NO IMPORTANCE	DETRIMENTAL	VERY DETRIMENTAL
Establishment of a central data storage facility (or several regional or disciplinary facilities) with wide public access (perhaps in the home) for general or specialized information retrieval primarily in the areas of library, medical and legal data.	J. Use of home terminals for education; growing competition between traditional teaching profession and advocates of programmed instruction.		⌂			⌂				
	K. Information storage becoming a salable service, resulting in change in business practices.	⌂				⌂				
	L. Improvement in social science research.	⌂				⌂				
	M. Individuals becoming proficient in law and medicine, through easy availability of relevant data at home.				⌂	⌂				
	N. The rise of new methods of computer–aided crime.		⌂						⌂	
	O. Information overload: the problem to select from plethora of information that which is important and relevant to the individual.	⌂							⌂	
	P. Revolution in library sciences, including greatly improved methods of searching for particular subjects.		⌂			⌂				
	Q. Invasion of privacy (assuming data associated with individual people can be retrieved).	⌂								⌂

Figure 8-3. (Continued)

NEW AUTOMATION AND COMMUNICATION TECHNIQUES										
IF THESE DEVELOPMENTS WERE TO OCCUR,	THEY MIGHT RESULT IN:	VIRTUALLY CERTAIN	PROBABLE	POSSIBLE	ALMOST IMPOSSIBLE	VERY FAVORABLE	FAVORABLE	LITTLE OR NO IMPORTANCE	DETRIMENTAL	VERY DETRIMENTAL
Availability of complex robots which are programmable and self–adaptive and capable of performing most household chores, such as machines which independently prepare meals and clean or otherwise dispose of dishes.	R. Increased demand for educational and recreational services.	△	△			□				
	S. More women entering the labor forces.		△	△		△	△			
	T. Re-orientation of certain industries (e.g., the electronic industry into the home appliance field and the latter diversifying into electronics service-mechanisms).	△	△				□			
	U. Robots replacing the automobile as the central feature of our economy			△	△		△			
	V. Development of counter-trend placing high value in "personally" done housework and menial tasks, e.g. home-cooked versus robot-prepared meals.			△			△			
Availability of a computer which comprehends standard IQ tests and scores above 150 (where "comprehend" is to be interpreted behavioristically as the ability to respond to questions printed in English and possibly accompanied by diagrams).	W. More precise understanding of how the human brain functions.	△	△			△				
	X. Self replicating computers and more advanced computers designed by other computers.		△				△			
	Y. Philosophical and speculative questions regarding human significance.			△				△		
	Z. Meaningful, or at least amusing, hardly ever boring, pastimes.			△			△			
	AA. The rise of a new elite: the "programmers".		△	△					□	

Figure 8-3. (Continued)

NEW AUTOMATION AND COMMUNICATION TECHNIQUES

IF THESE DEVELOPMENTS WERE TO OCCUR,	THEY MIGHT RESULT IN:	VIRTUALLY CERTAIN	PROBABLE	POSSIBLE	ALMOST IMPOSSIBLE	VERY FAVORABLE	FAVORABLE	LITTLE OR NO IMPORTANCE	DETRIMENTAL	VERY DETRIMENTAL
Development of sophisticated teaching machines utilizing adaptive programs which respond not only to the students' answers but also to certain physiological responses of the students (such as extreme tensions).	BB. Greatly increased rate of learning among students of all ages.		⌂	⌂		⌂	⌂			
	CC. Significant changes in the number and role of teachers.	⌂	⌂			⌂	⌂			
	DD. Significant decrease in those aspects of education transmitted uniquely by a human teacher (including, probably, humanistic values, and the stimulation of intellectual pursuits).				☐				⌂	
	EE. A more pervasive educational system which might end ignorance-induced poverty.		⌂	⌂		☐				
	FF. Increased research into physiological responses and relationship to learning.		☐				☐			
	GG. A more rebellious student population than the present.			☐					⌂	
Reliable use of ESP (such as telepathy) in communications.	HH. Replacement for normal communication modes.		⌂	⌂		⌂	⌂			
	II. Thought interferences becoming a form of aggression; thought shielding a social necessity.		⌂	⌂					⌂	
	JJ. Application to situations which demand absolute honesty; e.g., criminal justice, diplomacy.		⌂	⌂		⌂	⌂			
	KK. New modes of scientific collaboration.		⌂	⌂		⌂	⌂			

Figure 8-3. (Continued)

The Technological World of 2000

Several other breakthroughs in physical technologies will have occurred between 1985 and 2000. Complex programmable and self-adaptive robots capable of performing many chores will have found use in the households of advanced countries. With such devices available, discretionary time will also have increased and with it the demand for educational and recreational services. Computers will have been built which comprehend standard IQ tests and score above 150. On-the-spot communication will be increasingly available to the citizens of most advanced countries; individual portable two-way communication devices will be in use, much to the consternation of teenagers required to "call in" on dates and to regulatory authorities required to allocate and control frequencies.

The Technological World of 2025

In the first part of the 21st Century, research into the means of directly stimulating the cortex may have led to demonstration of a man-machine symbiosis in which certain men (perhaps with implanted electrodes or other, less repugnant devices) extend their intelligence by being connected to a computer. This development might have the effect of multiplying human intelligence manyfold.

It is worth reiterating here some of the earlier comments and reservations about the Delphi method. First of all it does not pretend to present future truth, but rather a scenario of potential futures based on current expertise. The questions are not only ambiguous, thus inviting multiple interpretations, but, more importantly, demand an interpreted future extrapolated from current trends as seen by scientists and engineers. One might make an equally valid extrapolation toward something considerably more hideous and less bland, as Ray Bradbury does in *Fahrenheit 451*.[16]

The predictions by technical experts tend to be neutral and objective, removed from human context, on the assumption that those who will make decisions based on these forecasts will somehow inject humanity into this impersonality. This has not happened because the decision maker has gradually shifted toward the neutral end of the spectrum, believing, possibly correctly, that objective decision is a better decision. It may as a matter of fact be a better decision, but its objectivity—if this is the right word—may not be the reason. In this context it would strengthen the Delphi capability if opinion could be sought from managers at the operating level who are intimately familiar with the recalcitrant nature of materials, people, and systems to be affected. It is at this latter level where real acceptance of innovation takes place, where it is decided whether a given technology will in fact have operational significance in 1985 or 2000.

But these caveats are mere carping. Of course this form of prediction is not perfect. It could not be, given the nature of the problem. These are approximations of the near future and, barring human catastrophe, they bear some real resemblance to what will be available to, possibly in use by, the library, communication, and information professions during the next half-century. This means that the students presently in those professional schools concerned with communication and information transfer will be living with, making decisions about, and controlling the application of these technological systems. The important question then is how well will they be prepared to deal with and make decisions about these systems, or, as in the recent past, will their real professional education accumulate from outside the schools, as it has for most of us.

EDUCATIONAL CONTEXT

Innovation flourishes in an atmosphere of anticipation of innovation. If the members of society expect something new, it is more likely to appear than if it is unforeseen and unheralded. It is like seeing ghosts at midnight. The greater the number of people who expect to see them, the more frequent they will be seen.

H. G. Barnett, *Innovations:*
The Basis of Change[17]

Libraries are part of at least three constituencies: the educational establishment, the communications establishment, and a profession called librarianship, which cynics might insist may not be part of either of the other two. All of these are part of a broader context—"The Knowledge Economy," a concept given form and body in Fritz Machlup's seminal work *The Production and Distribution of Knowledge in the United States,* in which he defines the problem.

We may designate as "knowledge" anything that is known by somebody, and as "production of knowledge" any activity by which somebody learns of something *he* has not known before even if others have. . . .
Thus if I tell you something you have not known, or only vaguely known, or had forgotten, I am producing knowledge, although I must have had this knowledge, and probably several others have too. In other word "producing" knowledge will mean, in this book, not only discovering, inventing, designing and planning but also disseminating and communicating.[18]

Peter Drucker also discusses this growing interconnection and interdependence in advanced societies. He does it almost wholly in economic and technological terms, and with a more restricting vocabulary. This description is worth listening to, because it poses the dilemma of a technological society.

> "Knowledge" as normally considered by the "intellectual" is something very different from "knowledge" in the context of "knowledge economy" or "knowledge work". For the intellectual, knowledge is what is in a book. But as long as it is in the book, it is only "information" if not mere "data". Only when a man applies the information to doing something does it become knowledge. Knowledge, like electricity or money, is a form of energy that exists only when doing work. The emergence of the knowledge economy is not, in other words, part of "intellectual history" as it is normally conceived. It is part of the "history of technology", which recounts how man puts tools to work. When the intellectual says "knowledge" he usually thinks of something new. But what matters in the "knowledge economy" is whether knowledge, old or new, is applicable, e. g., Newtonian physics to the space program. What is relevant is the imagination and skill of whoever applies it, rather than the sophistication or newness of the information.[19]

In fairness to Drucker, this is quoted out of context. There does exist in his book an extensive discussion of the problems associated with the utilization of knowledge. It is quoted here principally to emphasize the increasing pressure that society is generating to use knowledge in socially relevant ways. Who defines "socially relevant" is of course another question. It seems likely, however, that the economics and technological choices of the next decade will create the environment in which the pressures on the educational establishment, including such institutions as the library, may force the definition of objectives and means.

Is education at the threshold of great change? Will the formal educational process be significantly different in 1980 than it was, say in 1960? One can easily argue that the change has already taken place in the larger society, but that such change has not yet been reflected in the educational establishment. The external elements for major change appear to be present: communication and information technology, economic pressure to seek financially feasible solutions, the democratization of higher education, and a beginning willingness to experiment in the large sense. Educational change, however, based only on these ingredients will be shallow and peripheral, for it needs direction and boundaries. In the words of Lewis B. Mayhew,

> . . . Higher education must become more specific than ever before as to why society should support it and utilize its services. If it does this and acts on the findings, the future pattern could be much more different than present trends suggest it will be.[20]

Mere additional funds for education will not solve present problems. In fact large funding may perpetuate them. If the traditional faculty bureaucracy, including its expression in unionization, does not become too strong, and if imagination and creativity can accept and utilize power, then financial pressure can be a blessing, an opportunity to ask— and answer—fundamental questions about directions and structure.

William Tolley, former President of Syracuse University, made the following refreshingly candid and perceptive observation about the economic facts (or unfacts) of academic life.

> In a college or university we don't have featherbedding for the sake of featherbedding—as is so often true of industry. Rather we have it because of custom, tradition, limited experience or conventional wisdom. The waste and inefficiency have never been systematically or scientifically examined. The truth is that we don't know as much as we think we do about our own business. And this goes for all of us—teachers, administrators, and trustees alike.[21]

The danger exists of course that, in the glorious and refreshing process of defining objectives and goals, the present traditional establishment will either (a) view its present formalisms as the totality of society, as all things to all men, or (b) restrict its vision to the point where it becomes irrelevant to most people. The irony of this is that, in the "knowledge society," education in many formats will come close to being many things to all men, but in a context quite different from today's patterns of higher education. And the context is indeed changing. The recent rise in student unrest, partially directed toward educational stasis, may play a role here.

There is little doubt that student criticism will result in better teaching and more interdisciplinary directions. However, the student span of attention in these matters is inclined to be short. Consequently their power in a political sense is limited. This is rather a pity because students have displayed a refreshing and uninhibited ability to point at weaknesses, thereby stirring up latent feelings of guilt and masochism among faculty members. But because students require instant and visible change they are not able to give the long-term attention and sustained effort necessary to really affect change. They are, and this is an important role, change agents. That is they cause change, but do not control its institutionalization because they are not a body with continuing and permanent membership. At present, it is the faculty who performs this role. As the economics of education become increasingly important and the rate of change accelerates, however, faculties may gradually lose their traditional power in this area. If this happens it would happen principally because a body such as a faculty, with many competing interests, cannot exercise sufficient self-discipline and consequently has difficulty acting with one voice in decision-making situations. This does not mean that it never happens, but rather that, in a period of change, faculty conservatism will tend to dominate, with the result that educational innovation may move out of the academy.

Some of these changes are worth reviewing briefly here for they will have impact on the larger structure of the educational process and consequently on the environment within which libraries exist and operate. The first change, observable for some time but now becoming apparent as a break in past rigidities, is the questioning of the grading systems and the assumptions of course structure and duration. The significant point here is not that pass-fail systems or that shorter or longer courses will supplant traditional forms of grading and courses, but rather that acceptance of the legitimacy of these changes will extend the options open to both instructor and student. Related to this change is the increasing abandonment of the college parietal posture, with its cacophony of rules, procedures, forms, and associated absurdities. Together these changes begin to place more responsibility on the student to define his own education and to police his own adolescent life. There are elements of danger here. The growth in student power and personal responsibility also gives the student the power to bargain. This may work against the laudable objective of teaching students rather than teaching subjects. The result could be that individual faculty members may retreat to their subjects, offering them in highly competent fashion within a market economy, rather than directing their energies toward the students as individual learners and as people in their own right. This would be a peculiar return to pattern, but it could be one response to growing student power and to the possible growth of malfeasance suits at the elementary and secondary school level.

Another trend which will have profound implications for patterns and structure is the recently formalized idea of the University Without Walls.

It is called a *University Without Walls* because it abandons the tradition of a sharply circumscribed campus and provides education for students wherever they may be—at work, in their homes, through internships, independent study and field experience, within areas of special social problems, at one or more colleges, and in travel or service abroad. It abandons the tradition of a fixed age group (18–22) and recognizes that persons as young as 16 and as old as 60 may benefit from its programs. It abandons the traditional class room as the principal instrument of instruction, as well as the prescribed curriculum, the grades and credit points which, however they are added or averaged, do not yield a satisfactory measure of education. It enlarges the faculty to include knowledgeable people from outside the academic world and makes use of various new techniques for storage, retrieval and communication of knowledge. It places strong emphasis on student self-direction in learning, while still maintaining close teaching-learning relationships between students, teachers, and others. It aims to produce not "finished" graduates but life-long learners.[22]

Disregarding the sales pitch and special pleading, the direction is clear. Innovative activities which, in the past, took place on the periphery of the establishment are moving toward the center. This does not mean that there will be uninhibited development of these patterns, but rather that they will be accepted as legitimate options. Enough students, however, in fact probably a good majority, will insist on structure rather than the free-wheeling approach of the University Without Walls. The important point is that the range of educational options available will be broadened.

As a comment on the history of change, it is worth noting that adult programs of high sophistication and professionalism have flourished in Europe and England for some time. In this country several institutions, Syracuse University and Goddard College among others, have held adult degree programs of note since the mid-1960's.[23] Antioch College has long experimented with work-study programs, wrapping courses and credits around work experience. All of these movements, fueled by a general dissatisfaction with education during the 1960's, are now converging to combine with the process of democratization in higher education which has exploded in the past few years. Within the larger context of the knowledge economy, these changes have fortunately not yet solidified into a new orthodoxy. There are too many unknowns and too many volatile elements—economics, reaction to change, tax structures, unionization, student apathy—to allow quick and easy short-term prediction.

Even a modicum of success, however measured, with these programs will have a significant effect on the communication and information needs of students. Neither the traditional library nor the conventional audio-visual center will match those needs. It will be necessary to seek new responses in function, in packaging, and in style so that the library can become more effective. It might be worth considering, for example, if this new institution, which we call the library, might become the center for adult and nonresidential programs in higher education. This may seem an unusual setting, but this suggests a way of making better use of the library's resources and talents, of its organizational and systems sense, and of its generalist approach to the educational process. There are many responses possible, including that of pulling the blankets over one's head.

IMPLICATIONS

Essentially this report has been concerned with describing one response, not only to change, but to anticipation of change. This is an important difference, for response to change, already observed or felt, has a different quality and posture from preparation for anticipated change. In the former case one basically reacts, in the latter one both initiates and reacts. The objective here then is to suggest and to explore the implications of a redefinition of role, function, and organization so that the library (the reader should stumble here) can be designed to anticipate and adapt more quickly and more easily to developments in the future.

A second objective, equally important but somewhat more exhortatory, is to urge the profession to take the lead in initiating change rather than merely reacting to outside pressures. The profession has done little to anticipate the changes discussed in this book. Indeed the profession may be completely unprepared to adapt to the needs implied in the discontinuities of Peter Drucker. One must not necessarily believe in their complete validity to accept the thesis of discontinuity. The gradual formation taking place today, of business conglomerates combining publishing, television, communications, and computer and educational technology, is a signal that cannot be ignored even though these conglomerates may temporarily have lost their nerve.[24] The library's bias toward conservation of knowledge, toward collecting and historical perspective, may hinder its ability to adjust. Librarians may become the victims of "future shock," that sudden realization of a new and completely unfamiliar landscape; and the traumatic anxiety of transition may be too much. If that happens the profession and the institution of the library will have lost the opportunity to have any influence on the future.

> Future shock will not be found in *Index Medicus* or in any listing of psychological abnormalities. Yet, unless intelligent steps are taken to combat it, I believe that most human beings alive today will find themselves increasingly disoriented and, therefore, progressively incompetent to deal rationally with their environment. I believe that the malaise, mass neurosis, irrationality, and free-floating violence already apparent in contemporary life are merely foretaste of what may lie ahead unless we come to understand and treat this psychological disease.
>
> Future shock is a time phenomenon, a product of the greatly accelerated

rate of change in society. It arises from the super-imposition of a new culture on an old one. It is culture shock in one's own society. But its impact is far worse. For most Peace Corps men, in fact most travelers, have the comforting knowledge that the culture they left behind will be there to return to. The victim of future shock does not.[25]

These apocalyptic words do not tell us what specifically we should prepare for in the future—except change. And this is a most important point because our present biases for planning rest principally on an extrapolation of past data and experience. There is little doubt that we can plan 5 to 10 years in advance, and do this rather efficiently. But to plan further than this requires a frame of reference we are only beginning to understand. Yet this is the dilemma, for, in a period of change, to design for 5 or 10 years establishes the basis for operations and planning for the next decade. This of course tends to inhibit both adaptability and initiative. Consequently our efforts in this regard should be directed not toward the design of specific systems, because this is not where real change will occur. Rather, effort should be concerned with the institutional framework and structure which will decide how innovation will be used and how fast change will take place. As a society we are much too quick to translate "can do" into "should do" without consideration of the consequences. On this point Elting Morison has a very relevant observation. On the decision of the Naval Board in 1869 to scrap the *Wampanoag*, a ship of advanced design and power, Morison writes:

> What these officers were saying was that the *Wampanoag* was a destructive energy in their society. Setting the extraordinary force of her engines against their way of life, they had a sudden insight into the nature of machinery. They perceived that a machine, any machine, if left to itself, tends to establish its own conditions, to create its own environment and draw men into it. Since a machine, any machine, is designed to do only a part of what a whole man can do, it tends to wear down those parts of a man that are not included in the design. . . . This insight seems to me worth pondering.[26]

There appear to be three general criteria necessary to bring about fundamental change in an institution such as the library. First, the frame of reference of the policy and decision-making apparatus, both formal and informal, must be friendly to and knowledgeable about the process of innovation. This requires that the social and professional context in which decision-making takes place must also have the same attributes. At the same time, decision makers must not be trapped in an orthodoxy of faddish innovation. The line between faddism and substantive change is a delicate and subtle one. To know it and to use it requires good judgment. We rather suspect that the position of this line may be more easily located when we have a better appreciation of and agreement on the goals, objectives, and functions of communications-oriented institutions.

Second, there must be general agreement in the professions involved on goals, objectives, and functions. The difference between short- and long-term goals must be understood. In this context it will be necessary to separate and to analyze the different functions of the institution—archival storage, intellectual access, switching, dissemination, and physical access. These functions must be differentiated within the meaning of the broader and extended institution which we are, for convenience sake, calling "the library." Interrelationships between functions must be recognized. That is to say, it must be viewed as a total system. When perturbation takes place at one point, the potential for change in other parts of the system must be isolated and understood.

We cannot measure these potentials at this time, an observation which should stimulate, if not data gathering, at least problem-generation. Again, the reader should remind himself that by "systems," he should think total communications complex, from publishing to archives, from broadcasting to computer systems, from selling to lending. We must be able to view critically the shibboleth of tradition, determining what is worth saving and what should be discarded.

The third criterion is that the transition from laboratory or pilot operation to real world operation must be made with minimum loss and maximum reliability. This is by no means an easy problem as many designers have learned. So much innovation is moved to the real world with neither resultant improvement nor change, and certainly no acceptance—like a pebble dropped into a large puddle of concrete. Neither the context nor the people affected are taken into consideration. For example, many of the devices and systems developed over the last 20 years in the information-retrieval field have (fortunately) been forgotten. Their disappearance was almost guaranteed at the time because (a) the relationship between a researcher and the body of relevant printed knowledge was (and is) not understood; (b) there are very few cases where complete and exhaustive bibliographical search is necessary, yet most devices are designed on this basis; (c) the intellectual access to most systems is so artificial and difficult that they invite neglect. Most of these same criticisms can be made of conventional library systems. It may be that in the process of changing social institutions we must go through a probing and highly empirical stage, in the hope that wisdom will eventually become ours. The mistake is that we parrot what the physical researcher says he does and not what he really does.

The road to wisdom?—Well, it's plain and simple to express:
  Err
  and err
  and err again
  but less
  and less
  and less.

Piet Hein, Grooks[27]

FUNCTIONAL IMPLICATIONS

There are several possible organizational patterns which could emerge from restructuring and reorienting the college library. For reasons that should be apparent by now, the organizational pattern of the conventional library is no longer adapted to present or future needs. Many of the patterns for future development depend on a series of definitions of function and objective which at present are neither available in operable form nor perhaps desirable at this time. There are so many covert and tacit assumptions about the traditional library, however, let alone professional complaints about its image and, by implication, its functions, that one might suspect it is already rigorously, if unconsciously, defined.

This covert but accepted definition is no longer valid because it makes the institution it defines uneconomic, noninitiating, built around an obsolete ideal of self-sufficiency, and limited to an increasingly smaller corner of the communication spectrum; hence it becomes uncompetitive in comparison to other services. With the exception of some special libraries, the present organization is ill equipped to service highly current information and data; hence the growth of information centers serving the consumer directly. The inability of the present library to serve highly current book and media interests—except at very high cost with a form of permanent retention, cataloging—has led to the growth of many parallel dissemination systems, such as book and media clubs, supermarket book sales, direct mail. The present structure is ill equipped to provide service or to advise on nonprint media: hence the independent growth of audiovisual centers and instructional communications groups. The library, in its present structure, is unable to integrate computing, video, and audio systems: hence the growth of separate closed-circuit, dial-access, information-retrieval, and CATV systems.

On the other side of the coin it should be observed that faculties and academic administrations have done little to alleviate these problems. There has been no attempt until recently, for example, to define and project substantive or disciplinary interests of the institution, nor to understand the implications of growth and disciplinary change for the total system. Faculty are added, new programs are instituted; and there is shocked surprise that both the holdings and the staff of the library must also grow and change, the former doubling every 16 years because of uncontrolled growth of research and curricula. Another example of the failure to see the broader implications of academic decision-making may be illustrated in the design of dormitories and residence houses which put a premium, necessary in the narrow view, on economic construction, with resulting crowding and a significant rise in acoustic noise. While this approach has decreased the cost of student housing, it has increased library costs by demanding longer hours and all-night study rooms, and by requiring expensive forms of policing and control. The costs are still there; they have merely been shifted to the library.

These two factors—one generated by the library tradition and the other created by the limits of academic decision-making—conspire to make the present library not only uneconomic but much less useful than it could be. It is in part this belief which has spurred the writing, structure, and recommendations of this book. And because we do not know the answers to these complex and growing problems our subtitle—The Academic Library in Transition—has special import. The question then becomes how to design a functioning organization that can both provide service and engage in adaptive innovation.

One recent and growing idea, the library college,[28] though bold and challenging, is not the answer at this time. Basically the library-college idea states that the library, based on the "generic book," that is, all media, is truly the heart of the college, in fact *is* the college, and that faculty members are members also of the library staff. This is a neat reversal of status, but one that cannot be seriously argued *at this time*. We predict that something like this will come about in the next two decades, and the library-information-communication profession will become a "fourth estate" on the campus, joining the faculty, administration, and, that newest estate, the student body, as an equal partner. To some extent this is beginning to happen now with the appearance of an office on the vice-presidential level, in both industrial corporations and institutions of higher education, concerned with information processing and communications activities. Mere grouping of these seemingly disparate activities, however, will not alleviate the problems of each. What is necessary, and what these pages are all about, is the complete amalgamation of function. This sense of mix is not yet part of the library-college idea. It represents a basically naive and early—too early—attempt to solve a very large and complicated problem. It is a rhetorical rather than empirical approach.

Acceptance of the library-college idea requires that several specific conditions be met. First, the specialization of academic disciplines among faculty must be weaker than it is now. We do not see this happening soon, although there is at least one unknown factor in this equation: the effect of student dissatisfaction. How long this may last and to what effect has already been discussed.

A second assumption of the library-college idea is that the library has a true base of political power within academe. This does not now exist. Thus far the library has been fortunate in living within an intellectual climate which has revered the printed book. This form of piety has been sufficient to justify the library's existence for several millenia, using such rubrics as "a true university is a collection of books" and the library is "the heart of the university." The rhetoric of the library-college rests in this tradition. These days are near an end. The hollowness of these slogans will haunt librarians if they continue to rely solely on such arguments to justify their existence and their budgets. This is not to say that all judgment should or would be reduced to a purely cost-benefit process. In the budget squeeze to come, however, the library will have to justify itself on other than traditional rubric, and its existence may not be taken for granted.

The third requirement of the library-college is based on a certain stability of information resources. That is to say the library-college assumes the student and faculty member will be surrounded by all the necessary resources in many media—the "generic book." This is a natural and grand idea, this attempt to think of the totality of media—print, sound, and image—in one continuum. Though most librarians have not yet caught up with this concept, the marketplace is beginning to move beyond it and now supports a much broader range of resources and services. The consumer, the student in this case, is not only aware of this range but demands it. Information centers, paperbacks, data analysis centers, the underground press, television, educational television and radio, film groups, computer laboratories—all represent the broadening spectrum that must be drawn on. The library-college must be able to tap these resources as easily as it does the rows of tapes, books, and films on its own shelves. Although dynamic on the institutional side, proponents of the library-college idea do not appear to be aware of the much larger sea of information beyond the walls.

These caveats on the library-college do not deny its charm and appeal in an era of doubt, unrest, cultural revolution, and amoral technology. Its base, however, is in the traditional library. It is on this point that it will founder, because the library does not have the academic power to assert its position and argue its undeniable case with vigor and confidence. Nor does it represent the communication flood within which it swims. It is for these reasons, and with these inputs, that the first step in a realistic transition is to broaden the communications base by combining the library with other activities which have basically the same mission. Merely combining these activities as we have done at Hampshire College, however, will help neither the financial nor educational problems because each activity retains its autonomy and separate mission; but there should occur over time a gradual blurring of the divisions. It may take 5 to 10 years to reach the point where it can be said that a new institution is emerging, where there is a coalescing of these semiautonomous units into a different functional framework. The principal problems exist in the way people identify themselves with or distinguish themselves from other people in the organization, and in the way outsiders view the different activities. The difficulty lies principally in superimposing a communications-based organization on an environment, the undergraduate college, which is not yet prepared for it. From this present congeries of separately conceived activities, however, there is the expectation that they will break down eventually into several functional units, different from those we know today.

1. *Processing and Organization.* This function is primarily concerned with the development of resources, regardless of format *or eventual use,* and with their organization into an effective and useful media base. This is not only the acquisition, storage, and cataloging operation of the conventional library. Not only does this extend to other formats, such as films, slides, tapes, and objects of art, but it also includes the purchase and processing of materials for sale (in the bookstore),[29] with the acquisition and organized storage of a range of materials for exhibition such as paintings, three-dimensional objects, and equipment for display in all media. Consequently materials in all media, and their associated equipment, must not only be organized for browsing, lending, and circulation, but also for sale, display, and transmission.

2. *Distribution and Dissemination.* Within this general function the concern is with the movement of materials both in physical form (books, slides, tapes, projectors) and by electronic means (video or audio channels, terminal to a time-shared computer, or rear-screen projection). This includes such operations as circulation, bookstore sales, audiovisual services in the classroom, closed-circuit radio or television, and duplication services for both print and nonprint media. This functional opera-

tion then is principally concerned (a) with a user or group of users; (b) with the equipment, in some cases portable, necessary to support distribution; (c) with the duplication, or in some cases change of format, so that the user can walk away with his own copy; (d) with the reliability of the channels of distribution; and (e) with the repackaging of information to match specific instructional needs.

3. *Information and Instruction.* The title of this hypothetical function may be somewhat misleading. It combines reference, merchandising, and serendipitous display. The reference librarian may object to the combination of the reference and educational efforts of the library with advertising and sales promotion. In this regard, however, it is worth noting that, in the best sense, all of these operations are directed toward matching a user (buyer, borrower, listener, viewer) with some kind of package (book, film, disc, photograph, Xerox copy) or another person, using one of several modes (reference interview, card catalog, lecture, display, advertisement) in order to meet some kind of need the patron has described. In essence this is the middleman, or switching function, which ranges from the temptation of the advertisement to the lengthy negotiation of a wide and deep need for specifically defined knowledge.

4. *Educational Technology and Systems.* Under this general rubric, three functions are included.
1. The design, development, and operation of systems in support of instruction; for example, video and other display systems, telephone networks, and time-shared computer systems.
2. Assistance to the faculty in the design of small or large segments of specific courses, taking full advantage of the range of media from print to sound to image both inside and outside the classroom.
3. The creation and production of packages, such as film, video, print, computer programs, or any combination of these, useful to instruction and other community activities.

It is worth noting that this totality is considered a separate function *at this time.* Sometime in the future the purely systems aspects in the first function above might be considered normal enough as an activity to be merely one of the means supporting other functions. That day is not yet here. These systems are considered esoteric enough and are, in fact, unstandardized enough to demand separate attention for the present. However, direct collaboration with faculty in the design of instructional modules and the production of such unit modules should always be considered a separate function.

5. *Institutional Research and Evaluation.* Academic systems can

no longer be viewed as frozen. They are processes which, though we may not know how to define them, are highly dynamic. Any institution consciously concerned with message transfer must continually study itself, its operations, and its communities in order to be effective. All institutions occasionally ask "how are we doing?" Very few ask the question which should precede this. "What do we need to know in order to make judgment as to how we are doing?" These are important and continuing questions that may not always have the same answer. Because most evaluation has to do with the cost of transferring messages—in money, labor, and systems—our organization places this function within our hypothetical library.

6. *Management.* This function is obviously a thread running through and holding together the other functions. It is also related to institutional evaluation, except that it carries that activity one step further. It essentially must ask and answer the question: What do you do as a result of any data evaluation and analysis? It is therefore concerned with four activities: (a) definition of decision data; (b) collection and flow of those data; (c) evaluation of options and decisions based on those data; and (d) the effective translation of these decisions into action.

Although these precise divisions may not stand the test of time and operational experience, the six functions sketched above represent an early attempt to anticipate the reordering of labor and effort necessary if the library (or its equivalent) is to be able to adapt.

IMPLICATIONS FOR BUILDINGS

Without for the moment examining the implications for buildings of the functional complex just discussed, there does exist a primary design problem at this time if it is assumed that we must think in terms of maximum flexibility, and that a transition period is necessary during which it may be difficult to specify means and modes of use. Assuming the desirability, as we have in this report, of a variety of means of transmission and modes of use, how do we design a building to allow maximum flexibility (or adaptability) in the future? In approaching such a question, primary attention must be given two aspects. First, we are concerned with the transmission of messages electronically. There are other possible means of transmitting messages, such as fluidics, which may in time replace electrical information transmission.[30] It is too early, however, to design for such devices for at the present time they are limited to control and sensing mechanisms. This limits us then to the use of wired connections and to certain kinds of broadcast and receiving facilities.

A second point is that because the modes of use of these kinds of message transmission are only beginning to emerge we are unable to specify location and space requirements for their use. This means a period of trial and error until we are able to understand and to specify the needs of planned use as well as occasional and serendipitous use. For building design, this requires the capability to move computer terminals, video receivers, and other kinds of viewing and listening devices to locations seldom if ever foreseen in the original planning. For electrical connections we do this now as a matter of course with plugs and plug strips which allow electrical fixtures to be placed in multiple spots as we adjust to operational demands. That this is not always successful and cords must stretch across floors, does not deny the reasonableness of the argument. The point is that the opportunity to adjust the location of terminals and receivers to need should be considered on the same level as electrical fixtures. It is worth noting that we are coming close to this with the telephone jack; but we still consider this at a somewhat different level than we do the electric light. Our assumption is that in time accessibility to communication devices will be as ubiquitous as that now for electricity, and that this sort of open accessibility will exist throughout a campus.

To accomplish this kind of accessibility is expensive at this time. This capability is necessary, however, if we are to use communication devices with the ease and ubiquity implied in these pages. It requires not only vertical risers capable of carrying an unknown amount of cable or other carriers within the building, but also of having maximum accessibility to power and communication cable horizontally, so that devices may be placed at any point on a single floor. A hollow or cellular floor which allows access to cable at any point is one possible, and expensive, solution. A more practical, although aesthetically less desirable, solution is the hung ceiling. This provides a two- to three-foot ceiling space (larger if heating and air conditioning duct is included) allowing cable to be strung from the riser throughout the building, thereby providing easy access for maintenance and installation. In either case normal access requires drilling through the floor surface, although it is much easier with the cellular floor. With the hung ceiling the cable can be dropped along walls or columns. In an architectural sense use of the hung ceiling exclusively may place severe restraints on the variation of ceiling heights, a conceit which may be aesthetically desirable.

Consequently it appears necessary to be able to design some combination of hung ceiling and hollow floor which would allow flexibility for aesthetic purposes, combined with several vertical risers. The exact number of risers would depend on floor size and anticipated use. To utilize all the columns at the module corners as risers would tend to enlarge the columns to inordinate size. It may be possible to use risers on a selective basis, however, thus providing both aesthetic variation and a more accessible communication system. Using conduits, as in the Hampshire Library Center, requires specification three years before the building is opened which locates exactly where and how people 10 years hence will use devices which in some cases we cannot even describe yet. This approach places severe restrictions on the location of computer terminals, video screens, audio terminals, and the unknown devices now on the drawing boards.

The anticipated changes in function discussed in the last section also pose major design problems, especially at a time when we are not able to describe precisely what form those changes may take. An illustrative example, one which may soon pose a problem for the Hampshire College Library Center, is the differing requirements by the video transmission facilities and by the loan desk for the same materials—audio tapes, films, video tapes, discs. Users legitimately wish to borrow these over the desk for use in screening and listening rooms. At the same time there is a demand for their use in video production and transmission. In the present structure these facilities are two floors apart. A similar situation exists in the repair and maintenance of equipment for studio and for lending. Had we been able to anticipate these relationships a closer physical juxtaposition of these functions would have been foreseen in the original design. This type of change and overlap of function will occur more frequently in the next decade. They will not be easy problems to solve. Highly specialized spaces such as a television studio and control room, the loan desk, and listening rooms do not lend themselves easily to flexibility. Consequently, this requires a better understanding of and agreement about potentially related functions in any library which intends to combine a range of activities under one roof. We do not know whether the functional combinations we have suggested in the last section will have validity and viability 10 years from now. If they have, or if they are a reasonable facsimile, then a complete rethinking of building design is required.

It is too early at this stage to do more than call attention to these possible changes and to their implications for design. One such change has already been discussed above in the question of materials' use by various interests in the building. Another planning implication can be seen in the work in processing and organizing materials. As discussed earlier this function not only includes books and other usual media, but also media and supplies for sale, and the range of materials for display. As computerized shelf-lists and catalogs become increasingly possible, the location of this function is no longer limited by the requirement of proximity to the card catalog. Consequently both the location of processing operations and the kinds of space required can and should be reconsidered. That function discussed under the rubric "information and instruction" obviously has ties to all sections of the building. It is in a sense the switching center within the building to bookstore, gallery, media collections, and information centers. This therefore should be the most publicly accessible and centrally located area in the building. These are but a few of the planning and design problems that must be faced in the future. The next 10 to 15 years will be critical, not only for the redefinition of the library as a more significant part of an institution, but also for the process of translating these new operational arrangements into viable and functional spaces.

IMPLICATIONS FOR THE PROFESSIONS

> But goals are achieved by some *means*, and sooner or later even the most impulsive man of action will discover that some ways of achieving the goal are more effective than others. A concern for *how* to do it is the root impulse in all great craftsmanship, and accounts for all the style in human performance. Without it we would never know the peaks of human achievement.
>
> Yet, ironically, this concern for "how it is done" is also one of the diseases of which societies die. Little by little, preoccupation with method, technique and procedure gains a subtle dominance over the whole process of goal seeking. *How* it is done becomes more important than *whether* it is done. Means triumph over ends. Form triumphs over spirit. Method is enthroned. Men become prisoners of their procedures, and organizations that were designed to achieve some goal become obstacles in the path to that goal.
>
> John Gardner. Self-Renewal[31]

This book has discussed the renewal of a static, if not moribund organization—the library—and of a profession, that grows in numbers but dies in content and purpose. The objective of the book, however, is not to bludgeon—that's too easy—but rather (a) to pull together a series of decisions made in the process of designing a library, (b) to pose some rather fundamental questions about the assumptions that provided the context for those decisions, and (c) to suggest alternatives in objectives and organization for the profession and for its institutions.

Essentially the malaise of librarianship—and one merely needs to scan the incestuousness of the professional literature to sense this—is the result of an overconcern with "how" rather than "why." This attention to methods and processes has allowed the profession to talk only to itself. Others have been excluded, not because they may not be interested, but rather because the profession has not had much to say to them. Consequently others have decided what the profession should be like, what it should do, and what image it should have. The pragmatic vocationalism—the "how"—of Melvil Dewey has been the warp and woof of the profession since the late nineteenth century; and, with some mitigation but more rhetoric, this became enshrined as a graduate program in the 1940's. Together with others of equal stature, Dewey's step made sense at that time for it ended centuries of bibliographic and classificatory chaos. It enabled what became the great research libraries in this country to cope with the tremendous expansion their collections went through during the first half of this century. It also excluded the librarian, with some notable exceptions, from the company of intellectuals and from the academic seats of power. In short it made him a clerk and threatens now, as Leonard Freiser has implied, to make him "the biggest garbage collector in history."[32] Since the 1940's, however, the professional fringe—where innovation always starts—has questioned this acquisitive syndrome. The current attempt to develop library networks may be the last gasp of an acquisitive society, especially in the absence of subject specialization. These words are not meant to suggest that we burn the documents and books, but rather that we force faculties and institutional administrations to make choices. The networks, as they are designed, are posited on the need to support research, not education or public information needs. It is in the latter concerns where the primary problems exist today, especially if our society is to close the widening gap between the real implications of research and the need for an educated and informed public to establish priorities in a world of many voices.

The reactive tendency of academic libraries is a reflection of the present research requirements of a technical and scientific society (including the humanistic disciplines) the members of which are unable to control their own output, much of which is noise, obscuring the important and inflating the trivial, and using a seventeenth century dissemination system designed under different conditions and for different needs. It is this process of reacting to outside demands rather than initiating change or exercising control over the goals of libraries that really underlies the arguments of this section. It has been assumed in these chapters that not only is change desirable but inevitable, and that it is better to be prepared for and to be a part of that change—indeed to initiate it—than to sit and wait for the world to change around us.

This poses the dilemma that libraries will soon face—the break with a long tradition and a redefinition of objectives. This will not happen suddenly. It is happening, and one year the profession will realize that its purpose is no longer the theory and practice of bibliographical control. Rather the librarian will find that he has a different kind of institution, with different kinds of demands on it, with different kinds of processes in it—an institution he may not be prepared to deal with. It is a bit like the story of the railroad magnate who was approaching bankruptcy until one day he suddenly realized he was not in the railroad business, but in the transportation business. This changed his whole approach and his conception of the kinds of problems he had to solve. It may be that librarians are no longer in the book "business" but in the communications "business."

It may be necessary—in fact it may be happening now—to build a cocoon around the present library, allowing it to serve out its present limited functions, and to develop consciously a new institution. Such an institution, which will eventually absorb or transform the present library, would be separated enough from the library so that it can be truly dynamic in its approach to communications processes in a broad social setting. Librarians may consider these harsh words, but the sentiment underlies the suggestion earlier in the chapter that the reader should stumble a bit over the word "library." Nothing less is suggested than the planned formation of a new profession, a new institution, and a new geography of interests, concerns, and objectives. The members of this profession must be familiar not only with the regulations of the Federal Communications Commission pertinent to CATV but with the graphics and aesthetics of fifteenth century printing, not only with executive routines in time-shared computers but with print and nonprint classification and indexing, not only with microform technologies but with the economics and structure of management information systems, not only with the publishing and presentation of children's literature but with video and audio production and recording techniques. These are the true generalists of the future: a breed that will be—and indeed is—required to provide the vision, the systems, and the factual awareness necessary to sustain and to interconnect the knowledge society, and to give it human dimensions.

How do we get from "here" to "there"? First, it is necessary to encourage a broad social awareness of the existence and extent of common concerns in the library, computer, graphics, and communications fields. Until there is an unconscious societal acceptance of this mutuality among decision-makers and opinion-formers, such a combination as discussed here will not become reality. One can point to a few examples of this change in public consciousness. For example, the gradual movement of the *Saturday Review* over the last 25 years from what was principally, though not exclusively, a literary and book-oriented journal to a magazine of broad cultural and communications interest is a case in point.[33] In the 1940's regular columns were added to the basic literary content, on fine art by James Thrall Soby and on music and recordings by Irving Kolodin. In the 1950's and early 1960's, a continued broadening took place: film reviews by Hallis Alpert and Arthur Knight; radio and television coverage by Gilbert Seldes and Robert Lewis Shayon; photography as an art was introduced to *SR* readers first by Ivan Dmitri and later by Margaret Weiss. The Science Supplement, under John Lear, was started in 1956. The Education Supplement, under Paul Woodring, and the Communications Supplement, under Richard Tobin, were both initiated during the early 1960's.

Literature, fine art, music, recordings, film, radio, television, photography, science, education, communication—if such a grouping begins to make sense to an informed and educated public, it may be time to reflect that mix in a social institution such as the library which presumably (at least it is the assumption in these pages) should represent the culture surrounding it. This is not merely the shelving of packages about these subjects, but rather the use, the total use, of the artifacts and systems produced by these activities. This, in context, is the difference between stasis and dynamism. The danger, of course, is that we shall mistake rhetoric for action, that the "electronic revolution" will become merely a literary movement, a conceit of the new intellectual.

As one sees the growth and change of the *Saturday Review*, it is apparent that a cultural base and context is already building around the broader institution advocated in these pages. Its expression as a social institution and managerial unit especially on the campus, however, is inhibited by the insulated walls each profession builds around its specialty: books, fine art, media, music, educational technology, computers, film, and so on. As a rule these specialists communicate only within these walls, and the person who advocates crossing the barriers is labelled a traitor or, worse, impractical visionary. It is for these reasons that an accepted cultural combination is a necessary part of the context. Legitimacy depends a good deal on image.

This leads to the second path on the map from "here" to "there." We need a continuing dialogue among the professions concerned, not merely in friendly association but with the objective of breaking down the separating fences and ascertaining mutual areas of interest, not as philosophical issues but for economic and operational reasons. Such cross-talk is observable in societies like the American Society for Information Science (ASIS), at least at a beginning level. Conversations among computer specialists, librarians, microform specialists, and scientists have been nursed for some 20 years under its auspices.[34] Worth noting is the range of coverage in the ASIS sponsored *Annual Review of Information Science and Technology,* especially Volume 5:[35] information needs and uses; communications technology; library automation; management information systems; and others. Because of its growth and background ASIS has been restricted principally to the problems of research and development in science and technology, with concomitant limitations. A broader interest than this will be necessary if the goal of a true communications profession is to emerge. Mere talk is not enough. Mutuality must be reflected in the evolving institution. For, although at moments we may admire the chutzpah of Clyde, we really do not want to be caught out with the reputation, in Bonnie's words, that "your advertising's just dandy, nobody'd know that you don't have anything to sell."

PROFESSIONAL EDUCATION

A third path is through professional education, even though, as Jesse Shera has pointed out

> . . . many of the procedures of a profession are inevitably petty, and therefore, because professional education must reflect this pettiness, the prevailing attitude toward it is likely to be ambivalent. . . . This paradox of professional education arises from the need to reconcile, within its instructional program, the pragmatism of a John Dewey with the self-sufficient search for intellectual excellence of a Cardinal Newman, and the reconciliation of the duality must be effected in the absence of any real understanding of the mysteries of the learning process.[36]

The need for reconciliation of pragmatism and intellectual excellence that Dean Shera alludes to here is of course apparent in any stable profession. The profession proposed here, if we may dignify our incipient hopes by calling it such, is fortunately not stable and indeed should not be for years to come. It is in this very instability and inchoate probing that the excitement of new operational design and creative endeavor can be generated as we search for a new professional base. Any attempt to freeze a professional curriculum at this time would be dangerous. We can, however, explore its possible attributes.

In an earlier report by the author in developing a curriculum for the information sciences,[37] a broad spectrum of substantive content was discussed under five headings: system analysis, ecology of systems, media, organization of information, and the man-system interface. These five rubrics still appear to be valid, despite some of the specialized jargon, in discussing possible curricula for what we will call here the communications profession. Though the emphasis will vary from that in the earlier report, it is significant that it is possible to use that framework in the context we are concerned with here. That is to say, there is a broad base of common concern and knowledge necessary to information scientists as well as to graphic artists, to television producers as well as to librarians, to educational technologists as well as to publishers. This is a binding quality of prime importance, overarching all the artificial boundaries of present professional and intellectual preserves.

There is overlap among the areas sketched below. The only purpose of division at this moment is to provide some generalized pigeonholes for convenience of discussion. One caution however: the word "system" must be very loosely understood. It applies both to the highly structured apparatus of a computer system, and to the highly informal, that is, poorly explicated, social and cultural systems for communication, such as those among psychologists, among galleries, in the classroom, or among the residents of a racial ghetto.

System Analysis

This area is concerned principally with the formal analysis of men, machines, and processes into effective and economically feasible operations for the accomplishment of specific objectives. It may include the analysis of cybernetic systems, especially the problems of intermediate and probabilistic systems. Among the specific areas of interest are library systems, management information systems, data analysis centers, system simulation, cost and evaluation studies, artificial intelligence, computer systems, CATV systems, and similar formal types of systems. It is worth noting that systems analysis is not necessarily directed only toward those systems using computers. It is concerned with operational efficiency and systems modelling, regardless of the means used.

Social Ecology of Communications Systems

In studying ecology and environment we are principally interested in the historical and social contexts for the processing of knowledge, with the development and social function of different kinds of communication institutions, with the needs of various segments of society, and with different kinds of societies and levels of technological and social development. It is concerned (a) with the historical development of writing, printing, graphic arts, and their effect on culture, (b) with the development of libraries and other institutional memories and their roles, and

(c) with the explosion of sound and image in the media culture of the latter part of this century. Other areas of equal concern are, for example, legal constraints on information and communication systems, invisible colleges, formal and informal communication nets, the economics of the production and distribution of knowledge, and human behavior in organizations as an example of communications behavior.

Media

In this area we are concerned with the format and intrinsic organization of messages, including their effect and role in formal, and especially in informal, communication systems. As our culture begins to examine the bases of education and the uses of literacy, it may be necessary to challenge some of the assumptions that we cherish; for example, the assumption that the written word is the only base for literacy. Consequently this area of concern must ultimately ask what form a message should take in what kind of context. These forms, or packages, may range from natural languages to algorithmic languages, from audio messages to visual messages, from print to sound to image. This substantive area must therefore be concerned with the languages used; the shape, content, and reduction of messages; and their roles in different situations.

Organization of Information

This has been a traditional area of library interest, especially such problems as classification, coding, indexing, abstracting, bibliographic description, and thesaurus development. It is necessary, however, to understand something of the intent and depth of these concerns. Attention should be especially focussed on the organization of knowledge both for structured and specific use as in technology and scholarship and for serendipitous discovery as in the arts and the sciences. In the latter case we are reminded of Delbruck's principle of limited sloppiness—You should be sloppy enough so that the unexpected happens, yet not so sloppy that you cannot figure out what happened after it has happened.[38] Our concern must be directed toward increasing the probability that the unexpected will happen. This concern is therefore directed toward pragmatic answers to the question posed above: what kinds of messages are best for what kinds of people? For what kinds of situations? For what kinds of subjects? It must therefore be concerned with retrieval and display systems, with content analysis, with the "syntax" of film and graphic arts, with file structure and organization, with serendipity.

Man-System Interface

In contrast to the area of "ecology" discussed above which pertains to social systems, here attention is directed toward the interface between the individual and whatever face the communication system turns toward him: a shelf of books, a video screen, a multimedia display, a reference librarian, a computer printout, a gallery wall. Curriculum development in this area must be dependent on peripheral technologies, partially, but not entirely, at the intersection of engineering and the behavioral sciences. It has implications, of course, far beyond the design of better communication systems, for study of this area concerns the total educational and learning process, cognitive and perceptual processes, and a deeper understanding of the sociology of knowledge.

To some the descriptions of these five areas may seem highly technological. This is not altogether unintentional. If we are not to be buried in the informational effluent of our age then we must understand something of the society which produces it, being, as Philip Ennis has warned, neither Luddite nor Technocrat for

> . . . it will be recalled that the Luddites were all hanged, [and] the technocrats suffered a worse fate; they were soon forgotten.[39]

No, the objective here is that of consciously developing a profession dedicated to the understanding of the media and information revolution surrounding us and to the design of social institutions which will provide better channels, both formal and informal, for the selection, use, and enjoyment of the plethora of messages presently hurled at us. To wring hands, or to wish this cacophony silenced, or worse, to ignore it, is sheer nonsense. It will not go away but it can be channeled, muted, and used if we care to make the effort.

Mere curriculum revision may not be enough. A more important factor in changing a profession may be, as Jencks and Riesman point out in their book *The Academic Revolution,* the kind of person recruited into the profession.

> We have repeatedly argued [they write] that this sorting and certifying is considerably more important than what the schools actually try to teach. Just as it is easier to change the character of a college by changing the admission requirements than by changing the curriculum, so too it is easier to change a profession by recruiting new sorts of apprentices than by changing the rules of apprenticeship. Professional schools have their students for only a few years, and they can do only so much with whatever raw material they get. But to the extent that they are overapplied and can select their raw material according to some preconceived plan, they can influence the profession they serve decisively.[40]

Assuming the validity of this argument, it is discouraging to note that, in the present situation, selection is really one of self-selection on the part of the student, because the schools and associations put so little energy into recruiting and admissions. Consequently, the prospective recruit makes his choice based on his perception of the library and the profession and on the match of his own self-image with that perception. This underlines an argument made earlier that the profession has allowed others to define it.

With these caveats in mind it appears appropriate to suggest that the professional schools put effort into recruiting and admissions equal to that put into curricular design. A warning, however: recruitment and curriculum must change together, for new apprentices, with a livelier and less inhibited attitude, will not tolerate the stuffiness or the superficiality of the traditional library school course.

Despite this disparagement the institution of the library and the profession of librarianship carry the seed for renewal. Of all the social institutions the library was the first to have developed around the intellectual extensions of man—the alphabet, writing, print, the manuscript, the book. If, in a metaphorical sense, we can use Snow's analogy of the two cultures, then the library as a functioning institution lives in both. That is it lived there until recently, when it committed itself almost completely to the technology of libraries, to the "how" rather than to the "why." Neither the library profession, however, nor the newer technologically and communications-oriented professions have learned to commute easily between the two cultures. It is this capability that will define the new profession and its institutional reflections. There are at least two dimensions to this capability.

The first of these dimensions has to do with the library (stumble here) as an agent of change, as a catalyst inducing and nursing transition and adaptation. This implies eventually total use of computers, telecommunications, and media in all formats. It implies collaboration and even combination with computer and information scientists, educational technologists, communication scientists, graphic artists, publishers, producers, and distributors of print and nonprint media. The changes in the background and cultural experiences of the public, identified and unidentified, who require information and knowledge, in whatever formats, demand that libraries not only accept a different level of operation, but initiate the changes necessary to get there. Though one can argue with the McLuhan statements, the plethora of messages and pseudo-messages gives substance to his prophecy. Without attempting to destroy the incredible richness of portions of this varied and incandescent media culture, some form of filtering, structuring, and steering is necessary. *If it cares to make the effort and if it can make what may be a quantum leap, the library profession, and its social expression in the library, may be the only present institution that can accomplish this.* The elements for this effort exist not at the accepted core of librarianship, but rather at the periphery in the computer, media, behavioral, and communication fields. The alternative is that the library will return to the supply depot and housekeeping stage, abandoning its incipient efforts of the last 50 years in reference and information services. This may well be an answer, but it would cause a major breakup of the profession. Indeed a breakup of the profession may be necessary.

The second dimension for the library in working toward these objectives has to do with a fundamental faith and some assumptions about technology and humanism. As Franklin Patterson has so eloquently pointed out in discussing the media and technological revolution,

> . . . it is in the tensions between this revolution which produces information and the human condition which demands wisdom, that the library must not only find its home, but also point the way. . . . The library is not only a user of technology, it is an arbiter between technology and humanism. Or, to put it more positively, the library orchestrates many technologies for human ends. It is uniquely situated to combine electronic and communications technology with the intellectual and cultural enterprise called education. Borrowing from the language of the biologist, we can say that the library is dependent upon, host to, and symbiotic with all other disciplines and technologies.[41]

What is suggested here is a marriage of the almost buried humanistic tradition of the library with the technological restlessness and social impact of the new media and communications systems. If, in the next decade, this issue is dodged by the library profession, then it will have lost the last chance to affect and to temper the technological bias of the knowledge society.

REFERENCES

1. As quoted in A. Toffler, The Future as a Way of Life, *Horizon* 7(3):110 (Summer 1965).
2. As quoted in *IEEE Spectrum,* 3:150 (September 1966).
3. Bertrand de Jouvenal, *The Art of Conjecture.* New York, Basic Books, 1967, 177.
4. P. F. Drucker, *The Age of Discontinuity: Guidelines to Our Changing Society.* New York, Harper & Row, 1968, ix.
5. *Ibid.,* ix–xi.
6. See for example C. Reich, *The Greening of America: The Coming of a New Consciousness and the Rebirth of a Future.* New York, Random, 1970.

7. See, especially, O. Helmer, *Social Technology*. New York, Basic Books, 1966; O. Helmer, *Analysis of the Future: The Delphi Method*, Santa Monica, Calif., The RAND Corp., March 1967; and O. Helmer, *A Use of Simulation for the Study of Future Values*. Santa Monica, Calif., The RAND Corp., September 1966.

8. Helmer, *Analysis of the Future, op. cit.*, 4.

9. T. J. Gordon and Robert H. Ament, *Forecasts of Some Technological and Scientific Developments and Their Societal Consequences*. Middletown, Conn., Institute for the Future, September 1969 (IFF Report No. 6), 29.

10. *Ibid.*, 3–4.

11. *Ibid.*, 20–28.

12. *Ibid.*, 31–32.

13. *Ibid.*, 29.

14. *Ibid.*, 70–73.

15. *Ibid.*, 41–47.

16. R. Bradbury, *Fahrenheit Four Hundred Fifty One*. New York, Simon & Schuster, 1967.

17. H. G. Barnett, *Innovations: The Basis of Change*. New York, McGraw-Hill, 1953, 19–20.

18. Fritz Machlup, *The Production and Distribution of Knowledge in the United States*. Princeton, N.J., Princeton University Press, 1962, 7.

19. Drucker, *op. cit.*, 269.

20. Lewis B. Mayhew, The Future of American Higher Education, *Liberal Education*, 53:453–462 (December 1967).

21. William P. Tolley, The President's Bulletin Board, Syracuse University, December 1959. Quoted in J. D. Koerner, *The Parson's College Bubble*. New York, Basic Books, 1970, 81.

22. *University Without Walls, Summary Statement*, Yellow Springs, Ohio, Union for Experimenting Colleges and Universities, Antioch College, September 28, 1970, 1–2.

23. See, for example, Syracuse University, *Independent Study Program 1971;* and *ADP, The Goddard College Adult Degree Program*, Plainfield, Vt., The Goddard Bulletin, January 1971.

24. Robert W. Locke, Has the Education Industry Lost Its Nerve? *Saturday Review*, 56(3), 42–44, 57–58, January 16, 1971.

25. Alvin Toffler, The Future as a Way of Life, *Horizon*, 7(3):109 (Summer 1965).

26. E. E. Morison, *Men, Machines, and Modern Times*, Cambridge, M. I. T. Press, 1966, 119.

27. Piet Hein, *Grooks*, Cambridge, M. I. T. Press, 1966, 34.

28. See *The Library-College*, Louis Shores, Robert Jordan, and John Harvey (eds.), Philadelphia, Drexel Institute Press, 1966; and Louis Shores, *Library-College USA*. Tallahassee, South Pass Press, 1970.

29. Susan Severtson and George Banks, Toward the Library-Bookstore, *Library Journal*, 96 (2) (January 15, 1971).

30. Alexander Block, Fluidics: Development and Outlook, *Engineer*, 228:14–17 (Jan.-Feb. 1969).

31. John W. Gardner, *Self-Renewal: The Individual and the Innovative Society*. New York, Harper & Row, 1963, 47.

32. Leonard H. Freiser, The Threshold of Silence, *Library Journal,* **94** (12):2451 (June 15, 1968).

33. The material about the *Saturday Review* is drawn from Norman Cousins, *Present Tense, An American Editor's Odyssey*. New York, McGraw-Hill, 1967, especially 1–75.

34. See article "American Society for Information Science" in *Encyclopedia of Library and Information Science, Vol. 1*. New York, Marcel Dekker, 1968, 303–307. (The author was President of ASIS in 1968.)

35. *Annual Review of Information Science and Technology*, Carlos A. Cuadra (Ed.), Vol. 5. Chicago, Encyclopaedia Britannica, 1970.

36. Jesse H. Shera, *Libraries and the Organization of Knowledge*. Hamden, Conn., Archon, 1966, 174.

37. Robert S. Taylor, *Final Report: Recommended Courses and Curricula*. Report No. 12 in Curriculum for the Information Sciences, Bethlehem, Pa., Lehigh University, Center for the Information Sciences, September 1967 (NSF Grant GE-2569), 7–22.

38. Bernice T. Eiduson, *Scientists: Their Psychological World*. New York, Basic Books, 1962, 126.

39. Philip H. Ennis, Technological Change and the Professions: Neither Luddite nor Technocrat, *Library Quarterly,* **32** (3):198 (July 1962).

40. Christopher Jencks and David Riesman, *The Academic Revolution*. New York, Doubleday, 1968, 254.

41. Franklin Patterson, The Library as Arbiter, *American Libraries,* **1** (3):255 (March 1970).

Appendix One

Reports and Papers Published Under This Grant

Reports

Taylor, R. S., The Extended and Experimenting College Library: Configurations and Functions of the Academic Library in Transition. (February 1969).

———, Ed., Relationship of Information Transfer Systems and Experimentation to the Design and Function of the Library. (April 1969)

———, Ed., Planning for Automated Systems in College Libraries. (April 1969)

———, and R. W. Trueswell, A Study of the Impact of Hampshire College on the Libraries of the Five-College Community. (February 1969)

Papers

Taylor, R. S., "Toward the Design of a College Library for the Seventies," *Wilson Library Bulletin,* **43** (1):44–51. (September 1968)

———, "Planning a College Library for the Seventies," *Educational Record,* **50** (4): 426–431. (Fall 1969)

———, "Orienting the Library to the User," in Use, Mis-Use and Non-Use of Academic Libraries, *Proceedings of the New York Library Association,* College and University Libraries Section Spring Conference, Watertown, May 1–2, 1970. New York Library Association, 1970.

———, "Technology and Libraries," *EDUCOM Bulletin,* **5** (3):4–5. (May 1970)

Appendix Two

Consultants to the Project[*]

Harlan Anderson
Time Incorporated
New York, New York

Lawrence Auld
Oakland University
Rochester, Michigan

G. Putnam Barber
University of Massachusetts
Amherst, Massachusetts

Joseph Becker
Becker & Hayes
Bethesda, Maryland

Lawrence Buckland
Inforonics Inc.
Maynard, Massachusetts

Evelyn Clement
Indiana University
Bloomington, Indiana

Anne Curran
Inforonics Inc.
Maynard, Massachusetts

Richard Dougherty
University of Colorado
Boulder, Colorado

George Dunnington
Amherst College
Amherst, Massachusetts

Anne Edmonds
Mount Holyoke College
South Hadley, Massachusetts

Donald P. Ely
Syracuse University
Syracuse, New York

Stephen Furth
International Business Machines
White Plains, New York

Vincent E. Giuliano
State University of New York
Buffalo, New York

James Govan
Swarthmore College
Swarthmore, Pennsylvania

Richard Harwell
Smith College
Northampton, Massachusetts

Tom Henry
CBS Laboratories
Stamford, Connecticut

Margaret L. Johnson
Smith College
Northampton, Massachusetts

James Kennedy
University of Massachusetts
Amherst, Massachusetts

Frederick Kilgour
Ohio College Library Center
Columbus, Ohio

Patricia B. Knapp
Wayne State University
Detroit, Michigan

*Organizations at time of consultancy.

244

Charles T. Laugher
Amherst College
Amherst, Massachusetts

Newton F. McKeon
Amherst College
Amherst, Massachusetts

William Nugent
Inforonics Inc.
Maynard, Massachusetts

Anthony G. Oettinger
Harvard University
Cambridge, Massachusetts

Richard C. Oldham
Consultant
Dudley, Massachusetts

Carl F. J. Overhage
Project Intrex
Massachusetts Institute of
  Technology
Cambridge, Massachusetts

Anne Peters
Library Processing Systems Inc.
Allentown, Pennsylvania

George E. Piper
Store Operation Services
Norwood, Massachusetts

David Remington
Bro-Dart Industries, Inc.
Williamsport, Pennsylvania

Norman P. Ross
Yale University
New Haven, Connecticut

Morris Schertz
University of Massachusetts
Amherst, Massachusetts

William A. Smith, Jr.
Lehigh University
Bethlehem, Pennsylvania

Donald K. Stewart
SLATE Services
Westminster, California

Frances Thorpe
British National Film Catalogue
London, England

Richard Trueswell
University of Massachusetts
Amherst, Massachusetts

David Weisbrod
Yale University
New Haven, Connecticut

Lawrence Wikander
Forbes Library
Northampton, Massachusetts

Hubert Wilke
Consultant
New York, New York

Conrad Wogrin
University of Massachusetts
Amherst, Massachusetts

Index